THE COOKBOOK THAT COUNTS

Illustrations by Mrs. Daniel Davis

Copyright © 1972
Lawrence Country Day School
Hewlett, New York 11557

Library of Congress Catalog
Card Number 72-89450

ISBN
0-9601046-1-5
First Printing, November 1972
Second Printing, October 1973
Third Printing, December 1975
Fourth Printing, January 1978

Profit from the sale of this book
to benefit
The Lawrence Country Day School
Hewlett, New York 11557

Copies of this book may be obtained by sending $6.50
(plus 60¢ for handling and postage) to:
THE COOK BOOK THAT COUNTS
Box 24
Cedarhurst, New York 11516

Checks payable to: LCDS Cookbook Fund

TABLE OF CONTENTS

Foreword
RECIPES:
to serve 4 5
to serve 8 43
to serve 12 93
to serve 16 137

Each chapter includes:
    Hors d'Oeuvres
    Soups
    Meats
    Poultry & Game
    Seafood
    Cheese & Eggs
    Potatoes, Rice & Pasta
    Vegetables
    Salads
    Desserts

ACCOMPANIMENTS:
Breads 182
Cakes 189
Cookies 201
Pies 204
Squares 209
Salad Dressings 212
Sauces 216
EXOTICA 219
RECIPE CONTRIBUTORS 225
INDEX 230
Order Blank ....
Equivalency and Abbreviation Tables ....

FOREWORD

We sincerely thank everyone who contributed recipes to THE COOKBOOK THAT COUNTS. The recipes included have been carefully tested and thoughtfully evaluated. To establish the character and format of our cookbook we enlisted the help of interested friends, the indulgence of families and the advice of many professionals, all of whom have given generously of their time, patience and skills.

THE COOKBOOK THAT COUNTS has been compiled for the benefit of The Lawrence Country Day School, an independent co-educational school which has served an ever growing community on the South Shore of Long Island since 1891.

The Cookbook Committee

Mrs. Crowell Baker
Mrs. William B. Bowring
Mrs. Edward N. Carpenter
Mrs. Ryland E. D. Chase
Mrs. John H. Claiborne, Jr.
Mrs. John M. Emery
Mrs. Chalmers Handy
Mrs. Seton Ijams
Mrs. James B. Ketcham
Mrs. Peter Posmantur
Mrs. Edgar B. Robbins
Mrs. Bruce Tucker
Mrs. W. James Wade
Mrs. Martin F. Weiner

to serve

HORS D'OEUVRES
for 4

CHUTNEY CHEESE SPREAD

Preparation: 10 min.
Chilling: 2-1/2 hr.

6 oz. cream cheese, softened
4 oz. sharp Cheddar cheese,
2 tbsp. dry sherry
1/2 tsp. curry powder
1/4 tsp. salt
1/4 c. finely chopped chutney
1 tbsp. minced chives

Combine cheeses, sherry, curry and salt. Blend well. Stir in chutney. Chill. Turn into serving dish and top with chives.

CREAM CHEESE AND CAVIAR

Preparation: 5 min.

8 oz. cream cheese, softened
1/2 c. sour cream
1 tbsp. onion juice
4 oz. red caviar
Melba toast

Reserve 1 spoonful of the caviar as a garnish for the top. Mix cream cheese, sour cream, onion juice and lastly the caviar. Chill. Serve with Melba toast.

EGGS STUFFED WITH SALMON

Preparation: 30 min.
Chilling: 2 hr.

6 eggs, hard-boiled
6 oz. smoked salmon, minced
2 tbsp. lemon juice
1 tbsp. capers, chopped
1 tbsp. onion, grated
1/8 tsp. pepper
2 tbsp. mayonnaise
capers and green scallions

Cut eggs in half lengthwise and remove yolks. Mash yolks well. Mix salmon and capers with yolks, grated onion, salt, pepper, lemon juice and mayonnaise. Stuff egg whites with the mixture. Garnish with capers and chopped scallions. Chill.

FISH EYES

Preparation: 10 min.
Chilling: 2-1/2 hr.

2 cans beef consomme
3 env. unflavored gelatin
1 can (7 oz.) crabmeat
　or 1 carrot, slivered
　or 3 eggs, hard-boiled and sliced
12 Melba rounds
1/2 c. mayonnaise

Bring consomme to boil. Add gelatin, softened in cold water. Stir until dissolved. Put 1 tsp. in each section of a plastic egg carton. Refrigerate 1/2 hr. Add 1-1/2 tsp. crabmeat (or carrot or egg) to each and cover with remaining consomme. Refrigerate until firm, about 2 hr. Spread Melba rounds with mayonnaise and put 1 dome-shaped "fish eye" on each.

HORS D'OEUVRES
for 4

OYSTERS ROCKEFELLER

Preparation: 25 min.
Broiling: 10 min.

12 oysters in shells
3/4 c. sour cream
3 cloves garlic, crushed
salt and pepper to taste
3 tbsp. grated Parmesan cheese
bread crumbs
1 tbsp. butter
1/2 c. heavy cream, whipped
1 c. frozen chopped spinach

Remove oysters from shells, reserving bottom shell of each. Mix 1/4 cup sour cream with a little crushed garlic, salt and pepper and put 1 tsp. of mixture in each bottom shell. Cover with oysters, then with spinach which has been mixed with balance of sour cream, garlic, salt and pepper. Sprinkle with cheese and bread crumbs. Dot with butter. Broil about 5 min. Add a tbsp. or whipped cream and broil about 5 min.

NOTE: Clams can be substituted for oysters.

SPEEDY PATE

Preparation: 30 min.
Chilling: 2 hr.

1/2 lb. calf's liver, sliced
3 tbsp. oil
2 med. onions, chopped
2 eggs, hard-boiled
2 slices white bread
salt and pepper to taste
oil or brandy (optional)
cocktail rye bread slices

Saute liver and onions in oil for 10 min. Put in wooden chopping bowl with eggs, bread, salt and pepper. Chop finely. If too dry, add either oil or brandy until smooth. Chill. Serve with rye slices.

STUFFED CLAMS

Preparation: 10 min.
Baking: 30 min.

1 can (8 oz.) clams
1/2 c. bread crumbs
2 cloves garlic, chopped
1 tbsp. chopped onion
1 tbsp. chopped parsley
1 tbsp. olive oil
1/8 tsp. oregano
12 clam shells
 or 4 scallop shells
grated Parmesan cheese

Saute garlic, onions, parsley, oregano and 1/4 cup bread crumbs in olive oil (about 2 min.) until garlic and onions start to brown. Mix with clams, clam juice and salt, Spoon into shells. Sprinkle lightly with remaining bread crumbs and cheese. Bake at 350 degrees for 25-30 min.

SOUPS
for 4

COLD AVOCADO SOUP

Preparation: 15 min.
Chilling: 2 hr.

3 chicken bouillon cubes
2 c. boiling water
2 avocados, mashed
1 tbsp. lemon juice (approx.)
1 c. sour cream
4 slices bacon, cooked and crumbled
2 tbsp. chopped chives
salt and pepper to taste

Make broth of bouillon cubes and boiling water. Cool about 10 min. and pour into blender. Add avocado and lemon juice. Blend on low speed until smooth. Add sour cream 1/4 cup at a time, blending between each addition. Season to taste with salt and pepper. Chill for 2 hr. Serve garnished with chives and bacon.

CLAM CHOWDER

Preparation: 5 min.
Cooking: 15 min.

1 can (8 oz.) minced clams
1 can potato soup
1 clam-can milk
2 bay leaves
2 good grinds of pepper

Put all ingredients in double boiler. Stir over low heat.

CRABMEAT SOUP

Preparation: 10 min.
Cooking: 10 min.

1 can cream of tomato soup
1 can (7 oz.) crabmeat
1/2 soup-can milk or cream
1/4 c. sherry
dash Worcestershire

Drain crabmeat and mix with remaining ingredients in a saucepan. Heat, stirring, to serving temperature.

CREAM OF BROCCOLI SOUP

Preparation: 40 min.
Cooking: 10 min.

1 pkg. frozen chopped broccoli
1 c. white sauce (see index)
1 c. strong chicken broth
1/4 c. dry white wine
small sprigs of fresh broccoli
nutmeg or mace to taste
salt and pepper to taste

Cook broccoli according to pkg. directions. Puree broccoli and sauce together in blender. In a medium-sized saucepan, blend puree, chicken broth and wine. Heat to serving temperature and correct seasoning. Garnish with sprigs of fresh broccoli and a sprinkling of nutmeg or mace in each cup.

SOUPS
for 4

ESCAROLE SOUP

Preparation: 45 min.
Cooking: 10 min.

1 lb. escarole
2 tbsp. butter
1-1/2 c. chopped onion
4 c. chicken broth or stock
1 tsp. dried fines herbes
salt and pepper to taste

Wash escarole and discard thick center ribs. Break leaves. In large saucepan melt butter and saute chopped onions lightly. Add 2 cups broth and simmer onions until transparent. Add escarole and stir, coating leaves with broth and butter. Cover and simmer for 5 min. or until escarole has wilted. Season with herbs and pepper. Blend half the escarole mixture, including broth, in blender for 1 min. Pour into bowl and blend other half. Return both halves to saucepan. Add remaining broth. Heat and add salt.

GAZPACHO

Preparation: 1/2 hr.
Chilling: 8 hr.

1 c. chopped, peeled tomatoes
1/2 c. chopped green pepper
1/2 c. chopped celery
1/2 c. chopped cucumber
1/4 c. chopped onion
2 tsp. snipped parsley
2 tsp. snipped chives
1 sml. garlic clove, minced
2-3 tbsp. tarragon wine vinegar
2 tbsp. oil
1 tsp. salt
1/4 tsp. fresh pepper
1/2 tsp. Worcestershire
2 c. tomato juice
1/2-1 c. croutons

Combine all ingredients except croutons. Puree in blender. Chill 8 hr. Garnish with croutons.

SOUPS
for 4

ONION SOUP

Preparation: 10 min.
Cooking: 20 min.

3 med. onions, chopped
1 tbsp. shortening
1 tsp. flour
1 can beef bouillon
1-1/2 soup-cans water
1 tbsp. Worcestershire
salt and pepper to taste
sherry to taste
1/2 c. grated Parmesan cheese

Saute onions in shortening until deep brown. Stir in flour. In a saucepan bring remaining ingredients, except cheese and sherry, to a boil. Add onions and simmer covered for 20 min. Just before serving, add sherry. Garnish with cheese.

SPINACH CURRY SOUP

Preparation: 20 min.

1 pkg. frozen chopped spinach, cooked
2 c. chicken stock
2 tbsp. flour
1 tbsp. curry
salt and pepper to taste
2 cans (13-oz. size) evaporated milk

Blend drained spinach until pureed, gradually adding stock. Pour into saucepan and add other ingredients. Heat until thick stirring occasionally. Correct seasonings. Can be served hot or cold.

SPINICHICKEN SOUP

Preparation: 15 min.

1 c. cooked spinach, chopped and drained
1 can chicken and rice soup
1 can clear chicken soup
1-1/2 tbsp. flour
2 tbsp. butter
salt and pepper to taste

Blend butter and flour over low heat. Add remaining ingredients, stirring until smooth. Correct seasonings and heat to serving temperature.

STRIPED SOUP

Preparation: 20 min.

1 can cream of tomato soup
1 can pea soup
1-1/2 soup-cans water or milk
2 oz. sherry (opt.)

In separate saucepans, heat tomato soup, diluted with 1/2 can water or milk, and pea soup, diluted with 1 can water or milk. 1 oz. sherry can be added to each. To serve: Pour simultaneously and at equal speeds from opposite sides into a soup bowl. They will meet, but not blend, at the middle.

SOUPS
for 4

COLD TOMATO SOUP

Preparation: 10 min.
Chilling: 2 hr.

1 can cream of tomato soup
1-1/2 c. tomato juice
1/4 c. lemon juice
1/4 c. chicken broth
1 tbsp. Worcestershire
3 drops Tabasco
1 tbsp. chopped basil
salt and pepper to taste
2 c. cottage cheese
lemon slices and parsley

Blend all ingredients except cottage cheese. Chill. Just before serving, add cottage cheese. Serve garnished with lemon and parsley.

MEATS
for 4

BEEF AND NOODLES MILANESE

Preparation: 1 hr.
Cooking: 45 min.

1 med. onion, chopped
1 clove garlic, minced
2 tbsp. butter
1 lb. ground beef
1 can (4 oz.) mushrooms
1 can (8 oz.) tomato sauce
1 can (6 oz.) tomato paste
1 bay leaf, crumbled
2 tsp. salt
1 tsp. oregano
2 eggs
1 tbsp. salad or olive oil
1 pkg. (8 oz.) wide noodles
1 pkg. frozen chopped spinach, drained
1/4 c. chopped parsley
1 c. (1/2 lb.) pot cheese
1/4 c. grated Parmesan cheese
1 tsp. basil

Cook and drain noodles. Brown onion and garlic lightly in butter. Add ground beef and cook until brown. Stir in mushrooms and liquid, tomato sauce, tomato paste, bay leaf, 1 tsp. salt and oregano. Simmer 15 min. Beat 1 egg in medium size bowl and pour over the noodles, stirring well. Beat second egg in same bowl. Add spinach, olive oil, parsley, pot cheese, Parmesan cheese, 1 tsp. salt and basil. Mix well. Pour half of the tomato mixture into shallow baking dish, 8-10 cup size. Layer half of the noodles on the sauce. Spread with spinach-cheese mixture. Repeat noodle layer and top with the rest of tomato mixture. Bake covered at 350 degrees for 45 min.

BEEF-STUFFED ZUCCHINI

Preparation: 1 hr.
Baking: 30-40 min.

1 lrg. zucchini
1 lb. ground beef
2 onions, chopped
1 c. bouillon, or tomato juice
1/2 tsp. Worcestershire
1/4 tsp. garlic juice
1/4 c. chopped parsley
1/4-1/2 c. bread crumbs
1/4 c. butter, melted
1/4 c. grated Parmesan cheese
salt and pepper to taste

Halve zucchini lengthwise. Keeping the shells intact, remove and chop meat. In a large frying pan, saute beef, onions and zucchini meat. Add stock to keep mixture moist. Simmer about 15 min. Season with salt, pepper, Worcestershire, garlic juice and parsley. Fill the zucchini halves and sprinkle with bread crumbs, melted butter and Parmesan cheese. Bake uncovered in shallow baking dish at 350 degrees for 30-40 min.

MEATS
for 4

✓ **SAUCE-POT MEATBALLS** Preparation: 20 min.
                          Cooking: 25 min.

1 pkg. onion soup mix
1-1/4 c. water
2 cans (8-oz. size) tomato sauce
1 lb. ground beef
1/2 tsp. garlic salt
1/2 tsp. thyme
1/4 tsp. pepper
1 tbsp. chopped parsley

In deep, thick saucepan, bring quickly to boil onion soup mix, water and 1-1/2 cans tomato sauce. Simmer covered 10 min. Mix ground beef, seasonings, parsley and remaining tomato sauce. Shape into meatballs and add to sauce. Simmer gently uncovered 25 min. turning occasionally.

✓ **TURKISH MEAT LOAF**   Preparation: 25 min.
                          Baking: 1 hr.

1-1/2 lb. ground beef
1 egg, beaten
2 thin slices white bread *1/2 c. Matzah Meal*
1 onion, grated
1 tbsp. olive oil
2 garlic cloves, crushed
1 tsp. allspice
1 tbsp. ground caraway seed
2 tbsp. chopped dill
salt and pepper to taste
1/2 c. water

Soak bread slices in water. Squeeze dry and shred. Place meat and other ingredients, except water, in bowl and knead well. Form into meat loaf. Place in baking pan and add water. Bake at 350 degrees for 1 hr.

INEBRIATED BEEF ROAST Preparation: 10 min.
                           Marinating: 8 hr.
                           Broiling: 35 min.

2" thick beef roast
2 tsp. tenderizer
1 c. water
1/4 c. whiskey
2-1/2 oz. soy sauce
1/2 c. brown sugar
1/4 c. lemon juice
3 tbsp. cooking oil
1/4 lb. fresh mushrooms, sliced
2 tbsp. butter

Place roast in shallow bowl and apply tenderizer. Mix other ingredients and marinate in refrigerator overnight. Broil 5" above charcoal fire, basting and turning often, approximately 35 min. for rare. Saute mushrooms in butter. Slice meat in thin strips across the grain. Add mushrooms to heated marinade and pour over sliced meat.

MEATS
for 4

STUFFED BEEF ROLL

Preparation: 30 min.
Cooking: 1 hr.

1-1/2 lb. round steak
1/4 lb. pork sausage
1/2 c. soft bread crumbs
1 apple, very thinly sliced
1 tsp. salt
1/4 tsp. pepper
2 tbsp. shortening
1 c. red wine
2 tbsp. flour

Preheat skillet. Pound steak thin, but do not tear. Work sausage smooth and spread on top of beef. Place bread crumbs and apple slices over sausage. Season with salt and pepper. Roll up jelly-roll fashion and secure with toothpicks. Melt shortening and brown meat on all sides. Reduce heat and add wine. Cover and braise 1 hr. or until tender, adding water if necessary. Remove meat. Make paste of flour and a bit of cold water. Add to skillet. Stir until smooth.

QUICK DIP SANDWICH

Preparation: 10 min.
Cooking: 25 min.

2 cubed steaks
salt and pepper to taste
1 onion, chopped
1 tbsp. cooking oil
1 beef bouillon cube
1 c. hot water
1/2 c. ketchup
1/2 tsp. Worcestershire
4 onion rolls, split

Cut steaks in half and season with salt and pepper. Brown in cooking oil with onions. Combine bouillon cube, water, ketchup and Worcestershire sauce. Pour over steaks. Simmer covered 20-25 min. Dip cut sides of rolls in sauce and place steaks between halves to form sandwiches.

SALISBURY STEAK

Preparation: 30 min.
Cooking: 10 min.

1 lb. ground round steak
1 c. fine bread crumbs
2 eggs, lightly beaten
1/2 c. dry red wine
1/2 c. heavy cream
1/4 c. chopped onion
2 tbsp. finely chopped parsley
1 tsp. salt
1/4 tsp. black pepper
4 tbsp. butter
1/2 lb. mushrooms, sliced
2 c. canned beef gravy

Combine in large bowl meat, bread crumbs, eggs, half the wine, cream, onion, parsley, salt and pepper. Mix lightly and shape into 4 oval cakes. Melt butter in a heavy skillet and fry cakes until well-browned on both sides. Add the mushrooms and cook 3 min. longer. Add gravy and remaining wine. Bring to a boil, cover and simmer until meat is cooked through, about 10 min.

MEATS
for 4

SWEETBREADS

Preparation: 15 min.
Reheating 5 min.

1 lb. sweetbreads
4 c. water
2 tbsp. vinegar
2 cans cream of mushroom soup
    or 2 c. fresh mushroom sauce
salt and pepper to taste
4 slices toast

Boil sweetbreads in water and vinegar for 10 min. Drain and devein. Add mushroom sauce or soup. Season with salt and pepper. Heat. Serve over toast.

LAMB AND EGGPLANT CASSEROLE

Preparation: 20 min.
Baking: 30 min.

1/3 c. butter or oil
1 med. eggplant, peeled
2 c. cooked lamb, cut in bite-sized pieces
2 tbsp. chopped onion
salt and pepper to taste
1 tsp. oregano
1 can (8 oz.) tomato sauce
1/4 c. grated Parmesan cheese
1/4 lb. Mozzarella cheese

Cut eggplant into long slices about 1/2" wide. Brown in butter and place in buttered, shallow baking dish. Cover with lamb. Brown onion and sprinkle over lamb. Season with salt, pepper and oregano. Cover with tomato sauce. Sprinkle with Parmesan cheese. Bake at 350 degrees for 20 min. Put thinly sliced Mozzarella on top and bake uncovered for 10 min. or until cheese is melted and slightly browned.

LAMB KEBABS

Preparation: 5 min.
Marinating: 5 hr.
Cooking: 20 min.

1 c. yoghurt
1-1/2 tsp. salt
1/2 tsp. pepper
4 cloves garlic, crushed
1 lb. lean lamb, 1" cubes
1/4 lb. lamb fat, 1/2" cubes
Syrian bread
4 tomatoes, quartered
4 onions, quartered

Mix yoghurt, salt, pepper and garlic in large bowl. Marinate meat and fat cubes in yoghurt mixture for at least 5 hr. Skewer meat, fat and vegetable quarters to desired quantity. Cook over charcoal fire until meat is well-cooked and fat is crisp. Remove meat from skewers and eat by hand wrapped in Syrian bread with vegetables alongside.

MEATS
for 4

GREEK ROAST LEG OF LAMB

Preparation: 15 min.
Roasting: 2 hr. 20 min.

1/2 leg of lamb (4-lb.)
1 tbsp. salt
1 tbsp. black pepper,
3 tsp. oregano
2 cloves garlic, sliced
1/4 c. butter
juice of 1 lrg. lemon
2 onions, chopped
4 sprigs parsley
3 dried mushrooms
1-1/2 c. water

Preheat oven to 500 degrees. Place lamb, skin side up, on rack in open roasting pan. Rub meat with mixture of salt, pepper and oregano. Push slices of garlic 1/2" into meat in slashes made by knife all over meat surface. Melt butter, add lemon juice and pour over meat. Add onion, mushrooms, parsley and 1/2 cup water to pan. Place in oven and roast at 500 degrees for 20 min. Add remaining water and lower oven temp. to 350 degrees. Roast to desired degree of doneness, approximately 2 hr. for medium-well done. Baste occasionally.

CALF'S LIVER MILANESE

Preparation: 30 min.

4 slices calf's liver, 1/2"
flour
1 egg, lightly beaten
bread crumbs
1/4 c. butter
2 tbsp. safflower oil
4 lemons, thinly sliced
salt and pepper to taste

In a plastic bag, dust the slices of liver with flour. Add salt and pepper. Dip in the egg and then the bread crumbs. Fry in the oil and butter until golden brown and cooked through (5-6 min. each side). Do not overcook. Garnish with lemon slices.

PORK CUTLETS A LA CHARCUTIERE

Preparation: 1 hr.
Cooking: 25 min.

2 tbsp. butter
1 lrg. onion, chopped
1 tbsp. flour
1 c. beef bouillon
1/2 c. white wine
1/2 tsp. salt
4 peppercorns
4 tbsp. chopped gherkins
1 tsp. French mustard
4 pork cutlets

Melt butter in saucepan and add onion. Cook until tender, without burning. Add flour and mix well. Cook until yellow. Add stock, wine, salt and peppercorns. Boil gently for 30-40 min. then add gherkins and mustard. Grill or fry cutlets for 20-25 min. Place on warm serving dish and cover with sauce.

MEATS
for 4

VEAL CHOPS IN WHITE WINE

Preparation: 15 min.
Baking: 1 hr. 15 min.

4 lrg. veal chops
2 med. onions, chopped
20 med. size mushroom caps
3 tomatoes, cut-up
2-1/2 c. white wine
salt to taste
paprika to taste

Brown chops in hot, dry skillet, about 1 min. each side. Put into large open pan on top of onions, tomatoes and mushrooms. Add salt, paprika and enough wine to cover vegetables before adding veal. Bake at 375 degrees for about 1 hr. 15 min. Baste frequently. Add more wine if necessary.

VEAL CUTLETS IN SOUR CREAM

Preparation: 45 min.

1 lrg. veal cutlet
2 tbsp. butter
1/4 c. rye whiskey
3/4 c. beef consomme
1 pt. sour cream
salt and pepper to taste
cayenne to taste
paprika
parsley

Melt butter in large, heavy skillet. Brown veal on both sides. Add consomme, salt and cayenne. Cover and simmer for 35 min. or until tender. Remove cutlet to serving dish and add whiskey and pepper. Scrape pan drippings into sauce. Bring to boil and cover. Cook 5 min. Add sour cream, return almost to boil and pour over veal. Garnish with paprika and parsley.

ROGNONS DE VEAU EN CASSEROLE

Preparation: 25 min.
Heating: 10 min.

7 tbsp. butter
3-4 veal kidneys
 or 8-12 lamb kidneys
2 tbsp. minced shallots
 or scallions
1/2 c. dry vermouth
1 tbsp. lemon juice
3 tbsp. Dijon mustard
salt and pepper to taste
1 c. sour cream
3 tbsp. paprika (opt.)

In large skillet, heat 4 tbsp. butter until foam starts to subside. Roll kidneys in butter. Cook uncovered, turning often. Do not let butter brown. (Cooking time is approx. 10 min. for veal, 5 min. for lamb.) Remove kidneys. Cook shallots in same pan for 1 min. Add vermouth and lemon juice. Boil rapidly until sauce is reduced to about 4 tbsp. Remove from heat and swirl in mustard, mashed with 3 tbsp. butter. Add salt, pepper, sour cream and paprika, mixing well. Cut kidneys into crosswise slices about 1/4". Add with juice to pan. Stir over low heat until hot but not boiling.

POULTRY & GAME
for 4

BARBECUED CHICKEN

Preparation: 10 min.
Baking: 1-1/2 hr.

1 roasting chicken, cut-up
10 oz. Russian dressing
1 jar (12 oz.) apricot jam
1 pkg. onion soup mix

Blend Russian dressing, preserves and onion soup mix. Pour over chicken in ungreased 1-2 qt. baking dish. Bake uncovered at 350 degrees for 1-1/2 hr.

BERMUDA CHICKEN

Preparation: 10 min.
Baking: 1 hr. 5 min.

3-lb. broiling chicken, cut-up
2 lrg. Bermuda onions, sliced
1/4 c. white wine
salt
poultry seasoning
paprika

Using a large sheet of aluminum foil as a dish, lay onion slices on foil. Place chicken pieces (skin side up), on onions Fold foil up to hold wine. Add wine. Sprinkle top of chicken with salt, poultry seasoning and paprika. Fold foil over chicken. Bake at 400 degrees for 50 min. Open foil and bake for 15 min. more.

CHICKEN A L'ORANGE

Preparation: 15 min.
Cooking: 45 min.

1 chicken, cut-up
1/4 c. butter
1 c. orange juice
2 tbsp. slivered orange rind
1/4 tsp. ginger
1/4 tsp. nutmeg
2 tsp. currant jelly
salt and pepper to taste
paprika

Sprinkle chicken with salt, pepper and paprika. In large saucepan melt butter, brown chicken and remove from pan. Stir orange juice, rind, ginger, nutmeg and jelly into pan juices, loosening brown particles. Replace chicken and simmer uncovered about 45 min.

Bake 350 1 1/2 hr.

CHICKEN BREASTS AND CHIPPED BEEF

Preparation: 10 min.
Baking: 3 hr.

4 whole chicken breasts, boned and skinned
4 slices bacon
1 can cream of mushroom soup
1/2 soup-can milk
1 c. sour cream
1 jar (2-1/2 oz.) chipped beef
sherry (opt.)

Wrap each chicken breast in bacon and place in baking dish lined with chipped beef. Blend soup, milk and sour cream and add to casserole. Bake uncovered at 300 degrees for 2-1/2—3 hr. This can be cooked ahead and reheated. Add sherry or milk if gravy gets too thick.

POULTRY & GAME
for 4

✓ CHICKEN BREASTS PIQUANT

Preparation: 5 min.
Baking: 1-1/2 hr.

3/4 c. rose wine
1/4 c. soy sauce
1/4 c. salad oil
2 tbsp. water
1 tsp. ground ginger
1/4 tsp. oregano
1 tbsp. brown sugar
4 whole chicken breasts, split
1-2 tsp. arrowroot (opt.)

Combine all ingredients except arrowroot and pour over chicken breasts in baking dish. Bake covered at 375 degrees for 1-1/2 hr. Thicken sauce gently with a little arrowroot smoothly dissolved in cold water if desired.

CURRIED CHICKEN

Soaking: 1-1/2 hr.
Preparation: 20 min.
Cooking: 1 hr.

1 frying chicken, cut-up
2 tbsp. lemon juice
2-3 c. water
1/2 c. flour
1/4 c. oil
2 med. onions, sliced
1 scallion, chopped
1 stalk celery, quartered
1 tsp. curry powder
1/4 tsp. garlic powder
1/4 tsp. onion powder
1/4 tsp. thyme
salt and pepper to taste

Soak chicken pieces in lemon juice and salt for 1-1/2 hr. Rinse and season with salt and pepper. Rub with flour and brown on all sides in hot oil. Remove chicken and pour off hot oil, keeping brown drippings in skillet. Add onions, scallion, celery and curry powder to skillet. Saute a few minutes and add water and balance of ingredients, except chicken. Blend well and simmer 5 min. Add chicken and simmer covered about 1 hr. or until tender. Add more water during cooking if necessary.

CHICKEN HASH A LA RITZ

Preparation: 45 min.
Broiling: 15 min.

3 c. boiled and diced white
  chicken
1 c. light cream
2 c. milk
2 tbsp. butter
2 tbsp. flour
1/2 c. heavy cream
1 egg, beaten
2 tbsp. heavy cream, whipped
salt and pepper to taste

Put light cream in saucepan and cook until reduced by 1/2. Heat butter in another pan, add flour, then slowly pour in milk, stirring constantly to make sauce. Continue cooking until reduced to 1 cup. Stir in heavy cream. Add 1 cup of this mixture to the chicken and place in casserole. Add egg and whipped cream to remaining sauce and pour on top. Brown under broiler.

POULTRY & GAME
for 4

CHICKEN MARSALA

Preparation: 10 min.
Cooking: 15 min.

4 whole chicken breasts, boned and split
1/2 c. margarine
seasoned flour
1/4 lb. mushrooms
2 beef bouillon cubes
1/2 c. boiling water
2 oz. Marsala wine
3 tbsp. lemon juice

Melt margarine in skillet. Dredge chicken in seasoned flour (any seasoning you like, but do include oregano) and brown in margarine. Add mushrooms and brown. Stir bouillon cubes into boiling water. Add wine and lemon juice. Pour over chicken and simmer uncovered 12-15 min. or until tender.

CHICKEN TOUR D'ARGENT

Preparation: 30 min.
Cooking: 10 min.

1 chicken (3 lb.) or 2 whole chicken breasts, split
3 tbsp. butter, melted
1 tbsp. chopped shallots
1/2 c. dry vermouth
1/2 c. dry white wine
1/2 c. veal gravy
4 tbsp. chopped mushrooms
1 tbsp. chopped cooked ham
1/4 tsp. tarragon
4 slices bacon, fried
salt and pepper to taste

Brown chicken well in butter. Remove chicken. Add shallots to pan and cook slowly until transparent. Add mushrooms and cook 2 min. Deglaze pan with wine and vermouth. Add veal gravy and boil hard until slightly reduced. Return chicken to sauce and simmer uncovered 10 min. basting frequently. Add chopped ham and tarragon. Season with salt and pepper. Sprinkle with crumbled bacon. May be done well ahead and reheated uncovered.

CHICKEN LIVERS IN RED WINE SAUCE

Preparation: 20 min.
Cooking: 10 min.

1 lb. chicken livers
1-1/2 c. red wine
4 tsp. cornstarch
3 tbsp. lemon juice
2 tbsp. sugar
scant 1/4 tsp. cinnamon
rice or toast points

Brown chicken livers with *no fat* in stick-proof pan. Remove to side dish. Add wine to pan and bring to boil. Remove from heat and slowly stir in cornstarch, which has been smoothly dissolved in lemon juice. Return to heat and bring just to a boil. Add seasonings and chicken livers. Stir until almost boiling. Serve on bed of rice or toast points.

POULTRY & GAME
for 4

DEEDEE'S DUCKLING A L'ORANGE

Preparation: 10 min.
Baking: 1 hr. 30 min.

1 duckling (approx. 5 lb.)
1 jar (10 oz.) orange marmalade
1 c. sherry
1 tsp. marjoram
1/2 tsp. fresh pepper
1 tsp. salt
1 can (11 oz.) mandarin orange sections in syrup

Prick duckling skin and place in roasting pan. Mix together marmalade, sherry, marjoram, salt and syrup from orange sections. Heat until marmalade has liquefied. Blend well and pour over duckling. Roast for 1-1/2 hr. at 325 degrees basting every 15 min. To serve, garnish with orange sections. Cover with 1 cup pan juices and serve remainder separately.

GOURMET TURKEY RICE CASSEROLE

Preparation: 1 hr.
Baking: 45 min.

1 box (5-1/2-oz.) Minute Rice
4 tbsp. butter
4 tbsp. flour
1 c. chicken broth
1 c. cream
1/3 c. sherry
1/2 tsp. Worcestershire
salt and pepper
1-1/2—2 c. diced cooked turkey
1 can (4 oz.) sliced mushrooms
2 tbsp. chopped parsley
buttered, fine bread crumbs

Cook rice according to pkg. directions. Melt butter and stir in flour. Add cream and broth and cook, stirring constantly, until mixture is thickened and smooth. Add sherry, Worcestershire, salt and pepper. Combine sauce with rice, turkey, mushrooms and parsley, mixing gently but thoroughly. Turn into greased casserole and top with bread crumbs. Bake uncovered at 350 degrees for about 45 min.

PHEASANT NORMANDY

Preparation: 20 min.
Baking: 1-1/2 hr.

1 lrg. pheasant, quartered
1/2 c. flour
3/4 c. butter, melted
4 apples, thinly sliced
1/2 c. heavy cream
3 tbsp. brandy
salt and pepper to taste

Dredge pheasant in flour and brown in 6 tbsp. butter over medium heat. In bottom of a medium casserole, make 2" layer of apples. Pour 3 tbsp. melted butter over apples. Arrange pheasant on top, adding more sliced apples to completely cover pheasant. Pour 3 tbsp. melted butter over casserole. Cover and bake at 375 degrees for 1-1/2 hr. Remove pheasant and add cream and brandy to apples. Mix well. Season to taste and serve pheasant on bed of apple mixture.

SEAFOOD
for 4

CRAB HOLLANDAISE

Preparation: 20 min.
Cooking: 5 min.

1 c. lump crabmeat
1 egg, hard-boiled and grated
2 tbsp. sherry
1/4 c. butter
1/2 tbsp. lemon juice
1-1/2 c. hollandaise sauce (see index)
generous dash of Tabasco
4 baked patty shells (opt.)

Melt butter in saucepan. Add crabmeat, grated egg and seasonings. Heat thoroughly. Place in 1-1/2-qt. casserole and cover with hollandaise. Brown under broiler.
OR, mound heated crabmeat mixture into patty shells, cover with hollandaise, place on cookie sheet and brown under broiler.

CRAB IMPERIAL

Preparation: 10 min.
Baking: 20 min.

4 tbsp. butter
2 tbsp. minced onion
1 tbsp. minced fresh parsley
1 tbsp. minced green pepper
1 lb. crabmeat chunks
1 tsp. salt
1/8 tsp. pepper
1 tsp. dry mustard
1 tsp. Worcestershire
Dash of Tabasco
1 egg yolk, beaten
4 tbsp. mayonnaise

Simmer onion, parsley and green pepper in butter. Add crabmeat and other ingredients. Stir to blend well. Mound into scallop shells or ramekins. Bake at 450 degrees for 20 min.

CRABMEAT SOUFFLE

Preparation: 20 min.
Baking: 45 min.

4 tbsp. butter
1/3 c. flour
1-1/3 c. milk
2 tsp. salt
1/8 tsp. pepper
1/8 tsp. dry mustard
4 eggs, separated
1-1/2 c. crabmeat, flaked and drained

Melt butter in saucepan. Blend in flour, then milk and cook gently, stirring with a wire whisk until thick. Add salt, pepper and dry mustard. Blend well. Whisk in egg yolks, one at a time. Add crabmeat and stir. Set aside to cool slightly. Beat egg whites stiff, but not dry. *Mix* half of the egg whites into the crabmeat mixture, then *fold* in the other half. Turn mixture into buttered 2-qt. souffle dish and bake at 350 degrees for 40-45 min.

SEAFOOD
for 4

MARINATED GREEN HALIBUT

Preparation: 10 min.
Chilling: 1 hr.
Cooking: 20 min.

4 lrg. slices halibut
1/2 c. oil
1/4 c. lemon juice
3 tsp. minced water cress
3 tsp. minced fresh dill
2 tsp. minced chives
3 tsp. minced onion
salt and pepper to taste

Put fish in a casserole. It is important that the fish fits the dish exactly. Mix the oil with the herbs and spices. Pour this marinade on the fish and leave it covered with foil in the refrigerator for about 1 hr. Cook covered at 450 degrees for 20 min.

LOBSTER TAILS A LA BARBER

Preparation: 30 min.
Cooking: 20 min.

8 frozen rock lobster tails
   (4-5-oz. size)
1/4 c. butter
1/4 c. sherry
2 tbsp. flour
1 tsp. paprika
3/4 c. light cream

Boil lobster tails about 7 min. Cut membrane and remove meat, keeping shells intact. Cut meat into little pieces. Cover both shells and meat and refrigerate 20 min. Before serving heat lobster in butter and sherry about 3 min. Stir in flour, paprika and cream. Cook until thick. Stuff lobster tails.

TOPPING:

2 c. bread crumbs
1/4 c. melted butter
1/4 c. snipped chives
1/4 tsp. salt
1/8 tsp. pepper

Combine all ingredients and spread lightly over lobster tails. Brown under broiler.

GRILLED SHRIMP

Preparation: 20 min.
Marinating: 1 hr.

2 lb. shrimp, uncooked
1 c. olive oil
1 tsp. salt
1 clove garlic, minced
4 tbsp. minced parsley
1/2 tsp. black pepper
2-3 c. cooked rice,

Clean shrimp. Mix remaining ingredients in large bowl. Marinate shrimp for 1 hr. Remove shrimp and thread on skewers. Broil 10 min. basting frequently with marinade. Turn skewers while broiling so all sides brown evenly. Unthread shrimp on bed of hot rice.

SEAFOOD
for 4

MY FAVORITE FISH DISH

Preparation: 15 min.
Baking: 25 min.

4 lrg. sole fillets
2 cans Newburg sauce
2 cans (4-1/2-oz. size) tiny shrimp, drained
salt and pepper to taste
grated Parmesan cheese
bread crumbs
paprika
2-3 tbsp. butter

Place fish fillets in shallow, greased ovenproof dish. Mix Newburg sauce, shrimp, salt and pepper. Pour over fish. Sprinkle with cheese, bread crumbs and paprika. Dot with butter. Bake at 375 degrees for about 25 min.

EASY FILLET OF SOLE

Preparation: 5 min.
Baking: 15 min.

Spray dish with Pam.
Sprinkle fish with pepper + Lawry's salt

4 fillets of sole
1 c. herb stuffing mix *or seasoned crumbs*
2 tbsp. dry vermouth
4 tbsp. butter
parsley
lemon wedges

Lay fillets flat in buttered 13" x 9" baking dish. Cover with stuffing mix. Sprinkle with vermouth and dot with butter. Bake uncovered at 350 degrees for 12-15 min. Garnish with parsley and lemon wedges.

FILLET OF SOLE EAST INDIAN

Preparation: 45 min.
Baking: 20 min.

6 fillets of sole
1/4 lb. fresh mushrooms, quartered
1 scallion, chopped with greens
1/4 c. white wine
2 tbsp. flour
2 tbsp. butter
1/2 c. milk
1 tsp. curry powder
salt and pepper to taste

Put fillets and onion in buttered skillet. Season with salt, pepper and curry powder. Add wine and cook slowly on top of stove until fish is white about 10 min. Remove fillets to casserole. Make sauce of butter, flour and milk, using same pan in which fish was cooked. Pour over fish in casserole. Garnish with mushrooms and dot with butter. Bake uncovered at 350 degrees for 20 min.

SEAFOOD
for 4

BAKED SEAFOOD CASSEROLE

Preparation: 15 min.
Chilling: 8 hr.
Baking: 1 hr.

1/2 lb. shrimp, cooked
1/2 lb. crabmeat
6 slices white bread
1/2 lb. sharp Cheddar cheese
3 eggs, beaten
1/2 tsp. dry mustard
1/2 tsp. salt
dash of pepper
2 c. milk
2 tbsp. sherry
1/4 lb. butter, melted
1 tsp. chopped fresh dill

Cube bread and cheese and arrange in layers in greased 1-1/2—2 qt. casserole with shrimp and crabmeat. Finish with layer of cheese on top. Pour melted butter over all. Mix mustard, salt, pepper, milk, eggs and sherry. Pour mixture over casserole. Refrigerate 8 hr. Bake, covered, at 350 degrees for 1/2—1 hr. Garnish with dill.

CHEESE & EGGS
for 4

SWISS FONDUE

Preparation: 20 min.

1 clove of garlic, split
1 lb. Swiss cheese, diced
3 tbsp. flour
2 c. dry white wine
1 tbsp. lemon juice
6 tbsp. kirsch or brandy
dash of nutmeg
dash of cayenne
dash of paprika
2 loaves of French bread

Dredge cheese in flour. Rub fondue pot with garlic. Add wine and place over moderate heat. When wine is hot (not boiling), add lemon juice, and add cheese a little at a time. Stir constantly with a wooden spoon until melted. Bring mixture to bubbling for an instant. Add kirsch and spices, stirring in figure 8 pattern until blended. Serve by dipping skewered bread cubes into cheese.

COTTAGE CHEESE PANCAKES

Preparation: 10 min.

4 eggs, separated
1 c. fine curd cottage cheese
1/4 c. flour
1/4 tsp. salt
melted butter
maple syrup
   or honey

Beat whites until stiff but not dry. Beat yolks until lemon-colored. Beat in cheese, flour and salt. Fold in egg whites. Bake on well-greased griddle until golden brown, turning only once. Serve with melted butter and warm maple syrup or honey.

CHEESE HAM SOUFFLE

Preparation: 30 min.
Baking: 40 min.

6 tbsp. butter
6 tbsp. flour
2 c. half and half
1-1/2 c. shredded, extra
   sharp Cheddar cheese
1/4 tsp. dry mustard
1 c. ground cooked ham
6 eggs, separated
1/4 tsp. cream of tartar
salt and pepper to taste

Preheat oven to 375 degrees. Melt butter, add flour and stir. Add warmed half and half and whisk until thickened. Add cheese and stir until melted. Add ham. Beat egg yolks with whisk until lemon colored. Add a little of cheese mixture to yolks and mix. Return all to saucepan, blending well. Beat egg whites with cream of tartar until stiff. Fold into cheese mixture. Pour into greased 2 qt. souffle dish. Bake 35-40 min.

CHEESE & EGGS
for 4

EGGS BENEDICTINE

Preparation: 20 min.

2 English muffins, split
butter
4 eggs
1 can (1-lb.) salmon
3 c. hollandaise sauce
 (see index)
parsley sprigs
paprika

Drain and flake salmon and heat in colander over simmering water. Toast and butter English muffins. Poach eggs. Mound salmon equally onto each muffin half. Top with a poached egg and spoon about 3/4 c. hollandaise sauce on each. Garnish with parsley and paprika.

EGGS LISA

Preparation: 10 min.

2 English muffins, split
4 eggs
2 tbsp. vinegar
4 slices ham or bacon
4 slices American cheese
Tabasco
salt and pepper to taste
butter

Butter muffins and toast on one side only. Cover each with slice of ham or broiled bacon and keep warm. Poach eggs in water and vinegar. Place cooked eggs on ham and top with cheese slices. Add several drops of Tabasco. Salt and pepper each. Broil about 2 min. or until cheese melts.

MONTE CRISTO SANDWICH

Preparation: 15 min.
Baking: 20 min.

8 slices bread
5 eggs
1/2 tsp. vanilla
1-1/2 tbsp. sugar
1 tsp. cinnamon
1/4 tsp. salt
1/2 c. milk or cream
peanut or corn oil
8 thin slices turkey
8 thin slices ham
4 thin slices Swiss cheese
cranberry sauce

In a shallow bowl, mix eggs, vanilla, sugar, cinnamon, salt and milk or cream. Soak bread in liquid. Deep fry in oil and drain. On 4 of the slices, place 2 slices each of turkey and ham and 1 slice of cheese. Cover with remaining slices. Bake at 350 degrees for 15-20 min. or until cheese is well melted. Serve with cranberry sauce.

POTATOES, RICE & PASTA
для 4

POMMES DE TERRE

Preparation: 10 min.
Baking: 20 min.

12 new potatoes, pared
1/4 lb. butter

Melt butter in small baking dish. Add potatoes. Cover tightly. Bake at 400 degrees for 20 min. shaking frequently.

POTATO HASH

Preparation: 15 min.
Baking: 20 min.

4 boiled potatoes
4 eggs, hard-boiled
1/2 c. bread crumbs
2 onions, thinly sliced
4 tbsp. butter
salt and pepper to taste
1 c. cream
parsley

Line the bottom of greased oven-proof dish with bread crumbs, then a layer each of thin potato slices and egg slices. Add a layer of onions, and salt and pepper. Dot with butter. Repeat, finishing with layer of bread crumbs. Pour cream over all and bake at 350 degrees for 20 min. Garnish with parsley.

POTATO SALAD

Preparation: 30 min.
Chilling: 2 hr.

1-1/2 c. boiled potatoes
1/4 c. chopped green pepper
1 tsp. salt
1 tbsp. chopped onion
1 tbsp. vinegar
mayonnaise to taste

Peel and dice potatoes. Mix with remaining ingredients. Chill.

NOODLE SPINACH TOSS

Preparation: 20 min.
Cooking: 10 min.

8 oz. med. egg noodles
1 pkg. frozen chopped spinach
1-1/2 tsp. lemon juice
1/8 tsp. nutmeg
1 c. sour cream
salt and pepper to taste

Cook noodles and spinach separately according to pkg. directions. Drain both. Combine with lemon juice, nutmeg, sour cream, salt and pepper. Toss lightly. Over low heat, bring to serving temperature, but do not boil.

POTATOES, RICE & PASTA
for 4

GREEK PILAF

Preparation: 10 min.
Cooking: 35 min.

- 3 tbsp. butter
- 1 med. onion, chopped
- 1 clove garlic, crushed
- 1/2 lb. sliced mushrooms
- 1 c. uncooked rice
- 2 c. chicken broth
- 1 tsp. salt
- 1/4 tsp. black pepper
- 3 tbsp. raisins
- 1/2 c. toasted slivered almonds

Saute onion in butter. Add garlic and mushrooms and saute briefly. Add rice and mix well, browning over high heat about 3-5 min. Add broiling broth, salt and pepper. Cover tightly and simmer over low heat for 20 min. Stir in raisins and nuts and continue cooking 10 min. or until raisins are heated through.

NOTE: Cooked peas, diced pimento, diced tomatoes or sliced, cooked sausage may be added.

GUATEMALAN SWEET POTATOES

Preparation: 20 min.
Baking: 20 min.

- 4 sweet potatoes
- 2 bananas
- 1/2 c. butter
- 1/2 c. milk
- 1 egg, beaten
- 1/3 tsp. salt
- 1/4 tsp. nutmeg

Boil sweet potatoes. Peel and mash with bananas. Season with salt and nutmeg. Add milk and egg. (Add more milk, if needed.) Place in greased 2-qt. baking dish. Bake at 350 degrees for 20 min.

SWEET POTATOES IN ORANGE SHELLS

Preparation: 10 min.
Baking: 20 min.

- 3 or 4 sweet potatoes
- 2 tbsp. melted butter
- 1/2 c. chopped walnuts
- 1/4 tsp. cinnamon
- 1/4 c. orange juice
- 4 orange shells (scooped out halves)
- 4 tbsp. butter
- 4 tbsp. brown sugar

Add melted butter to potatoes and mash well. Add chopped nuts and flavor with cinnamon and enough orange juice to make mixture the consistency of stiff dough. Spoon into orange shells and add a dab of butter and a little brown sugar to each one. Bake at 400 degrees until brown, approximately 20 min.

VEGETABLES
for 4

ARTICHOKES AND PEAS

Preparation: 5 min.
Baking: 30 min.

1 pkg. frozen artichoke hearts
1 pkg. frozen peas
1/3 c. lemon juice
1 clove garlic, minced
2 tbsp. water
2 tsp. dried thyme
1 tbsp. butter
salt and pepper to taste

Place all ingredients in 1-1/2-qt. baking dish. Bake uncovered at 350 degrees for 15 min. Separate artichokes hearts with fork. Bake 15 min. more or until tender.

ASPARAGUS EN CASSEROLE

Preparation: 15 min.
Baking: 45 min.

1/4 c. butter
2 c. canned asparagus
1 tsp. salt
1/8 tsp. pepper
3 eggs, beaten
1 c. grated American cheese
1-1/4 c. Ritz cracker crumbs
1 c. milk

Drain asparagus and cut into 2" pieces. Mix with other ingredients except butter. Pour into greased casserole. Melt butter and pour over top. Bake uncovered at 350 degrees for 45 min.

LIVELY GREEN BEANS

Preparation: 15 min.

1 tsp. prepared mustard
2 tsp. Worcestershire
1/4 c. butter, softened
1 pkg. frozen green beans or 1 can green beans

Cook and drain beans according to directions. Blend mustard and Worcestershire into butter and add to hot green beans.

BEETS IN SOUR CREAM

Preparation: 10 min.
Cooking: 15 min.

12 beets, cut in strips or,
1 can (1 lb.) shoestring beets
salt and pepper to taste
2 tbsp. vinegar
2 tbsp. sugar
2 tbsp. flour
2 tbsp. butter
1/2 c. sour cream

Cook beets if fresh. Drain if canned. In top of double boiler combine all other ingredients and heat, stirring constantly, until thick. Add beets and bring to serving temperature.

VEGETABLES
for 4

BRUSSELS SPROUTS SOUFFLE

Preparation: 40 min.
Cooking: 35 min.

4 tbsp. butter
1/4 c. flour
1/2 tsp. salt
1 c. milk
4 eggs, separated
4 oz. shredded sharp Cheddar cheese
1 pkg. frozen Brussels sprouts

Cook Brussels sprouts according to pkg. directions. Drain and chop. Melt butter. Blend in flour, salt and milk. Stir over low heat until thickened. Beat egg yolks until thick and lemon colored. Stir some of the sauce into egg yolks, then return to pan. Stir vigorously. Add cheese and continue stirring until melted. Add chopped sprouts. Stir to mix. Remove from heat. Beat egg whites until stiff but not dry, and fold into cream mixture. Turn into greased 1-1/2 qt. souffle dish. Bake at 350 degrees for 35 min.

CARROT SOUFFLE

Preparation: 35 min.
Cooking: 45 min.

1 bunch carrots (about 1 lb.)
1 c. white sauce (see index)
1/4 c. sugar
1/2 tsp. salt
4 eggs, separated

Preheat oven to 350 degrees. Pare carrots, cook in salted water until tender. Drain and mash. Combine with white sauce, sugar, salt and egg yolks. Cook about 1 min. longer. Remove from heat. Beat egg whites until stiff, but not dry, and fold into carrot mixture. Turn into 3 qt. souffle dish. Bake about 45 min.

BAKED CAULIFLOWER

Preparation: 45 min.
Baking: 15 min.

1 head cauliflower
1 can chicken bouillon or broth
1 onion, grated
salt and pepper to taste
1/2 c. shredded Cheddar cheese

Boil cauliflower in chicken broth until tender, 30-40 min. Mash in food mill or blender. Season with salt, pepper and grated onion. Put in 1-1/2 qt. ungreased baking dish. Sprinkle with cheese. Bake uncovered at 350 degrees for 10-15 min.

VEGETABLES
for 4

ZESTY CORN

Preparation: 5 min.
Cooking: 25 min.

3 slices bacon
1 pkg. frozen corn
2 tbsp. chopped parsley
1/4 tsp. salt
dash pepper
1-1/2 tbsp. chopped onion

Cut bacon into 1" pieces and fry until crisp. Remove bacon. Saute onion in 2 tbsp. bacon fat until delicately browned. Add frozen corn. Cover and cook until corn is thawed, stirring occasionally. Cook 5 min. longer. Add parsley and seasonings. Garnish with crumbled bacon.

BRAISED ENDIVE

Preparation: 15 min.
Cooking: 15 min.

6-8 heads of endive
dash of pepper,
    freshly ground
1/4 c. butter
1 tbsp. lemon juice
1 tsp. salt
2 tbsp. water

Slice endives in half, lengthwise, and put in skillet with 1" boiling water. Cover and simmer 6-7 min. Remove endive. Pour off water and dry pan. Melt butter in saucepan and lightly brown endives, cut side down. Add rest of ingredients. Cover and cook over very low heat about 15 min.

STUFFED MUSHROOMS

Preparation: 20 min.
Cooking: 5-10 min.

16 lrg. mushrooms
1 sml. onion, chopped
1/2 green pepper, chopped
2 oz. grated Parmesan cheese
2 tbsp. sherry
1 c. white sauce (see index)
2 tbsp. chopped parsley
4 tbsp. butter, melted
salt and pepper to taste

Remove stems from mushrooms and chop. Lightly saute onion, green pepper and chopped stems in 2 tbsp. melted butter. Add parsley, sherry, cheese and sauteed vegetables to white sauce. Place mushroom caps cup side down on ungreased baking sheet and brush with melted butter. Broil for 2 min. Invert and fill with stuffing, brush with melted butter and broil about 3 min.

VEGETABLES
for 4

MUSHROOM SOUFFLE

Preparation: 30 min.
Baking: 40 min.

1/4 c. butter
1/4 c. chopped onions
1/4 c. flour
3/4 c. milk
1/4 c. dry white wine
1 tsp. salt
1/8 tsp. pepper
4 egg yolks
1/2 lb. fresh mushrooms, finely chopped
5 egg whites
1/4 c. chopped parsley

Preheat oven to 375 degrees. Melt butter in saucepan, add onions and cook until tender. Add flour, blend and let it froth for 1-2 min. Stir in milk, beat with wire whisk and heat until hot and thick, whisking to keep smooth. Whisk in wine. Add salt, pepper and egg yolks, stirring between each yolk. Add mushrooms and blend well. Remove from heat and allow to cool. Beat egg whites until stiff, but not dry. Stir half of them into cooled mushroom mixture and carefully fold in other half. Pour into greased and floured 1-1/2 — 2-qt. souffle dish. Bake at 375 degrees for 35-40 min. Sprinkle with parsley. Serve immediately.

CREAMED ONIONS DELUXE

Preparation: 20 min.
Baking: 20 min.

6 lrg. onions, sliced
1/4 c. & 2 tbsp. butter
2 tbsp. flour
1 c. milk
4 tbsp. grated sharp Cheddar cheese
1/4 c. fresh bread crumbs
salt to taste

Saute onions in 1/4 cup butter until clear. Melt remaining butter and blend in flour and milk. Stir over low heat until thickened. Add 2 tbsp. cheese and salt. Pour sauce over onions in shallow dish. Sprinkle with bread crumbs and remaining cheese. Bake uncovered at 350 degrees for 20 min.

DUTCH TOMATOES

Preparation: 35 min.

2 pkg. frozen Welsh rarebit
4 tomatoes, halved
1/2 tsp. salt
4 slices bacon, cooked and crumbled
parsley sprigs

Prepare Welsh rarebit according to pkg. directions. Meanwhile, sprinkle tomatoes with salt and broil about 10 min. Pour rarebit over broiled tomatoes in ovenproof serving dish. Broil about 5 min. Sprinkle bacon on top and garnish with parsley sprigs.

VEGETABLES
for 4

TOMATO PUDDING

Preparation: 15 min.
Baking: 45 min.

8 slices bread,
  cut in sq.
1 can (1-lb. 12-oz.)
  tomatoes, sieved
1/2 tsp. salt
1/8 tsp. pepper
1 c. brown sugar
1/3 c. butter, melted

Combine and bring tomatoes, salt, pepper and sugar to a boil. Put bread squares in buttered deep dish (2-3 qt. size). Pour melted butter over squares and toss lightly. Pour hot tomato mixture over bread and bake uncovered at 350 degrees for 45 min. or until thick like a pudding. Halfway through cooking, push down bread with fork.

VEGETABLE PATTY

Preparation: 30 min.
Baking: 20 min.

2 boiled potatoes
1 c. cooked string beans
1 c. cooked peas
1/2 c. cooked carrots
1/2 c. cooked celery
2 eggs, beaten
1 onion, sliced and sauteed

Put vegetables through coarse grinder or blender at slow speed. Mix in eggs and shape into patties. Bake on greased baking sheet at 350 degrees until brown.

VEGETABLES ORIENTAL

Preparation: 5 min.
Cooking: 15 min.

1/2 c. thinly sliced onion
2 tbsp. oil
2 c. celery, sliced
  diagonally
1 c. frozen peas, uncooked
2 cans (3-oz. size) sliced
  mushrooms
1-1/2 c. chicken stock or broth
3 tsp. cornstarch
1 tsp. salt
1 tbsp. soy sauce
1/2 tsp. ground ginger

In large skillet, cook onion in oil until transparent. Stir in celery. Cook for 1 min. Stir in peas, cover and simmer 4-5 min. Dissolve cornstarch in small amount of cold water. Add to vegetables with broth, salt, soy sauce and ginger. Cook, stirring constantly, until sauce thickens slightly. Stir in mushrooms and serve.

VEGETABLES
for 4

ZUCCHINI WITH MUSHROOMS AND PEPPERS

Preparation: 20 min.
Cooking: 20 min.

1 lb. zucchini
2 peppers (red or green)
1/2 lb. fresh mushrooms
 or 1 oz. dried mushrooms
2 cloves garlic, crushed
1 tbsp. oregano
1 can (16-oz.) tomato puree
2 c. boiling water or stock
4 tbsp. olive oil
1 lrg. onion, sliced
2 tbsp. cornstarch
1/4 c. lemon juice
salt and pepper to taste

Wash zucchini thoroughly and cut into 1" cubes. Coarsely chop peppers. Wash, dry and slice mushrooms. (If dried are used, soak 10 min. in water to cover.) Heat oil in deep saucepan or skillet. Brown garlic and onions slightly. Add puree and boiling water or stock. When this comes to a boil, add zucchini, peppers and mushrooms. Cover and cook slowly for 20 min. Just before serving, add cornstarch smoothly dissolved in lemon juice and season with salt and pepper. Serve piping hot.

SALADS
for 4

NOTE: *A selection of Salad Dressings for tossed green or mixed salads appears in the Accompaniments Chapter.*

AVOCADO MOUSSE

Preparation: 25 min.
Chilling: 3-1/2 hr.

1 env. unflavored gelatin
1/2 c. cold water
3/4 c. boiling chicken broth
1 tsp. Worcestershire
1 tbsp. lemon juice
1 tsp. onion juice
1/2 tsp. sugar
1/2 tsp. salt
cayenne to taste
1/2 c. heavy cream, whipped
   or 1/2 c. sour cream
1/2 c. mayonnaise
1 c. ripe avocado, sieved
lettuce leaves
stuffed green olives

Soften gelatin in cold water. Add broth, Worcestershire, lemon and onion juices, sugar, salt and cayenne. Chill about 30 min. until slightly thickened. Fold in whipped or sour cream, mayonnaise and avocado. Whip with rotary beater and correct seasonings. Pour into 4-cup mold. Chill at least 3 hr. Unmold onto bed of lettuce. Garnish with sliced olives.

CELERY ROOT REMOULADE

Preparation: 40 min.
Chilling: 2 hr.

2 med. knobs celery root
1 tbsp. Dijon or
   Dusseldorf mustard
lemon juice to taste
3/4 c. mayonnaise
4 leaves Bibb lettuce

Pare celery knobs well. Cut into slices about 1/16" thick and cut slices into strips thinner than toothpicks. Combine mayonnaise, mustard and lemon juice. Add celery knob strips and chill until serving time. Serve individually on a leaf of lettuce. Good also as an appetizer.

SALADS
for 4

CUCUMBER ONION MOLD

Preparation: 1 hr.
Chilling: 2-3 hr.

2 cucumbers
1 med. onion, thinly sliced
1-1/2 c. sour cream
1/4 c. sugar
1/4 c. red wine vinegar
1 env. unflavored gelatin
1 tsp. chopped dillweed
2 tbsp. salt
1/4 tsp. white pepper
paprika
cherry tomatoes

Wash cucumbers and flute skins lengthwise with tines of a fork. Slice paper thin and place in layers in a medium bowl, sprinkling each layer liberally with salt. Put a smaller bowl on top to act as weight. Set aside for 1 hr. pouring off liquid as it accumulates. Add onion, sour cream, sugar, dillweed and pepper. Stir to blend. Soften gelatin in vinegar, and heat until dissolved. Mix well with cucumber mixture. Correct seasoning. Pour into oiled 3-cup mold and refrigerate until set. Serve on lettuce garnished with paprika and cherry tomatoes.

LIMA ROQUEFORT SALAD

Preparation: 15 min.
Chilling: 2 hr.

2 pkg. frozen baby lima beans
2 c. tangy French dressing
1 onion, chopped
4 oz. Roquefort cheese
tomato wedges
lettuce leaves

Cook limas according to pkg. directions. Drain. Add chopped onions to French dressing, and marinate. Just before serving add softened cheese and toss. Place on lettuce leaves and surround with tomato wedges.

PISSENLIT SALAD
(Dandelion greens)

Preparation: 20 min.
Cooking: 15 min.

1 lb. dandelion greens
6 slices bacon
2 tsp. sugar
1 tsp. salt
1/8 tsp. fresh black pepper
1/4 c. minced shallots
1/4 tsp. dry mustard
3 tbsp. red wine vinegar
1 tsp. mixed salad herbs
1/4 c. croutons

Remove roots or stems from greens. Wash in several changes of cold water. Dry well. Saute bacon until crisp. Remove, drain and crumble. Saute shallots in bacon grease until transparent. Add remaining ingredients except croutons and heat, stirring until sugar is dissolved. Put greens and bacon in salad bowl. Pour hot dressing over and toss lightly. Add croutons.

SALADS
for 4

SALMON MACARONI SALAD

Preparation: 30 min.
Chilling: 1 hr.

4 oz. macaroni
1 can (3-3/4-oz.) salmon
1/4 c. chopped dill pickle
1 sml. onion, minced
1/2 c. diced celery
1 c. cooked peas
1 tsp. salt
1/4 tsp. pepper
1/2 c. mayonnaise
salad greens

Cook macaroni according to pkg. directions. Drain and flake salmon with all ingredients except salad greens. Toss lightly and chill at least 1 hr. Serve on greens.

SATURDAY LUNCH

Preparation: 30 min.

1 green pepper
2 c. celery, including as many leaves as possible
1 c. Port du Salut cheese
1/2 c. raw broccoli
7 med. size mushrooms
2 eggs, hard-boiled
2 c. lamb, tongue, ham, turkey or duck
2 tsp. caraway seeds
1 bottle (8oz.) French dressing
4 tbsp. hot barbecue sauce
1 pinch of horseradish
radishes, tomatoes, water cress, scallions, red onion as garnish

Chop all ingredients and combine. Mix well and serve.
NOTE: No lettuce.

SPINACH-MUSHROOM SALAD

Preparation: 20 min.

1/2 lb. fresh young spinach
1/2 lb. fresh mushroom caps
1 sml. onion, thinly sliced
2 eggs, hard-boiled
10 slices bacon, cooked
1-1/2 c. Crowell's salad dressing (see index)

Destem spinach leaves and tear into bite-size pieces. Slice mushrooms and add to spinach in large salad bowl, along with onion and chopped eggs. Refrigerate covered with damp cloth if not serving immediately. Just before serving, add crumbled bacon and salad dressing. Toss well.

SALADS
for 4

MOLDED TUNA RING

Preparation: 15 min.
Chilling: 2 hr.

- 2 cans (7-oz. size) tuna, drained and flaked
- 1/2 c. chopped black olives
- 1/2 c. slivered almonds
- 1 env. unflavored gelatin
- 2 eggs, hard-boiled and chopped
- 1 c. sour cream
- 1-1/2 c. mayonnaise
- 1 tbsp. grated onion
- 1 tbsp. lemon juice
- 1/2 tsp. salt
- 1/2 c. oil and vinegar dressing

Soften gelatin in 1/2 cup cold water and mix over hot water until dissolved. Stir in 1 cup mayonnaise and sour cream. Add remaining ingredients. Turn mixture into 4-cup mold. Refrigerate until set. Mix remaining mayonnaise and dressing and serve alongside.

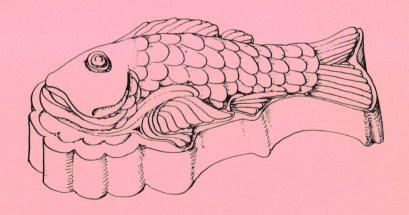

DESSERTS
for 4

NOTE: A large selection of Cakes, Pies, Cookies and Squares appears in the Accompaniments Chapter.

APPLE BETTY

Preparation: 10 min.
Baking: 1 hr.

8 sour apples, peeled and thinly sliced
3/4 c. sugar
1/2 tsp. cinnamon
1 tbsp. butter
1/2 c. bread crumbs

Arrange apples in layers in baking dish. Over each layer sprinkle blended sugar and cinnamon and dot with butter. Over top layer spread bread crumbs. Bake covered at 350 degrees for 1/2 hr. Continue baking uncovered for 1/2 hr. or until apples are soft and bread crumbs brown.

HARD SAUCE:

1/4 c. butter
3/4 c. sugar
a few drops vanilla

Cream butter and gradually add sugar, continuing to beat until thoroughly mixed. Add vanilla and blend.

APPLE PANCAKE

Preparation: 1/2 hr.
Baking: 10 min.

5 tbsp. granulated sugar
1 tsp. ground cinnamon
2 tbsp. butter
1-2 McIntosh apples
3 tbsp. all-purpose flour
1/4 tsp. baking powder
dash of salt
2 eggs, separated
3 tbsp. milk
sour cream
  or vanilla ice cream

Combine 2 tbsp. sugar and cinnamon and set aside. Melt butter in 10" oven-proof skillet and sprinkle sugar/cinnamon mixture evenly over it. Pare and core apples. Slice in 1/4" slices and arrange in mixture in skillet. Cook over low heat 5 min. Combine flour, baking powder, salt, egg yolks and milk. Beat egg whites, adding 3 tbsp. sugar gradually, until they form soft peaks. Fold into flour mixture. Pour batter over apple pieces, spreading evenly with spatula. Bake at 400 degrees for 10 min. or until golden and puffy. Loosen edges with spatula and invert onto plate. Serve with sour cream or vanilla ice cream.

DESSERTS
for 4

CHOCOLATE WAFFLES

Preparation: 10 min.
Baking: 3 min.
(per waffle)

1/2 c. shortening
3/4 c. sugar
2 eggs, beaten
1 tsp. vanilla
1-1/4 c. flour
1 tsp. baking powder
6 tbsp. cocoa
1/2 tsp. cinnamon
1/2 tsp. salt
1 pt. vanilla ice cream
 or 1 pt. heavy cream, whipped

Cream shortening. Add sugar slowly continuing to beat. Add eggs, flavoring and sifted dry ingredients. Mix well. (Mixture will be stiff.) Heat waffle iron, not as hot as for breakfast waffles. Place tablespoonful of mixture in each section Bake approximately 3 min. Serve with ice cream or whipped (sweetened) cream.

CREAMY CUSTARD

Preparation: 15 min.
Chilling: 2 hrs.

1/2 pt. heavy cream
1/2 c. sugar
1 env. unflavored gelatin
1 c. sour cream
1/2 tsp. vanilla

Mix heavy cream, sugar and gelatin in small saucepan. Set on low heat and stir until dissolved. Cool until slightly thickened and at room temperature. Fold in sour cream and vanilla. Turn into small, oiled mold and chill about 2 hr.

EASY PEACH MELBA

Preparation: 5 min.

4 cling peach halves
4 scoops vanilla ice cream
8 tbsp. raspberry jam
peach syrup

Drain peach halves, reserving syrup. Put a scoop of vanilla ice cream in each dessert bowl. Top with inverted peach half. Spoon on generous amount of raspberry jam, thinned with peach syrup.

GRAPES GLACEE

Preparation: 15 min.
Chilling: 8 hr.

1 lb. white seedless grapes
1/2 c. sour cream
1/2 c. light brown sugar

Stem and wash grapes. Mix with sour cream and brown sugar. Cover and refrigerate 8 hr. Serve in sherbet glasses.

DESSERTS
for 4

LEMON BLUFF

Preparation: 10 min.
Cooking: 20 min.
Chilling: 2 hr. (opt.)

1 c. sugar
1/4 c. flour
1/8 tsp. salt
juice and grated rind of 1 lemon
2 egg yolks, beaten
2 egg whites, stiffly beaten
1 c. heavy cream, whipped

Mix sugar, flour, salt, juice, grated rind and egg yolks together. Fold in egg whites. EITHER: Cook mixture in double boiler until thickened. Chill and serve with whipped cream. OR: Bake for 20 min. at 350 degrees in baking pan, surrounded by hot water. Serve with whipped cream.

QUICK CHOCOLATE MOUSSE

Preparation: 10 min.
Chilling: 1 hr.

1 egg plus 1 egg yolk
1 pkg. semi-sweet chocolate bits
1 tsp. vanilla
1 tsp. brandy
1 c. hot milk
pinch of salt

Place all ingredients in blender. Blend 1 min. Pour into glasses (or pots de creme) and chill.

SAINTE EMILION au CHOCOLAT

Preparation: 30 min.
Chilling: 12 hr.

1/4 lb. butter
1/2 c. sugar, plus a little
1 egg yolk
8 oz. bitter chocolate
1 c. milk
12-16 macaroons
rum or brandy

Cream butter and sugar together until well blended. Scald milk and let cool. Mix with yolk of egg. Melt chocolate over low flame with very little water. Stir in milk/egg mixture, then butter/sugar mixture. Stir carefully until absolutely smooth. In 1-1/2 qt. souffle dish arrange layer of macaroons soaked in a little rum or brandy. Over these pour layer of chocolate mixture, then another layer of macaroons, and so on, until dish is full, finishing with macaroons. Refrigerate for at least 12 hr.

to serve

8

HORS D'OEUVRES
for 8

CHEESE BALL

Preparation: 15 min.

16 oz. cream cheese
8 oz. cracker barrel
  cheese, sharp
8 oz. Old English cheese
8 oz. smoky cheese
6 oz. blue cheese
1 tbsp. Worcestershire
1/2 tsp. onion salt
1/2 c. pecans
1/2 c. chopped almonds
1 tbsp. chopped parsley

Let cheeses come to room temperature. Mix first 7 ingredients together and form into large ball. Roll in pecans, almonds and parsley. Can be frozen.

CHEESE BITS

Preparation: 10 min.
Baking: 6 min.

1 lb. Cheddar cheese
5 tbsp. blue cheese,
  crumbled
1 pkg. refrigerator
  buttermilk biscuits

Cut cheese into 16 1/4" cubes. Open and halve each biscuit. Fold half biscuit around each cube topped with 1 tsp. blue cheese. Pinch edges together. Bake at 475 degrees for 6 min. or until browned.

NOTE: Brick or Swiss cheese can be substituted for Cheddar.

HOT CLAM DIP

Preparation: 5 min.
Cooking: 15 min.

12 oz. cream cheese
  and chives
2 cans (8-oz. size)
  minced clams
1 tbsp. lemon juice
salt to taste
1 tsp. paprika
potato chips
  or corn chips

Mix cream cheese, clams (drained), a little clam juice, lemon juice, salt and paprika. Heat over low flame until smooth. Serve in small chafing dish over warmer with potato or corn chips.

HORS D'OEUVRES
for 8

CURRIED CHICKEN BALLS

Preparation: 20 min.
Chilling: 2 hr.

1 can (4-3/4 oz.) chicken spread
2 tbsp. chutney, chopped
1 tsp. curry powder
dash of salt
2 tsp. mayonnaise
1/3 c. coarsely chopped, toasted almonds or parsley

Blend chicken spread, chutney, curry powder and salt. Add enough mayonnaise to moisten. Form into 3/4" balls. Roll each ball in chopped almonds or parsley. Chill. To serve: Spear with toothpicks. Arrange picks in apple or orange for pretty effect.

CRAB RAVIGOTE

Preparation: 30 min.

1-1/2 c. lump crabmeat
1/4 c. tarragon vinegar
salt and pepper to taste
2 tbsp. capers
2 tbsp. chopped chives
1 tbsp. minced onion
1/2 c. mayonnaise
2 eggs, hard-boiled and chopped

Flake the crabmeat. Moisten with vinegar and marinate for 15-20 min. Drain and season crabmeat with salt and pepper. Add capers, chives, onion and mayonnaise. Mix well. Taste for flavor and correct seasoning. Fill crab shells or ramekins and cover with a coating of mayonnaise. Sprinkle liberally with egg.

CRABMEAT AND CREAM CHEESE

Preparation: 10 min.
Baking: 15 min.

8 oz. cream cheese
1 tbsp. milk
1 can (6-1/2 oz.) crabmeat
2 tbsp. onion, chopped
1/2 tsp. horseradish
1/4 tsp. salt
dash pepper
1/3 c. toasted, sliced almonds
crackers

Blend all ingredients except almonds. Put in small baking dish. Sprinkle with almonds. Bake uncovered at 375 degrees for 15 min. Serve hot with crackers.

HORS D'OEUVRES
for 8

CHINESE MEAT AND VEGETABLE PUFFS

Preparation: 15 min.
Baking: 15 min.

1 c. bean sprouts, drained
1 can (7-oz.) water chestnuts, drained and chopped
2 tbsp. chopped onion
1 pkg. beef-flavored mushroom soup mix
1/2 lb. chopped beef
2 pkg. refrigerator crescent rolls

Cook first 5 ingredients in pan until meat is brown. Open crescent dough and cut each perforated roll into thirds. Put 1 tsp. meat mixture on each piece of dough. Put another piece of dough on top and seal edges with a fork. Place on ungreased cookie sheet and bake at 375 degrees for 15 min.

MUSHROOM CANAPES

Preparation: 20 min.
Broiling: 1 min.
Baking: 12 min.

3 tbsp. butter
1/2 lb. mushrooms, minced
1 tsp. salt
1/4 tsp. pepper
1 tsp. paprika
2 egg yolks, hard-boiled and chopped
2 tsp. lemon juice
4 tsp. grated Gruyere cheese
1/2 tsp. brandy
Melba toast

In a skillet saute mushrooms in butter for 10 min. Drain any remaining liquid. Add salt, pepper, paprika, egg yolks, lemon juice, cheese and brandy. Mix well. Pile on unbuttered Melba toast and place under broiler for 1 min. Bake at 350 degrees for 12 min.

YIELD: 24

SNAILS IN MUSHROOMS

Preparation: 15 min.
Broiling: 6 min.

24 sml. fresh mushrooms
1/2 c. butter
1 clove garlic, minced
1 lrg. onion, finely chopped
2 cans (6-oz. size) snails (24 snails)
1/2 c. chopped parsley
1/2 tsp. pepper
Parmesan cheese, freshly grated
paprika

Grease shallow baking dish. Arrange destemmed mushroom caps in dish. Rinse snails, drain and place 1 in each mushroom cap. Add to each a good dab of butter (1 tsp.), parsley, a dash of pepper, and a sprinkling each of Parmesan cheese and paprika. Broil about 6" from flame for about 6 min.

HORS D'OEUVRES
for 8

SNOW CAP SPREAD

1 can (4-1/2 oz.) deviled ham
2 tbsp. minced onion
4 oz. cream cheese
2 tbsp. sour cream
1-1/4 tsp. hot mustard
1/2 c. chopped parsley
crackers

Preparation: 30 min.
Chilling: 3 hr.

Mix ham and onion. Form into ball and refrigerate for 2 hr. Frost with a blend of cream cheese, sour cream and mustard. Refrigerate at least 1 hr. Roll in parsley and serve with crackers.

PATE MAISON

1/4 c. butter
1 lb. chicken livers
1/4 c. finely chopped onion
1 tsp. salt
1/4 tsp. dry mustard
1/4 tsp. black pepper
1/4 tsp. thyme
1/8 tsp. mace
1/4 c. heavy cream
French bread
  or crackers

Preparation: 20 min.
Chilling: 2 hr.

Heat butter in skillet and add chicken livers and onion. Cook over medium heat for 10 min. stirring frequently. Put into blender adding seasonings and cream. Blend until mixture is smooth. Turn into serving dish or mold. Chill. Serve with French bread or crackers.

YIELD: 1-1/4 cup

PINEAPPLE SALAMI

24 chunks of pineapple, drained
24 chunks of salami
4 tbsp. soy sauce
2 tbsp. brown sugar
2 tbsp. vinegar

Marinating: 3 hr.
Preparation: 10 min.
Broiling: 5 min.

Marinate salami in soy sauce, brown sugar and vinegar for several hours. String pineapple and salami alternately on skewers. Broil until brown about 5 min.

SOUPS
for 8

ALMOND SOUP

Preparation: 2 hr.
Chilling: 8 hr.
Cooking: 30 min.

1-1/2 lb. smoked pork, butt end
2 qt. water
1-1/2 c. almonds shelled and skinned
2 c. white bread crumbs, with crusts removed
1/2 c. chopped onions
6 c. chicken broth
1 tsp. dried fines herbes
1/2 tsp. pepper
1 c. sherry
salt to taste

In large saucepan, simmer pork in water for 2 hr. adding water if necessary in order to have 2 cups of broth. Remove meat from pan and refrigerate 8 hr. Skim off congealed fat. Cut enough meat from bone to make 1/2 cup when chopped. Blend with a little pork broth in blender. Add to remaining pork broth in top of double boiler. Blend almonds and onions with a little chicken broth in blender. Add to pork mixture. Blend bread crumbs and remaining chicken broth. Add herbs, pepper and sherry and stir into pork/almond mixture. Heat through, stirring occasionally. Correct seasonings.

COLD AVOCADO SOUP

Preparation: 10 min.
Chilling: 2 hr.

3 ripe avocados
4 c. chicken stock or broth
2 c. heavy cream
salt to taste
cayenne to taste
salted or curried whipped cream

Slice avocados into blender. Add a little chicken stock and blend. Add more stock until blender container is almost full. Blend well. Pour into a large jar and add cream, salt and cayenne. Chill and serve with a tsp. of whipped cream on top.

CARROT SOUP

Preparation: 10 min.
Cooking: 40 min.
Chilling: 4 hr.

6 tbsp. butter
1 lb. carrots, thinly sliced
1 lb. tomatoes, peeled and chopped
1-1/2 c. chicken broth
1 c. light cream
sugar to taste
salt and pepper to taste
chopped parsley

Melt butter in heavy saucepan and saute carrots. Add tomatoes and cook about 2 min. Add stock or broth, bring to boil, cover and simmer until carrots are soft, about 30 min. Add sugar if necessary, cream, salt and pepper. Return to boil and pour into blender and puree. Serve hot or chill thoroughly. Garnish with parsley.

SOUPS
for 8

BILLI BI CLAM SOUP

Preparation: 25 min.

40 oz. bottled clam juice
1/2 c. dry white wine
4 chicken bouillon cubes
1 sml. onion, chopped
1/2 c. chopped celery
2 tsp. dried fines herbes
1/2 tsp. fresh ground pepper
1 can (7-1/2 oz.) minced clams
4 egg yolks, lightly beaten
1 pt. heavy cream
1/2 c. chopped parsley

Simmer first 7 ingredients for about 10 min. Strain, reserve liquid and blend solids in blender with minced clams and juice from clams. In top of double boiler put the puree, egg yolks and cream. Add warm liquid, reserved from first step. Heat over boiling water. Garnish with chopped parsley. Serve hot or cold.

CHICKEN BROTH

Preparation: 20 min.
Cooking: 3 hr.

1 chicken (2-1/2 lb.) cut-up
1 leek, sliced
2 lrg. onions, quartered
1/4 c. chopped chives
1 bay leaf, whole
1/2 tsp. thyme
1/4 tsp. powdered clove
1/4 tsp. nutmeg
1 tsp. crushed peppercorns
2 tsp. salt

Place chicken in 2-3 qt. cold water. Bring to boil. Skim off foam until it stops appearing to assure clear broth. Add rest of ingredients and simmer covered for 2-1/2—3 hr. Remove chicken from broth. Strain broth into a bowl. Chill. Pour into ice trays and freeze. Seal in freezer bags. 4 cubes average 2/3 cups broth.

CURRIED EGGPLANT SOUP

Preparation: 45 min.
Heating: 20 min.

2 med. unpeeled eggplants, cubed
salt and pepper to taste
5 tbsp. butter
1/2 c. chopped onion
1 tsp. mashed garlic
1 tbsp. curry
1/2 tsp. rosemary
bouquet garni
1/2 tsp. crushed chervil
5 c. chicken or beef stock
1 c. heavy cream
2 egg yolks
parsley

Melt 2 tbsp. butter in heavy saucepan. Add eggplant, salt and pepper and cook until golden brown. In another pot saute onion and garlic with salt and pepper in 2 tbsp. butter until onion is well wilted. Add seasonings, bouquet, stock, eggplant and herbs. Cover and simmer 15-20 min. Discard bouquet. Blend eggplant mixture in blender. Cool. Add cream which has been mixed with egg yolks. Blend in blender or mix with wire whisk. Serve hot, garnished with parsley.

SOUPS
for 8

MAINE FISH CHOWDER

Preparation: 30 min.
Heating: 30 min.

2 lb. haddock fillets
3 c. chopped onions
6 c. potatoes, diced
1/2 lb. salt pork, diced
2 bay leaves
8 c. water
5 c. milk
1 c. cream
2 tsp. salt
1/2 tsp. pepper
Westminster or pilot biscuits

In large saucepan or kettle cook fish in water with salt, pepper and bay leaves for 15 min. Drain, reserving liquid. Cook pork in skillet until brown. Remove from pan and drain fat, retaining enough to cook onions until soft. Add to strained liquid and potatoes. Bring to boil and cook 15 min. Add fish, milk and cream and heat to serving temperature. Test for seasoning. Add pork scraps and serve with biscuits floating on top.

MINESTRONE MILANESE

Preparation: 2 hr.
Soaking: 8 hr.
Cooking: 2 hr.

STOCK:

2 lb. shank beef
1 shank bone
3 sprigs parsley
1 tomato
1 carrot
1 onion
1 potato
3 qt. water
salt and pepper to taste

Place all stock ingredients in large pot. Bring to boil and simmer covered for 2 hr. Remove meat and bone. Add bone marrow to broth and put through food mill.

SOUP:

1/2 c. kidney beans
1/2 c. rice
1/4 c. olive oil
1 can (20-oz.) tomatoes
2 c. chopped spinach
2 qt. soup stock
1 onion, sliced
1 tbsp. chopped parsley
2 stalks celery, diced
2 c. shredded celery
2 c. chopped carrots
1/4 c. grated Parmesan cheese
salt and pepper to taste

Soak kidney beans in water 8 hr. In soup pot, saute fresh vegetables in oil. Stir, add rice, beans, salt, pepper, stock and tomatoes. Cover and simmer for 1-1/2 hr. until rice and beans are tender and most of the liquid is absorbed. Add cheese and mix thoroughly.

SOUPS
for 8

CLEAR MUSHROOM SOUP

Soaking: 3 hr.
Preparation: 15 min.
Cooking: 35 min.

3-4 oz. dried mushrooms
2 qt. chicken broth
1/2 tsp. mixed dried herbs
1 tsp. salt
pepper to taste
1 tsp. arrowroot or
   cornstarch
1/2 c. sherry (opt.)

Place mushrooms in strainer and run warm water over them, shaking frequently to clean. Place in bowl, add broth and let stand, stirring occasionally to allow grit to sink to bottom. Remove and drain mushrooms. Chop and put in large saucepan with broth. Simmer 30 min. uncovered. Strain through cheesecloth for extra clarity. If desired, thicken with arrowroot or cornstarch dissolved in a little cold water. Add sherry. Serve with a few chopped mushrooms in bottom of each cup.

FRENCH ONION SOUP

Preparation: 15 min.
Cooking: 1 hr.

2 lb. yellow onions
3 tbsp. butter
1 tbsp. cooking oil
2 qt. brown stock
   or beef broth
1/2 c. dry vermouth
5 tbsp. cognac
salt and pepper to taste
croutons
Parmesan cheese

Mince onions and cook over moderate heat until golden brown. Heat brown stock. Add onions to stock. Add vermouth. Simmer for 40-60 min. partially covered, skimming top occasionally. Season to taste. Add cognac prior to reheating or serving. Serve with croutons and/or Parmesan cheese.

VICHYSOISSE

Preparation: 15 min.
Cooking: 40 min.
Chilling: 2 hr.

3 stalks celery, sliced
8 med. onions, diced
6 potatoes, peeled and diced
1/2 c. chopped parsley
salt and white pepper
   to taste
2 c. water
2-1/2 c. chicken stock or broth
1-1/2 c. heavy cream
chopped chives

Cook vegetables, parsley, salt and pepper in broth and water until soft and tender. Puree in blender. Add cream and stir. Chill. Serve garnished with chives.

MEATS
для 8

BEEF ROLL-UPS

Preparation: 30 min.
Baking: 1 hr. 30 min.

2 lb. tenderloin, sliced across the grain, paper thin
3 c. herb stuffing mix
1 med. onion, chopped
4 cans cream of mushroom soup
4 tbsp. oil
2 tsp. Kitchen Bouquet
5-6 tbsp. flour
salt and pepper to taste

Prepare stuffing according to pkg. directions. Place meat on floured board. Put 1-2 heaping tbsp. stuffing on each slice. Roll each slice up and fasten with a toothpick. In a large skillet, brown rolled beef in oil on all sides. Remove to ungreased baking dish, 15" x 8". Mix mushroom soup, Kitchen Bouquet (or Gravy Master), onion, salt and pepper into oil in skillet. Pour over roll-ups and bake covered at 300 degrees for 1-1/2 hr.

BEEF EGGPLANT PARMIGIANA

Preparation: 45 min.
Cooking: 30 min.

3/4 lb. ground round steak
1 c. olive oil
1 med. onion, chopped
1 clove garlic minced
1/4 tsp. pepper
1 tsp. marjoram
1/2 tsp. basil
2-1/2 c. tomatoes
1/2 tsp. salt
1/4 c. flour
1 lrg. eggplant, peeled and sliced 1/2" thick
1/2 lb. Mozzarella cheese
1 c. grated Parmesan cheese

Cook beef in large saucepan until brown and crumbly. Remove meat. Add 1/4 cup oil to pan and cook onion and garlic until transparent. Return meat, add seasonings and tomatoes and simmer gently about 30 min. Dip eggplant in flour mixed with salt. Heat remaining oil and brown eggplant slightly on both sides. In a large casserole, place alternate layers of eggplant, sauce, sliced Mozzarella and Parmesan. Top with remaining Parmesan, dot with butter and bake covered at 350 degrees for 30 min.

BEEF STUFFED CABBAGE

Preparation: 30 min.
Cooking: 3 hr.

1 head cabbage
3 lb. chopped beef
1 onion, grated
1 egg
2 tbsp. rice
1 bottle (12 oz.) chili sauce
1 can (8 oz.) whole cranberries
salt and pepper to taste

Remove core of cabbage and boil cabbage for 5 min. Let stand so leaves come off easily. Mix meat, onion, salt, pepper, egg and rice. Stuff each cabbage leaf with mixture. Place a few leaves of cabbage on bottom of pot. Put chili sauce and cranberries in pot. Arrange stuffed cabbage on top of this and simmer for about 3 hr.

MEATS
for 8

BEEF STEW

Preparation: 30 min.
Baking: 4 hr.

2 lb. beef chunks
1/4 c. bacon fat
seasoned flour
1-1/2 cloves garlic, chopped
1 lrg. onion, chopped
2 beef bouillon cubes
1 c. hot water
8 oz. tomato sauce
12 peppercorns
3 whole cloves
1/4 c. chopped parsley
1/2 bay leaf
1/2 c. sherry or white wine
6 potatoes, pared
   and quartered
12 carrots, pared
2 celery stalks, chopped
1/4 lb. mushrooms, sliced
1/4 lb. white onions, peeled

Brown beef chunks in hot fat. Sprinkle with seasoned flour. Combine garlic, onion, bouillon cubes, hot water, tomato sauce, peppercorns, cloves, parsley and bay leaf, and heat to boiling. Pour over meat in heavy saucepan. Cover and simmer for 4 hr. After 3 hr. add sherry and remaining ingredients.

GASTON BEEF STEW

Preparation: 1 hr.
Cooking: 3-1/2 hr.

1/2 lb. salt pork, in 1" cubes
2 lb. stew beef, in 1" cubes
1/2 c. flour, seasoned
   with salt and pepper
1-1/2 cloves garlic, chopped
1 lrg. onion, chopped
1 c. beef broth
1 can (8 oz.) tomato sauce
12 peppercorns
3 whole cloves
1/4 c. chopped parsley
1/2 bay leaf
1/2 c. sherry
6 med. potatoes, pared
   and quartered
6 carrots, pared and
   quartered
1 celery stalk, chopped
salt and pepper to taste

Saute pork over low heat in a large heavy skillet. Add beef and brown at high heat. Sprinkle with flour. In a separate pan, combine garlic, onion, broth, tomato sauce, peppercorns, cloves, parsley and bay leaf. Heat until boiling and pour over meat. Cover and simmer for 3 hr. Add sherry. Continue simmering covered. In a separate pan, cook potatoes, carrots and celery until nearly tender. Add to meat for last 15-20 min. of cooking.

MEATS
for 8

DINAH'S POT ROAST

Preparation: 30 min.
Baking: 3 hr.

1 beef brisket (4-1/2 — 5 lb.)
1 tbsp. cooking oil
1 onion, coarsely chopped
3 celery stalks, sliced
1/2 green pepper, chopped
3 carrots, sliced
3 tomatoes, chopped
3 potatoes, peeled & chopped
1 bay leaf
1 c. beef broth
1 c. red wine
basil to taste
marjoram to taste
Kitchen Bouquet
garlic salt to taste
salt and pepper to taste

Brown roast in oil in a large kettle or Dutch oven. Add vegetables, broth, wine, salt, pepper, basil, marjoram and bay leaf. Bring to a boil and cover. Bake at 325 degrees for 3 hr. Remove meat to platter and keep warm. Strain vegetables and pan juices. Puree vegetables and return to kettle with pan juices. Add enough Kitchen Bouquet to color and flavor. Add salt, pepper and garlic salt. Pour sauce over the sliced brisket.

GOULASCHE-SUPPE

Preparation: 1-1/2 hr.
Cooking: 2-1/2 hr.
Chilling: 8 hr.

2 tbsp. butter
2 tbsp. oil
4 lb. beef chuck, cubed
2 lb. onions, diced
6 c. beef broth or stock
2 cloves garlic, crushed
3 green peppers, chopped
3 red peppers, chopped
1 lb. tomatoes, peeled
   and diced
1 tsp. caraway seed
1 tsp. ginger
3 tbsp. paprika
1 tsp. Tabasco
1 tsp. soy sauce
1/2 tsp. sugar
1 tbsp. ketchup
1 tbsp. tomato paste
salt and pepper to taste
1/2 lb. green beans, cut up
1/2 lb. mushrooms, quartered
1 c. sour cream

Heat 1 tbsp. butter and oil together in large enamelled pot. Brown meat on all sides. Remove. Add onions and brown, adding more butter if necessary. Return meat to pot, cover with broth or stock and let simmer while preparing vegetables. Add next 12 ingredients, cover and simmer about 2 hr. or until meat is tender. In a skillet saute mushrooms in 1 tbsp. butter and add with beans to stew. Simmer 30 min. Add sour cream. Correct seasoning. Cover and refrigerate 8 hr. Reheat slowly just to boiling point.

MEATS
for 8

SWEET AND SOUR MEATBALLS

Preparation: 15 min.
Cooking: 1 hr.

3 lb. ground beef
3 tbsp. fat
2 cans (20-oz. size) pineapple chunks
1/2 c. brown sugar
3 tbsp. cornstarch
1/2 c. cider vinegar
2 tsp. soy sauce
2 green peppers, coarsely chopped
salt and pepper to taste

Shape beef into balls. Brown in large skillet in fat. Drain pineapple, reserving syrup. Combine brown sugar and cornstarch and blend in pineapple syrup and 1 cup water. Add vinegar and soy sauce and stir over medium heat until thick. Add meatballs and simmer covered for 50 min. Add green pepper and pineapple chunks. Season to taste. Cover and simmer 10 min. longer.

PICCADILLO

Preparation: 25 min.
Cooking: 1 hr.

2 med. onions, diced
2 green peppers, diced
30 sml. stuffed olives
1 jar (2-1/4 oz.) capers
4 tbsp. olive oil
1 c. seedless raisins
1-1/2 lb. chopped beef
1 can (29 oz.) tomato sauce
2 tsp. Worcestershire
1/2 tsp. MSG
1/4 tsp. oregano
1/2 tsp. salt
1/4 tsp. pepper
1/2 tsp. garlic powder
1/2 tsp. celery salt
1/2 tsp. paprika

Saute onions and green peppers in 2 tbsp. olive oil. Set aside. Saute meat in remaining olive oil. Drain. Stir in remaining ingredients and cook covered over low heat for 40-60 min.

HAM AND SPINACH CASSEROLE

Preparation: 30 min.
Baking: 1 hr.

2 lb. creamed cottage cheese
2 c. cooked diced ham
2 pkg. frozen chopped spinach, thawed
5 eggs
6 tbsp. flour
1/2 lb. Cheddar cheese, coarsely chopped
salt and pepper to taste

Combine cottage cheese, eggs, undrained spinach. Add flour mixed with 3/4 cup cold water making a smooth paste. Add cheese and ham and blend thoroughly. Place in buttered 2 qt. casserole. Bake uncovered at 350 degrees for 1 hr.

MEATS
for 8

HAM AND EGGPLANT CASSEROLE

1 lrg. eggplant
2 med. onions, sliced
2 sprigs parsley, chopped
2 garlic cloves, chopped
2 celery stalks, chopped
1/2 green pepper, chopped
2 tbsp. oil or shortening
2 c. diced ham, cooked
1/2 tsp. thyme
5 bay leaves
1/2 c. seasoned bread crumbs
1 egg, beaten
1/2 c. Parmesan cheese

Preparation: 25 min.
Baking: 30 min.

Pare eggplant and cut into 3" cubes. Steam in 1" water for 10 min. Drain in colander. Saute onions and chopped vegetables in oil over low heat until lightly browned. Add ham and drained eggplant and simmer 10 min. Add seasonings, half the bread crumbs and egg. Mix well. Turn into buttered 2 qt. casserole. Cover with rest of bread crumbs. Sprinkle with Parmesan cheese. Bake uncovered at 325 degrees about 30 min.

LAMB CURRY

1/2 c. flour
1 tbsp. curry powder
3 lb. lean lamb, cubed
2 tbsp. shortening
2 cans onion soup
1 c. sliced celery
1 unpeeled, tart red apple, cubed
1/2 c. seedless white raisins
salt and pepper to taste

Preparation: 15 min.
Cooking: 1 hr.

Combine curry powder and flour. Roll the lamb in the flour mixture. In a skillet, brown the lamb in the shortening and blend in any remaining flour. Add the soup, celery, apple and raisins. Cook covered over low heat for about 1 hr. or until lamb is tender. Stir several times while cooking.

MOUSSAKA

2 lb. ground lean lamb
1 eggplant (2-1/2 lb.)
1 med. onion, chopped
3 tbsp. olive oil
2 tsp. salt
1 tsp. pepper
1/2 tsp. garlic powder
2 cans (6-oz. size) tomato paste
1 container (6 oz.) yoghurt
4 egg yolks
1/2 c. flour

Preparation: 30 min.
Cooking: 1 hr. 15 min.

Peel and cut eggplant into 1/2" slices. Salt and set aside for 1 hr. Pour off collected liquid. Saute chopped onion in 1 tbsp. oil. Add lamb, salt, pepper, garlic and tomato paste. Cook until meat is slightly brown. Put some oil in another skillet. Dip eggplant slices in flour and brown on both sides. In large casserole, arrange alternate layers of eggplant and meat mixture, finishing with eggplant. Bake uncovered at 350 degrees for about 1 hr. Blend yoghurt, egg yolks and flour and mix well. Pour over top of casserole and bake 15 min. more or until brown.

MEATS
for 8

LEG OF LAMB WITH MUSTARD COATING

Marinating: 2 hr.
Baking: 1-1/2 hr.
Broiling: 40 min.

1/2 c. Dijon mustard
2 tbsp. soy sauce
1 clove garlic, mashed
1 tsp. crushed rosemary or thyme
1/4 tsp. powdered ginger
2 tbsp. olive oil
6 lb. leg of lamb

Blend first 5 ingredients, and add olive oil by drops to make thick and creamy dressing.

FOR ROAST LEG OF LAMB:
Paint leg of lamb with dressing. Refrigerate for 1 hr. and at room temp. 1 hr. before cooking. Roast at 350 degrees for 1-1/4 hr. for rare, 1-1/2 hr. for medium.

FOR BARBECUE:
Have butcher bone lamb. You will have 4-5 lb. meat. Flatten meat so it is all about same thickness. Paint one side with dressing and let stand 1 hr. Paint other side and let stand 1/2 hr. Barbecue or broil about 20 min. on each side.

ORIENTAL PORK CHOPS

Chilling: 3 hr.
Cooking: 30 min.

8 thick (1") pork chops
3/4 c. dry sherry
3/4 c. soy sauce
4 tsp. ground ginger
1 garlic clove, mashed
3 tbsp. honey
3/4 tsp. dried rosemary

Combine all ingredients except chops. Blend well. Pour into heavy-duty plastic bag. Add chops. Remove as much air as possible and secure with tie. Refrigerate 1-3 hr. Broil chops, basting with marinade, about 15 min. per side.

PORK CHOPS IN VERMOUTH

Preparation: 10 min.
Baking: 1-1/2 hr.

8 med. thick pork chops
4 tbsp. prepared mustard
4 tbsp. ketchup
salt and pepper to taste
Worcestershire to taste
8 onion slices
8 tomato slices
1/2 c. dry vermouth
1/4-1/2 c. water

Place pork chops in shallow baking dish. Spread with mustard and ketchup, then sprinkle with salt, pepper and Worcestershire. Top each chop with a slice of onion and a slice of tomato. Pour vermouth and water over to half cover. Cover and bake at 350 degrees for 1 hr. Uncover, baste and bake 30 min. longer.

MEATS
for 8

SWEETBREADS SUPREME

Preparation: 1 hr. 30 min.
Cooking: 10 min.

3 pair sweetbreads
2 tbsp. lemon juice
2 tsp. salt
8 slices pineapple
1/4 c. butter, melted
8 slices bacon, cooked and crumbled
2 cans mushroom soup
1-1/2 c. heavy cream
paprika

Soak sweetbreads in cold water to cover for 1 hr. Drain. Cover with fresh water, add lemon juice and salt and cook 15-20 min. Drain. Plunge sweetbreads into cold water, split, remove membrane and slice or break into small pieces. Place pieces on pineapple and brush with melted butter. Broil until delicately browned, about 10 min. Garnish with bacon. Serve with mixture of mushroom soup, cream and paprika, heated.

VEAL BIRDS

Preparation: 20 min.
Cooking: 45 min.

16 slices veal scallopine
1/2 c. chopped cooked ham
1/4 c. chopped onion
1/2 c. chopped raw carrots
1/2 c. chopped raw celery
1/2 c. Mozzarella cheese, cubed
3/4 c. chopped fresh parsley
salt and pepper to taste
1 c. (approx.) seasoned flour
4 tbsp. butter
4 tbsp. oil
2 c. chicken broth
1/2 c. dry white wine or dry vermouth
2 c. sour cream

Mix ham, cheese, vegetables, including 1/4 cup chopped parsley, salt and pepper. Mound evenly on the veal slices. Roll up and secure with toothpicks or string. Roll in seasoned flour. Brown in oil and butter in a large skillet. Add chicken broth to skillet. Cover and simmer for 30 min. Turn birds occasionally to ensure cooking throughout. Remove birds to serving platter and keep warm. Add wine to pan and boil down to about half its original amount (about 8-10 min.). Remove from heat. Stir in sour cream and remaining parsley. Warm over low heat, stirring constantly, until it almost boils, but do not boil. Pour over veal birds.

MEATS
for 8

VEAL WITH LEMON

Preparation: 15 min.
Cooking: 8 min.

2 lb. veal scallopine
1/2 c. flour
salt and pepper
1/4 c. oil
2 chicken bouillon cubes
1-1/2 c. boiling water
1/2 c. dry white wine
1-1/2 tbsp. lemon juice
1 lemon, thinly sliced
16 sml. sprigs parsley

Dip veal slices in flour, salt and pepper mixed together. Heat oil in large skillet. Brown veal quickly, several pieces at a time. Remove. Stir in bouillon cubes mixed with boiling water. Add wine and lemon juice. Scrape drippings into liquid and boil down slightly (leaving 2/3 starting amount). Return veal to pan and cook over high heat for about 8 min. or until tender. Pour sauce over veal. Garnish with lemon slices and parsley.

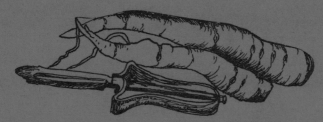

VITELLO TONNATO

Preparation: 30 min.
Cooking: 1-1/2 hr.
Chilling: Overnight

1 leg of veal, boned (2-1/2 lb.)
8 anchovy fillets
1 can (7 oz.) tuna fish, drained
3/4 c. mayonnaise
3 tbsp. capers
1 onion
1 carrot
1 celery stalk
3 sprigs parsley
2 cloves
pinch salt
4 c. stock
2 tbsp. lemon juice
dash pepper

Tie veal into an evenly shaped roll. Pierce meat in various spots with a sharp knife and insert small pieces of 4 anchovy fillets. Place roll in deep saucepan with onion, carrot, celery, parsley, cloves and salt. Add stock to cover, bring to boil and simmer covered for 1-1/2 hr. Let cool in stock. Drain, saving liquid. Mash tuna, 4 anchovy fillets, 1/2 tsp. capers, lemon juice and pepper. Mix with mayonnaise. Thin mixture with stock until it has the consistency of cream. Cover veal with sauce and refrigerate overnight. To serve, remove veal from sauce and slice paper thin. Cover again with sauce and sprinkle with extra capers. Serve with extra sauce on the side.

NOTE: Can substitute 2 cups dry white wine for vegetables and stock.

POULTRY & GAME
for 8

STUFFED BANTAMS

Preparation: 25 min.
Broiling: 20 min.

8 whole chicken breasts, boned and skinned
salt
MSG. (opt.)
1 egg
1 pkg. herb-seasoned stuffing
2 cans cream of mushroom soup
1 can (7 oz.) crabmeat, drained, flaked and boned
1/4 c. chopped green pepper
1 tbsp. lemon juice
2 tsp. Worcestershire
1 tsp. prepared mustard
1/4 tsp. salt
1/2 c. salad oil
2 tsp. Kitchen Bouquet
1/2 tsp. onion juice
dash pepper

Sprinkle inside of chicken breasts with salt and MSG. Make filling of egg, stuffing, 1/2 cup of soup, crabmeat and next 5 ingredients. Divide mixture equally between 8 breasts, fasten each closed with toothpicks or skewers. Broil about 10 min. per side, basting with sauce made of rest of soup, oil, flavor enhancer, onion juice and pepper.

NOTE: This dish may also be broiled on the barbecue. Broil over hot coals for about 30 min. or until tender. Turn frequently, basting after the first 10 min.

CHICKEN BREASTS IN SAUCE

Preparation: 35 min.
Baking: 30 min.

4 whole chicken breasts, boned, skinned and split
1/2 c. diced carrots
1/2 c. diced celery
1/4 c. diced onions
1/4 c. diced green pepper
1/2 c. mild Cheddar cheese shredded
1/4 lb. butter
1 can beef consomme
1/2 c. dry vermouth
1 c. heavy cream
1/2 c. chopped parsley
paprika

Stuff each half breast with mixture of raw vegetables and cheese. Secure with toothpicks. Put into buttered baking dish. Dot with butter and bake at 400 degrees for about 30 min. or until chicken does not show dent when pressed with back of spoon. Drain cooking liquid into large frying pan. Add consomme and vermouth and boil hard until reduced by half. Add cream and boil again until slightly thickened. Add parsley and stir. Pour over chicken or place chicken back into sauce to reheat before serving. (Remove toothpicks or warn your guests!)

POULTRY & GAME
for 8

CHICKEN AND ARTICHOKE AU GRATIN

Preparation: 20 min.
Cooking: 20 min.

2 pkg. (9-oz. size) frozen artichoke hearts
4 tbsp. butter
1 c. milk
4 tbsp. flour
1 c. chicken broth
3 tbsp. sherry
3/4 c. grated Cheddar cheese
salt and pepper to taste
4 c. diced, cooked chicken
paprika

Cook artichoke hearts as directed on pkg. and drain. In a saucepan melt butter. Stir in flour and gradually blend in milk and chicken broth, stirring until thick and smooth. Remove from heat. Stir in sherry and 1/4 cup cheese. Season with salt and pepper. Arrange artichoke hearts around edge of a shallow baking dish, with chicken in the center. Pour on cheese sauce. Sprinkle with remaining Cheddar and a light dusting of paprika. Bake uncovered at 375 degrees for 20 min. or until nicely browned.

CHICKEN CASSEROLE

Preparation: 15 min.
Chilling: 8 hr.
Baking: 1 hr.

4 c. cooked, diced chicken
1 pkg. (8 oz.) wide egg noodles
2 c. milk
2 cans cream of mushroom soup
1 onion, chopped
1/2 lb. Velveeta cheese, cubed
1 c. bread crumbs (approx.)

Mix all ingredients in a 3 qt. casserole. Cover and refrigerate 8 hr. Top casserole with bread crumbs. Bake uncovered at 350 degrees for 1 hr. or until well heated.

NOTE: Do *not* pre-cook noodles since standing softens them.

CHICKEN ROSEMARY

Preparation: 40 min.
Baking: 45 min.

4 whole chicken breasts, boned and skinned
3 pkg. frozen asparagus
1 c. mayonnaise
1 can cream of celery soup
1/4 lb. almonds, chopped
1 tsp. rosemary
1 c. white wine
salt and pepper to taste

Boil chicken 30 min. drain and dice. Cook asparagus according to pkg. directions and arrange on bottom of 3 qt. buttered baking dish. Mix chicken with mayonnaise, celery soup, rosemary, wine, salt and pepper and put over asparagus. Sprinkle almonds on top. Bake uncovered at 325 degrees for 45 min.

POULTRY & GAME
for 8

CHICKEN IN ROSE WINE

Preparation: 10 min.
Baking: 2 hr.

8 whole chicken breasts, split
1-1/2 c. rose wine
1/2 c. soy sauce
1/4 c. water
2 cloves garlic, crushed
2 tsp. ground ginger
2 tsp. oregano
2 tbsp. brown sugar
2 tsp. arrowroot or cornstarch, dissolved in 1/4 c. cold water

Combine ingredients. Cover. Bake at 350 degrees for 2 hr.

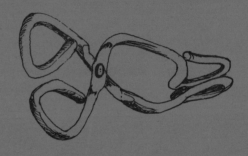

CHICKEN AND LAMB ALGERIQUE

Preparation: 1-1/2 hr.

4 chicken breasts, boned skinned and diced
2 lb. lamb cubes (1-1/2")
2 onions, chopped
2 tbsp. oil
2-1/2 c. water
1/2 c. white wine
3 or 4 carrots, pared and cut into 1" slices
4 tsp. salt
1/2 tsp. pepper
1/2 tsp. ground ginger
1/2 tsp. cinnamon
4-5 sml. zucchini, cut into 1/2" slices
2 fresh tomatoes, skinned and chopped
1 pkg. frozen lima beans
1 c. seedless raisins
1 lb. box couscous
1/4 lb. butter, melted
salt
parsley
1/2 c. almonds

In a skillet, brown lamb chunks in oil and transfer to large kettle. Saute onions until golden, about 5 min. and remove to kettle. Add water to skillet and bring to boil, scraping bits from pan. Pour into kettle. Add chicken, wine, carrots, salt, pepper, cinnamon and ginger. Bring to boil. Cover and simmer 40 min. Add zucchini, tomatoes, lima beans and raisins. Cover and simmer 30 min. more or until meat is tender. Meanwhile, prepare 1 box of couscous, according to directions, and spoon it into a deep platter. Drizzle melted butter over it and stir lightly. Make a deep well, pushing couscous to edges. Pour stew into center and garnish with parsley and almonds.

POULTRY & GAME
for 8

COTELETTES A LA TOUREL

Preparation: 35 min.
Chilling: 2 hr.
Cooking: 15 min.

3 whole chicken breasts, skinned and boned (about 1 lb.)
1/2 lb. raw lean pork
2 eggs, well beaten in 1 tbsp. chicken stock
1/8 tsp. salt
1/8 tsp. pepper
2 slices white bread, crusts removed, cubed and soaked in 1 c. milk
1/2 tsp. ginger
1 med. onion, grated
2 tsp. dillweed
1-1/2 c. bread crumbs
1/2 c. butter

Chop chicken and pork. Put through fine blade of meat grinder. Place in blender with eggs and bread (squeezed nearly dry), salt, pepper, ginger, onions and dillweed. Blend on low speed until smooth. Test for seasoning. Shape into cotelettes (patty) and roll in bread crumbs. Refrigerate 1-2 hr. Heat butter in skillet. Saute cotelettes slowly until cooked and golden brown on both sides. Serve with sour cream sauce.

SOUR CREAM SAUCE:

1/2 c. minced chives
2 tbsp. chopped parsley
1 c. sour cream
salt and pepper to taste
1 tbsp. dillweed

Combine sour cream with chives and parsley. Season with salt, pepper and dillweed.

CHICKEN LIVER CASSEROLE

Preparation: 30 min.
Broiling: 3 min.

2 lb. chicken livers
1/2 c. flour
3 tbsp. butter, melted
1/4 c. Madeira wine
4 lrg. tomatoes, peeled and diced
1 c. grated Cheddar cheese
slivered almonds

Roll chicken livers in flour and saute in butter. Add wine and tomatoes and simmer 3 min. Put in 2-qt. casserole and sprinkle with cheese. Place under broiler until cheese melts, about 3 min. Sprinkle with almonds and serve immediately.

POULTRY & GAME
for 8

ROCK CORNISH HEN VERONIQUE

Preparation: 15 min.
Baking: 1-1/2 hr.

8 Rock Cornish game hens
4 c. white sauce (see index)
1 lb. seedless grapes, halved
3/4 c. butter
1 tbsp. tarragon
1/2 tsp. paprika
salt and pepper to taste
8 onions, quartered
4 c. white wine or dry vermouth

Place quartered onion in each hen. Combine tarragon, paprika, salt and pepper and sprinkle on hens. Put large dab of butter on each hen and bake at 300 degrees for 1 hr. 15 min. After first 30 min. pour wine over hens and baste several times afterwards. Meanwhile, prepare white sauce. At last minute combine grapes, and white sauce and pour over hens.

PHEASANT IN SOUR CREAM

Preparation: 30 min.
Baking: 3 hr.

3 pheasants, whole or pieces
1/2 c. flour, seasoned with salt, paprika and pepper
8 tbsp. butter
2 c. sour cream
2 c. light cream
1/2 c. chopped parsley

Roll pheasant in seasoned flour. Brown in a skillet in butter and put pheasant in a casserole. Add 1 tbsp. seasoned flour to butter in skillet and mix well. Add sour cream mixed with light cream and stir until smooth. Pour over pheasant. Bake covered at 275 degrees for 2-1/2 — 3 hr. Remove pheasant from casserole. Stir sauce with a wire whisk until smooth. Pour over pheasant. Add parsley as garnish.

NOTE: If whole pheasants are used, the baking time will be 3 hr. or more.

POULTRY & GAME
for 8

LEMON TURKEY

Preparation: 15 min.
Baking: 2-1/2 hr.

1 turkey (7-8 lb.)
1/2 c. lemon juice
1 c. white wine
1/4 lb. butter
2 cloves garlic, minced
1/2 tsp. crushed rosemary
1/2 tsp. thyme
1 med. onion, sliced

Cut turkey into serving pieces. Place on a large square of heavy duty aluminum foil. Fold up edges to form a bowl and add other ingredients. Fold foil over and close it. Bake at 350 degrees for 2 hr. Open foil and fold back to expose turkey pieces. Baste with liquid and bake 15-20 min. more or until turkey is nicely browned. Baste again. Remove turkey pieces to serving platter and pour juices etc. over turkey.

LES OISEAUX SAUVAGES A LA FRANCAISE

Preparation: 1-2 hr.
Baking:
Geese: 1-1/2 hr.
Ducks: 1 hr.
Pheasant: 1/2 - 3/4 hr.

2 wild geese, ducks or pheasants
14 sml. white onions, peeled
2 c. water
4 chicken bouillon cubes
1 c. red wine (opt.)
14 sml. mushrooms (opt.)
1/4-1/2 c. instant flour
1 tbsp. Gravy Master (approx.)
1-2 tsp. salt
1/4 tsp. celery salt
1/4 tsp. garlic salt
1/4 tsp. onion salt
1/2 tsp. herbs (tarragon, basil and/or marjoram)

Wash birds and sprinkle with salt. Place in Dutch oven, or an ovenproof covered casserole. Cover bottom of pan with water, bouillon cubes and wine. Cover and bake at 350 degrees. Add onions and mushrooms halfway through cooking. Baste occasionally, adding more liquid if needed. When bird is tender, remove lid. Remove onions and mushrooms to platter. Brown birds under broiler, turning to expose all sides. Browning will be very quick. Remove birds to platter and keep warm. Make pan gravy by skimming off fat, adding instant flour pre-mixed with water, Gravy Master, salt, celery salt, garlic salt, onion salt, herbs, and a little more wine.

SEAFOOD
for 8

CLAMS CATAPLANA

Preparation: 20 min.
Cooking: 15 min.

8 doz. sml. hard-shell clams
8 tbsp. olive oil
6 med. onions, thinly sliced
1 tsp. paprika
1/2 tsp. crushed hot
   dried red peppers
2 lrg. cloves garlic, minced
4 bay leaves, broken
1 c. dry white wine
2 med. tomatoes, chopped
6 oz. smoked ham, chopped
6 oz. linguica, chorico
   or other garlic sausage,
   cut from casing
   and crumbled
1/2 c. finely chopped
   fresh parsley

Scrub clams and soak in cold water at least 1 hr. Drain and rinse well. Heat oil in cataplana or heavy casserole with tight lid, for top of stove cooking. Add onions, paprika and red peppers and cook over low heat until onions are limp and golden. Stir in garlic, wine, bay leaves, tomatoes, ham, sausage and parsley. (NOTE: This is where you stop if you are doing this ahead of time.)

Add clams, pushing them down into mixture. Cover tightly. Cook on top of stove over medium heat about 15 min. or until clams open. DO NOT uncover until ready to serve.

NOTE: Serve in soup bowls and use crusty bread to mop up sauce.

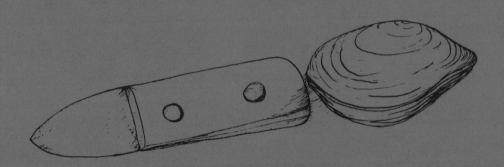

CLAMS LINGUINE

Preparation: 10 min.
Cooking: 15 min.

1-1/2 lb. linguine
   (flat spaghetti)
1 c. olive oil
2 cloves garlic, minced
1 tbsp. thyme
garlic salt to taste
pepper to taste
4 cans (10-oz. size) clams

Cook linguine according to pkg. directions. Drain. Heat oil in large skillet. Add garlic and cook for 1 min. Add clam juice (drained from can), thyme, garlic salt and pepper. Cook about 10 min. Add clams and heat through. Pour hot sauce over linguine.

SEAFOOD
for 8

MEETING STREET CRAB

Preparation: 20 min.
Baking: 30 min.

2 lb. crabmeat
1/2 c. butter
1/2 c. flour
2 c. heavy cream
1/2 c. sherry
salt and pepper to taste
1 c. grated, sharp
   Cheddar cheese

Melt butter in top of double boiler. Blend in flour, add cream and stir with wire whisk until thick. Add sherry, salt and pepper. Remove from heat and add crabmeat. Pour mixture into buttered 2-qt. casserole. Sprinkle with grated cheese. Bake uncovered at 350 degrees for 30 min. or until cheese is melted and mixture is bubbly. Do not overcook.

NOTE: Shrimp may be substituted for or combined with crabmeat.

CRABMEAT MOUSSE

Preparation: 15 min.
Chilling: 2 hr.

2 env. unflavored gelatin
2 tbsp. dry sherry
1 c. chicken broth
2 egg yolks
1 c. heavy cream
3 tbsp. lemon juice
5 drops Tabasco
2 c. crabmeat, flaked
2 sml. celery stalks,
   cut-up
2 tbsp. finely
   chopped scallions
4 sprigs parsley
1/4 tsp. marjoram
1/4 tsp. thyme
1/2 c. mayonnaise
lettuce leaves (field,
   Bibb, oakleaf or Boston)

Place gelatin and sherry in blender and set aside. Bring broth to boil and add to blender. Blend at low speed until gelatin is dissolved, about 10 seconds. Continue blending and add egg yolks, cream, lemon juice, Tabasco, crabmeat, celery, scallions, parsley, marjoram and thyme. Blend until mixture is smooth. Add mayonnaise to blender for a few seconds, or mix in bowl with wire whisk if blender is too full. Pour into lightly oiled 6-cup mold and chill at least 2 hr. Unmold onto bed of lettuce leaves.

SEAFOOD
for 8

BOILED SALMON

Preparation: 35 min.
Chilling: 2 hr.

2 lb. fresh salmon
2 qt. water
2-3 tbsp. white vinegar
1 tbsp. salt
7 peppercorns (white)
5 whole allspice
1 bay leaf
1 onion
1 carrot
4-5 fresh dill sprigs
lemon slices
cucumber slices
dill or parsley

Combine ingredients except fish, garnish, mayonnaise or sauce, in a kettle and boil covered 15 min. Place fish in stock, bring to boiling point, uncovered. Skim. Simmer covered 15-20 min. Remove fish carefully and drain. Garnish with dill or parsley, lemon and cucumber slices.

NOTE: Serve hot with hollandaise or cold with mayonnaise.

COQUILLES ST. JACQUES

Preparation: 1 hr.
Baking: 10 min.

2 c. sauterne
1 bay leaf
3 sprigs parsley
1 tsp. dried thyme
2 lb. sea scallops
1/2 tsp. salt
1/2 lb. fresh mushrooms, finely chopped
1/4 c. minced onions
1 tbsp. minced parsley
3 tbsp. butter
2 tbsp. water
1 tsp. lemon juice
1/4 c. butter, melted
1/4 c. flour
2 tbsp. grated Swiss cheese
2 egg yolks, lightly beaten
1/4 c. heavy cream
1 c. buttered bread crumbs

Heat sauterne, bay leaf, parsley sprigs and thyme. Add scallops to wine and simmer covered about 10 min. Remove bay leaf and parsley. Drain scallops, reserving liquid. Cut scallops into small pieces. Saute mushrooms with onion and minced parsley in butter, water and lemon juice for about 7 min. Strain liquid into reserved wine. Add mushroom mixture to scallops. Blend melted butter and flour. Cook over low heat until bubbly. Gradually stir in wine mixture. Bring to boil stirring constantly. Add cheese and cook, stirring until cheese is melted. Cool. Mix egg yolks and heavy cream. Combine with cool sauce. Add scallops, mushrooms and onions. Fill ramekins or scallop shells with mixture and sprinkle with bread crumbs. Bake at 450 degrees about 10 min. or until browned.

SEAFOOD
for 8

JAMBALAYA

Preparation: 45 min.
Baking: 20 min.

1 lb. raw shrimp, cleaned and deveined
1/2 lb. ham, cooked and cubed
1/2 lb. bacon, in 1-1/2" strips
1/2 c. chopped onion
1 green pepper, chopped
1 c. uncooked rice
1/2 clove garlic, crushed
1 lb. tomatoes, chopped
1 bay leaf
1/2 tsp. thyme
2 c. chicken broth
salt and pepper to taste
chopped parsley

Fry bacon until crisp in a large skillet. Remove and set aside. Saute onion in bacon fat until limp. Add green pepper and saute for 1 min. Add rice and cook 3-4 min. Add garlic, tomatoes, bacon, salt and pepper, bay leaf and thyme. Stir to blend. Pour in chicken broth and bring to a boil. Add ham and shrimp. Cover and bake at 350 degrees for 15-20 min. Check after 15 min. Rice should have absorbed all liquid and be soft. Garnish with parsley.

SHRIMP CASSEROLE

Preparation: 30 min.
Marinating: 6 hr.
Baking: 50 min.

2 lb. shrimp, cooked
1 tbsp. lemon juice
3 tbsp. salad oil
1/4 c. uncooked rice
2 tbsp. butter
1/4 c. minced green pepper
1/4 c. minced onion
1 tsp. salt
1/8 tsp. pepper
1/8 tsp. mace
dash of cayenne
1 can cream of tomato soup
1/2 c. sherry
1/2 c. slivered almonds
paprika

Marinate shrimp in lemon juice and oil. Refrigerate 6 hr. Cook, drain and chill rice. About 1 hr. before serving, saute green pepper and onions in butter for 5 min. Add to shrimp with all other ingredients except almonds and paprika. Mix lightly. Top with almonds. Bake uncovered at 350 degrees for 50 min. or until bubbly. Sprinkle with paprika.

SEAFOOD
for 8

BROILED FILLET OF SOLE

Preparation: 5 min.
Broiling: 20 min.

8 lrg. fillets of sole
1/2 c. butter
1/4 tsp. rosemary
1/4 tsp. thyme
1/4 tsp. chervil
1/4 tsp. dillweed
1/4 tsp. fennel weed
1/4 tsp. MSG (opt.)
salt and pepper to taste
12 lemon wedges

In large baking pan, melt butter and stir in herbs and seasonings. Place fillets in mixture and baste liberally. Broil 4"-5" from heat for 15 min. or until fish is white with brown flecks and no longer shows depression when pressed with back of spoon. Baste at least 3 times during cooking. Be sure to baste liberally just before serving. Garnish with lemon wedges.

MOUSSE DE SOLE

Preparation: 20 min.
Baking: 1 hr.

1-1/2 lb. sole
  or flounder fillets
2 c. light cream
5 eggs
4 egg whites
2 tbsp. butter melted
salt and white pepper
  to taste
3 c. hollandaise sauce
  (see index)

In a blender, combine fillets, eggs, egg whites, butter and half the cream. Blend for 3 min. or until smooth. Combine with rest of cream. Add salt and pepper and transfer to buttered 2 qt. casserole. Place in pan of water and bake uncovered at 350 degrees for 45 min. to 1 hr. or until a knife inserted in center comes out clean. Serve with hollandaise sauce.

NORWEGIAN FISH PUDDING

Preparation: 30 min.
Baking: 1 hr.

6 tbsp. butter
6 tbsp. flour
2 tsp. salt
white pepper to taste
2 c. milk, heated
1-1/2 lb. sole or
  flounder fillets
6 egg yolks, beaten
  until thick
6 egg whites, stiffly
  beaten

In large saucepan make cream sauce of first 5 ingredients. Boil fish for a min. or two in water and flake. Mix egg yolks and fish into cream sauce. Fold in egg whites. Put into a well-greased casserole, set in pan with 1" water. Bake at 350 degrees for 1 hr. or until a knife comes out clean.

NOTE: Serve as is or with hollandaise or chili sauce.

SEAFOOD
for 8

DEVILED SEAFOOD CASSEROLE

Preparation: 35 min.
Chilling: 8 hr.
Baking: 30 min.

8 tbsp. butter
1 can (6-oz. size) crabmeat
1 lb. lobster, cooked
1 lb. shrimp, cooked
9 tbsp. flour
1 c. evaporated milk
1-1/2 c. milk
1 c. beef consomme
1 tbsp. cornstarch
1 tbsp. lemon juice
1 tbsp. Worcestershire
4 tbsp. ketchup
1 tbsp. horseradish
1 lrg. clove garlic, crushed
1 tsp. prepared mustard
1/2 tsp. salt
1 tsp. soy sauce
2 tsp. MSG (opt.)
1/4 tsp. cayenne
4 tbsp. parsley, chopped
1/4 c. sherry
1/2-1 c. bread crumbs

Melt butter in top of double boiler and blend in flour. Heat milks and consomme together. Blend into flour mixture slowly. Add cornstarch dissolved in a little milk and cook until thick. Add seasonings and stir well. Add seafood and sherry and stir gently to blend. Put in greased 3-4 qt. casserole. Sprinkle top with bread crumbs. Refrigerate 8 hr. Bring to room temperature. Bake uncovered at 400 degrees for 30 min.

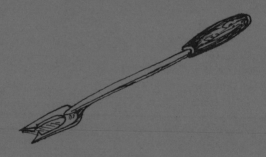

SPANISH PAELLA

Preparation: 30 min.
Baking: 30 min.

1 chicken (3-lb.), cut-up
2 med. onions, chopped
1 green pepper, chopped
1 jar (4 oz.) pimentos
1 can (8 oz.) tomatoes
2 c. uncooked rice
4 c. seafood stock
1/2 pkg. frozen peas
1 doz. sml. clams, steamed until opened
1 lb. shrimp, cooked and cleaned
1/2 lb. sml. sausages, fried
salt and pepper to taste
saffron

Brown chicken in oil. Brown onions and pepper. Add half the drained pimentos and blend thoroughly. Add tomatoes and cook well. Add rice, clam juice, peas, clams, shrimp and pinch of saffron. Bring to a boil. Arrange in casserole and garnish with remaining sausages and pimentos, cut in strips. Bake at 350 degrees for 30 min. or until rice is tender.

CHEESE & EGGS
for 8

CHEESE NOODLE OMELET

Preparation: 15 min.
Cooking: 20 min.

8 eggs
1 tsp. salt
1/8 tsp. pepper
2 tbsp. chopped green pepper
1 tbsp. pimento
2 tbsp. butter, melted
2 c. cooked noodles
1 c. shredded Cheddar cheese

In a bowl beat eggs, salt and pepper. Stir in noodles, cheese, green pepper and pimento. Melt butter in large skillet and pour over egg mixture. Cover and cook over medium heat 15-20 min. Do not stir. Cut into wedges and remove from skillet with spatula. Serve immediately.

ONION CHEESE CAKE

Preparation: 5 min.
Baking: 1 hr.

4 eggs
1 c. cottage cheese
1 c. skim milk
6 tbsp. flour
2 tbsp. dried parsley
1/4 c. sliced onions
1 tsp. prepared mustard
1 tsp. salt
1/4 tsp. pepper
pinch garlic powder

TOPPING:
2 tbsp. bacon bits
chopped chives

Blend all ingredients at high speed until creamy. Pour into 9" greased (or non-stick) cake or pie pan. Sprinkle with mixed bacon and chives. Bake at 325 degrees for 1 hr. until top is browned. (Puffiness will settle when removed from heat.)

SOUR CREAM SOUFFLE

Preparation: 10 min.
Baking: 35 min.

1/2 c. freshly grated Parmesan or Romano cheese
1-1/2—2 c. sour cream
1/2 c. flour
5-6 eggs, separated
2 extra egg whites
1 tsp. salt
1/4 tsp. cayenne
2 tbsp. chopped chives

Coat a buttered 2 qt. souffle dish with grated cheese and refrigerate. In a large bowl combine sour cream and flour. Beat well with whisk to blend. Add egg yolks, one at a time, whipping after each addition. Stir in salt, pepper, chives and remaining cheese. Beat all egg whites until firm and fold gently into cream/yolk mixture. Bake at 350 degrees for 30-35 min.

CHEESE & EGGS
for 8

QUICHE LORRAINE

Preparation: 15 min.
Cooking: 55 min.

1 pie shell (10")
    unbaked and chilled
1 tbsp. butter, softened
12 bacon slices, cooked
    and crumbled
4 eggs
2 c. heavy cream
3/4 tsp. salt
pinch nutmeg
pinch cayenne pepper
1/8 tsp. pepper
1 c. grated Swiss cheese

Preheat oven to 425 degrees. Rub butter over surface of pie shell. Combine eggs, cream, salt, nutmeg, cayenne and pepper. Beat with eggbeater to mix thoroughly. Sprinkle pie shell with bacon and cheese and pour in cream mixture. Bake at 425 degrees for 15 min. Reduce oven heat to 300 degrees and bake 40 min. or until knife inserted in center comes out clean.

TOMATOES BENEDICT

Preparation: 30 min.
Cooking: 5 min.

5 or 6 fresh beefsteak
    tomatoes
2-1/2 c. minced cooked ham
16 eggs
2 tbsp. vinegar
6 c. hollandaise sauce
    (see index)
16 slices bacon,
    cooked and crumbled

Slice tomatoes crosswise to obtain 16 slices, no ends. Poach the eggs in simmering water with a little vinegar added. Mound about 2 tbsp. ham on each tomato slice. Add a drained poached egg to each and pour hollandaise over (about 1/3 cup each). Top with bacon.

WELSH RAREBIT

Preparation: 15 min.

1/2 lb. sharp Cheddar
    cheese, cubed
2 egg yolks
2 tsp. butter
1 tbsp. Worcestershire
1 tsp. dry mustard
1 tsp. salt
1 tbsp. flour
2 c. milk
garlic salt to taste (opt.)
toast
    or English muffins

Dissolve flour in a little cold milk. Add remaining milk and beat in egg yolks. Add other ingredients and cook over low heat, stirring constantly. Add garlic salt if desired. Cook until cheese is well-melted, stirring until it boils. Serve over toast or muffins, plain or with choice of garnish. Can be frozen.

POTATOES, RICE & PASTA
for 8

FETTUCINE ALFREDO

Preparation: 15 min.
Cooking: 10 min.

1 lb. med. egg noodles
1/4 lb. butter, softened
1 c. heavy cream
freshly ground black pepper
1/4 lb. Parmesan cheese, grated

Cook noodles according to pkg. directions and drain. Put noodles over low heat, add butter and stir gently until butter is melted and coats noodles well. Add cream and grind in generous amounts of pepper. Continue stirring and tossing noodles gently until cream thickens and clings to noodles. Add cheese and stir to mix well.

GOLDEN POTATO CASSEROLE

Preparation: 15 min.
Baking: 50 min.

6 potatoes, baked
1 pt. sour cream
10 oz. sharp Cheddar cheese, grated
1 bunch green onions, finely chopped
3 tbsp. milk
1 tsp. salt
1/4 tsp. pepper
2 tbsp. butter
1/2 c. soft bread crumbs

Scoop out potatoes and put through grinder or ricer. Add sour cream, cheese, green onions, milk, salt and pepper. Mix well and transfer to a greased pan or baking dish, 9" x 13". Melt butter in a small pan. Add bread crumbs and mix well. Scatter over potato mixture. Bake uncovered at 300 degrees for 50 min. or until piping hot and golden brown. Cut into squares.

POTATO PIE

Preparation: 30 min.
Baking: 30 min.

1 unbaked 10" pie shell
1 lb. cottage cheese
2 c. unseasoned mashed potatoes (instant or fresh)
1/2 c. sour cream
2 eggs
2 tsp. salt
1/8 tsp. cayenne
1/2 c. thinly sliced scallions
3 tbsp. grated Parmesan cheese

Put cottage cheese through sieve to make it smooth. Beat mashed potatoes into it. Beat in sour cream, eggs, salt and cayenne. Stir in scallions and spoon into pie shell. Sprinkle top with grated cheese and bake at 425 degrees for 30 min. or until golden brown and puffy.

POTATOES, RICE & PASTA
for 8

POTATO SOUFFLE GRUYERE

Preparation: 1-1/2 hr.
Baking: 1 hr.

6 med. potatoes, baked
1/2 c. butter, softened
2 oz. Gruyere cheese, minced
2 tsp. minced chives
1 tsp. salt
1/8 tsp. pepper
pinch of savory
4 eggs, separated
1 c. heavy cream, whipped

Cool potatoes, discard skins, and put through ricer. (Should amount to about 3-1/2 cups.) Add butter, cheese, seasonings and mix well. Fold beaten egg yolks into cream. Fold in potatoes. Beat egg whites until peaks form and gently fold into potato mixture. Spoon into buttered 3 qt. souffle dish, or casserole with straight sides. Bake at 350 degrees for about 1 hr. or until browned on top and "set" inside.

CAMELOT POTATO SALAD

Preparation: 30 min.
Chilling: 4 hr.

15 med. potatoes, boiled
1/3 c. chopped chives
1 tsp. salt
1/8 tsp. freshly ground pepper
2 tbsp. grated onion
3/4 c. garlic salad dressing (oil and vinegar type)
1/4 c. Rhine wine
1/2 c. chopped celery
1/2 c. sour cream
1/2 c. mayonnaise

Garnish:
  salad greens
  parsley
  radishes
  sliced tomatoes
  sliced hard-boiled eggs
  black olives
  green olives

Pare and slice potatoes while still warm. Combine with chives, salt, pepper, onion and 1/2 cup salad dressing. Stir well and chill. Combine wine, celery, sour cream, mayonnaise and remaining salad dressing. Chill. Just before serving, combine 2 mixtures and mix well. Garnish.

POTATOES, RICE & PASTA
for 8

GERMAN POTATO SALAD

Preparation: 20 min.
Cooking: 10 min.

10 med. potatoes
2/3 c. salad oil
6 tbsp. vinegar
8 slices bacon
1/2 c. minced onion
1/2 c. minced green pepper
2 tsp. salt
1/4 tsp. pepper

Boil potatoes and cool. In large skillet, fry bacon until crisp then drain and crumble. In same pan, heat all ingredients, except potatoes and bacon. Peel and slice potatoes into large bowl. Pour heated ingredients over potatoes and mix well. Sprinkle bacon on top.

SWEET POTATO CASSEROLE

Preparation: 25 min.
Boiling: 1 hr.
Baking: 20 min.

6 sweet potatoes or yams
1 can (8 oz.) diced pineapple
1/4 c. juice from pineapple
1/3 c. sugar
6 tbsp. shortening
dash cinnamon
marshmallows

Boil peeled potatoes and mash. Add other ingredients (except marshmallows) and mix. Put in a 2-qt. casserole. Top with marshmallows and bake at 350 degrees until marshmallows brown (about 20 min.).

NOODLE PUDDING

Preparation: 20 min.
Baking: 30 min.

1/2 lb. noodles
1/2 c. butter
6 McIntosh apples, pared and sliced
1/2 c. shredded coconut
2 c. sugar
1/2 tsp. cinnamon
1/2 c. white raisins
3 eggs, well-beaten
juice of 1/2 lemon
1 tsp. vanilla

Cook noodles according to pkg. directions and drain. Add butter. Mix apples with coconut, sugar, cinnamon and raisins. Add noodles and butter to fruits and spices. Add eggs, lemon juice and vanilla and blend well. Pour into greased shallow baking dish and bake at 350 degrees-375 degrees for 1/2 hr. or until top is browned.

POTATOES, RICE & PASTA
for 8

RICE CASSEROLE

Preparation: 30 min.
Baking: 45 min.

1/2 c. chopped onion
3 tbsp. butter
2 c. cooked rice
1 tsp. salt
1/2 c. chopped celery
1/2 c. minced parsley
1 can (4 oz.) chopped mushrooms, including liquid
2 carrots, grated

Saute onion in butter. Put all ingredients in a buttered 2 qt. casserole, mixing with two forks. Bake covered at 300 degrees for 45 min.

WILD RICE CASSEROLE
(Minnesota's Chippewa)

Preparation: 15 min.
Baking: 1-1/2 hr.

1 c. grated American cheese
1 c. chopped ripe olives
1 can (20 oz.) tomatoes
1 can (3 oz.) mushrooms
1/2 c. chopped onion
1 c. wild rice, washed and drained
1/2 c. olive oil
1-1/2 c. boiling water
1-1/2 tsp. salt
1/4 tsp. pepper

Layer all ingredients in listed order in 2 qt. casserole. Bake at 350 degrees for 1-/2 hr.

GARLIC GRITS

Preparation: 10 min.
Baking: 30 min.

2 c. grits
1/2 c. milk
2 rolls garlic cheese
4 eggs, beaten
1/4 lb. butter
salt and pepper to taste
1 tsp. Worcestershire
Parmesan cheese
paprika

Cook grits according to pkg. directions. Add other ingredients. Pour into buttered casserole. Sprinkle with Parmesan cheese and paprika. Bake uncovered at 300 degrees for 30 min.

VEGETABLES
for 8

BANANA FRITTERS

Marinating: 1 hr.
Cooking: 10 min.

6 bananas, sliced 1"
2 c. light rum
1 egg, lightly beaten
1/4 c. milk
1-1/2—2 c. cornflake crumbs
1/2 tsp. salt
oil for deep frying

Marinate bananas in enough rum to cover for 1 hr. turning occasionally. Dip slices in egg mixed with milk. Then dip in crumbs mixed with salt. Drop into hot (375 degree) oil and fry for 1-2 min. until nicely browned. Drain on absorbent paper and salt lightly.

ITALIAN BEANS

Preparation: 30 min.
Cooking: 10 min.

3 pkg. frozen Italian beans
4 tbsp. butter
2 tbsp. chopped scallions
4 tbsp. flour
1-3/4 c. water
1/4 c. Marsala wine
1/2 tsp. chopped basil
1/2 tsp. chopped oregano
3/4 c. shredded Parmesan cheese
salt and pepper to taste

Cook beans as directed on pkg. Drain. Melt butter and saute scallions until golden. Sprinkle with flour and blend. Cook 1 min. so that it froths. Add water and wine and stir constantly until smooth and thick. Stir in herbs and cheese. Cook until cheese is melted. Add salt and pepper. Pour sauce over beans.

PUREE OF STRING BEANS

Preparation: 30 min.

4 lb. string beans
  or 4 pkg. frozen cut beans
2/3 c. milk
2 tbsp. butter
1/2 c. heavy cream
salt and pepper to taste
nutmeg

Cook fresh beans in boiling salted water about 10 min. until just tender. (If using frozen beans, cook according to pkg. directions.) Cut into small pieces. Puree beans and milk in blender, a little at a time. Add butter, cream, salt, pepper and nutmeg.

BEETS A LA SCHULTZ

Preparation: 15 min.
Cooking: 45 min.

3 cans (1-lb. size) beets
3/4 pt. sour cream
3 tbsp. vinegar
3 tbsp. butter
3 tbsp. flour
3 tbsp. sugar
salt and pepper to taste

Put beets through food grinder. Add sour cream, vinegar, butter, flour, sugar, salt and pepper. Stir well. Put in top of double boiler and cook for 45 min.

VEGETABLES
for 8

BRUSSELS SPROUTS AND CAULIFLOWER

Preparation: 10 min.
Cooking: 15 min.

1 lb. Brussels sprouts
1 med. head of cauliflower
2 tsp. salt
paprika
4 tbsp. butter

Break cauliflower into flowerets and cook in boiling, salted water with Brussels sprouts for about 10 min. Drain and toss with butter and paprika.

MARINATED CARROTS

Preparation: 20 min.
Chilling: 6 hr.

6-8 lrg. carrots, in 3" sticks
1/2 c. water
3/4 tsp. salt
1/4 c. olive oil
3 tbsp. vinegar
white pepper to taste
1 clove garlic, crushed
1 bay leaf
2 tbsp. minced parsley

Cook carrots rapidly in wide-bottomed pan with boiling water and 1/4 tsp. salt. Turn once and cook until tender but still crisp (8 min. or less). Drain. Place carrots in 1-1/2 qt. casserole. Mix oil, vinegar, 1/2 tsp. salt, pepper, garlic, crushed bay leaf and parsley and pour over carrots. Chill 6 hr. covered turning once or twice. Serve at room temperature.

CAULIFLOWER CHOPIN

Preparation: 15 min.
Cooking: 20 min.

1/2 c. butter, melted
1/2 c. croutons
1/4 tsp. onion salt
1/4 tsp. garlic salt
1/8 tsp. dried thyme
3 tbsp. lemon juice
1 lrg. cauliflower (about 2-1/2 lb.)
2 tsp. salt
4 thinly sliced lemons
1 tbsp. chopped parsley
1 egg, hard-boiled and chopped

In a medium skillet, melt butter and saute croutons with onion salt, garlic salt, dried thyme and lemon juice. Trim leaves and stem from cauliflower. Place in large pot, stem side down, and cover with boiling salted water. Add lemon slices. Simmer covered 20 min. or until tender. Drain. Sprinkle with egg and parsley. Pour crouton mixture over cauliflower.

VEGETABLES
for 8

CELERY AMANDINE

Preparation: 40 min.

6 c. diced celery
salt and pepper to taste
3/4 c. butter
3 tbsp. minced chives
3 tbsp. grated onion
1-1/2 c. blanched shredded almonds
1 tsp. minced garlic
3 tbsp. dry white wine

In a saucepan season celery lightly with salt and pepper and add 6 tbsp. butter. Cover and cook slowly until celery is tender, shaking frequently. During cooking, sprinkle celery with chives and onion. Arrange in a serving dish. Combine almonds and remaining butter and brown. Add garlic, salt, pepper and wine. Cook for 1 min. Pour over celery.

CORN PUDDING

Preparation: 15 min.
Cooking: 1 hr.

1 can (12 oz.) whole kernel corn
3 eggs
2 c. light cream
1/4 c. all-purpose flour
2 tbsp. butter, melted
1 tsp. salt
1/2 tsp. nutmeg
1/4 tsp. black pepper

In a large bowl, beat eggs until foamy. Beat in 1-1/2 cups of cream. In a small bowl, blend remaining 1/2 cup cream into flour until mixture is smooth. Beat into egg mixture. Add corn, butter, salt, nutmeg and pepper. Mix until well-blended. Pour into buttered 1-1/2 qt. baking dish. Put baking dish in a pan placed on oven rack. Pour boiling water to depth of 1" into pan. Bake at 325 degrees for 1 hr.

FRIED EGGPLANT WITH YOGHURT

Preparation: 30 min.
Cooking: 30 min.

1 c. yoghurt
3 cloves garlic, minced
1 tsp. salt
1 lrg. eggplant, peeled and cut in 1/2" slices
1 c. vegetable oil
1 lrg. onion, sliced
3 tomatoes, sliced

Mix together first 3 ingredients and set aside. Score eggplant with crisscrosses with point of knife and sprinkle with salt. Lay in a pan and let stand 10-15 min. Drain off excess water and wipe dry. Heat oil in large skillet. Fry eggplant slices until lightly browned and set aside. Brown onion slices until crisp. Drain and place between 2 slices wax paper and crush with rolling pin. Return eggplant to skillet and place sliced tomatoes on top. Sprinkle crushed onions over tomatoes. Simmer uncovered until hot. Spread half of yoghurt garlic mixture on a platter, place eggplant/tomatoes on top and cover with remaining yoghurt mixture.

VEGETABLES
for 8

EGGPLANT STUFFED WITH ITSELF

Preparation: 20 min.
Baking: 15 min.

1 lrg. eggplant
1/2 c. bread crumbs
1 can (28-oz.) tomatoes, drained
6 green olives, chopped
1 tbsp. chopped parsley
2 cloves garlic, minced
4 tbsp. olive oil
10 anchovies (opt.)
tomato sauce

Remove calyx of eggplant. Parboil whole for 10 min. and let cool. Cut in half lengthwise and remove pulp, keeping skin whole. Chop pulp and saute in olive oil with garlic and parsley for 5 min. turning constantly. Add tomatoes and bread crumbs. Mix. Add olives and anchovies and mix. If too soft a mixture, add extra bread crumbs. Fill shells and bake at 350 degrees for 15 min. Top with heated tomato sauce to cover.

MUSHROOMS PAPRIKA

Preparation: 20 min.
Cooking: 15 min.

2 lb. mushroom caps
2 med. onions, chopped
1/4 c. butter
4 tbsp. paprika
2 tsp. salt
1/2 c. sour cream

In a large skillet, melt butter and fry onion until brown. Add mushrooms to frying pan and add water to cover. Simmer until mushrooms are tender and water has evaporated, about 10 min. Stir in sour cream, paprika and salt. Heat, stirring constantly, but do not boil.

CHOUCROUTE ALSACIENNE

Preparation: 30 min.
Baking: 4 hr.

2 lb. sauerkraut
1 onion, finely chopped
2 carrots, finely chopped
1 lrg. sweet apple,
  pared and sliced
8-10 slices lean bacon
10 peppercorns, bruised
salt to taste
4 thin slices smoked
  or baked ham
  or prosciutto
3 tbsp. butter
1 c. beef consomme
1-2 c. domestic champagne

Wash sauerkraut in several changes of water and drain well, pressing to remove all water. Cover bottom of large earthenware casserole with bacon slices. Add a layer of onions, carrots and apples (about 1/2 of each). Sprinkle peppercorns over and salt lightly. Add another thin layer of sauerkraut, 2 slices ham, another layer of vegetables and apple slices, another layer of sauerkraut, 2 more slices of ham, and a topping layer of sauerkraut. Dot with butter, and cover with consomme (undiluted) and champagne. Bake covered at 300 degrees for about 4 hr. If more moistening is needed, add a little more champagne.

VEGETABLES
for 8

SPINACH CASSEROLE

Preparation: 10 min.
Baking: 20 min.

2 pkg. frozen chopped spinach
1/2 pt. sour cream
2 cans (4-oz. size) sliced mushrooms
2 tomatoes, sliced
Parmesan cheese, grated

Cook spinach according to pkg. directions. Drain. Add mushrooms and sour cream. Place in casserole and cover with sliced tomatoes and cheese. Bake uncovered at 350 degrees for 15-20 min.

SPINACH RING WITH MUSHROOMS

Preparation: 15 min.
Baking: 15 min.

4 pkg. frozen, chopped spinach
1 lb. fresh mushrooms, sliced
2 tbsp. butter
2 tsp. flour
1 c. light cream
salt and pepper to taste

Cook spinach according to pkg. directions. Drain thoroughly and pack into oiled ring mold. Place in a pan of hot water and bake at 350 degrees for 15 min. Saute mushrooms in butter until tender. Add light cream and season with salt and pepper. Thicken sauce with a little flour smoothly dissolved in a little cold water. Unmold spinach ring onto a heated platter and fill center with mushrooms.

STUFFED TOMATOES

Preparation: 30 min.
Baking: 20 min.

8 ripe tomatoes
1/2 c. bread crumbs
1/2 c. chopped fresh mushrooms
1/2 c. chopped onions
2 tbsp. powdered beef broth mix
2 cloves garlic, minced
2 tsp. chopped fresh basil
1 tbsp. chopped parsley
salt and pepper to taste
butter

Take a thin slice off the top of each tomato. Scoop out insides, leaving a thick shell. Mix tomato meat with all other ingredients except butter. Fill tomato shells with equal amounts of mixture. Dot each with butter and bake at 350 degrees for 15-20 min.

VEGETABLES
for 8

ZUCCHINI IN TOMATO SAUCE

Preparation: 20 min.
Baking: 40 min.

6 c. unpeeled zucchini, in 1/4" slices
1 med. onion, sliced
4 slices bacon, cooked and crumbled
1/2 c. Parmesan cheese, grated
1/4 tsp. oregano
1/4 tsp. paprika
1/2 c. chopped parsley
1/8 tsp. garlic powder
2 cans (8-oz. size) tomato sauce
1/4 tsp. bovril (opt.)
salt and pepper to taste

In large skillet brown zucchini and onion lightly in bacon fat. Place in layers in 2 qt. casserole, sprinkling each layer with mixture of cheese, oregano, paprika, salt, pepper, chopped parsley, garlic powder and bacon. Mix the tomato sauce with the bovril and pour over casserole. Bake uncovered at 375 degrees for about 40 min.

BAKED ZUCCHINI

Preparation: 20 min.
Baking: 40 min.

2 lb. unpeeled zucchini, (each about 5" long)
3 slices prosciutto, finely diced
3 slices bacon, minced
3 tbsp. chopped parsley
1/2 med. onion, minced
1/4 c. butter, melted
salt and pepper to taste

Cook zucchini in boiling water for 3 min. and drain. Slice each in half lengthwise and put in buttered baking dish in a single layer. Mix prosciutto, bacon, parsley, onion and seasonings. Sprinkle on top of zucchini. Pour butter over all and bake uncovered at 350 degrees for 30-40 min.

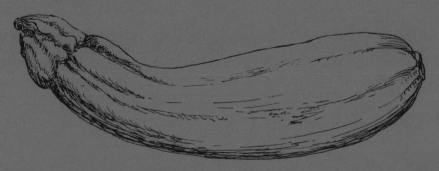

SALADS
for 8

NOTE: *A selection of Salad Dressings for tossed green or mixed salads appears in the Accompaniments Chapter.*

ANTIPASTO SALAD

Preparation: 20 min.

1 head iceberg lettuce
1 jar (6 oz.) artichoke hearts, drained
1 jar (4 oz.) pimento slices,
1 tin Norwegian sardines drained
1 can (7-1/4 oz.) black olives
1 can (3-1/2 oz.) tuna fish, flaked and drained
1 tin rolled anchovy fillets
16 slices salami
16 slices prosciutto or boiled ham, rolled
2 c. sliced celery
2 c. oil and vinegar dressing

Line a large bowl with lettuce. Arrange other ingredients spoke-wheel fashion. Cover with plastic wrap and chill until ready to serve. Place salad dressing on the side.

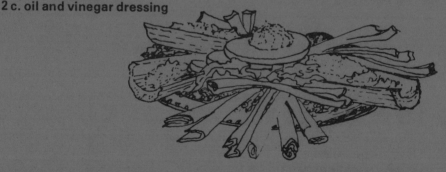

AVOCADO MOLD

Preparation: 10 min.
Chilling: 2 hr.

2 pkg. (3-oz. size) lemon gelatin
1 avocado, peeled and diced
1 c. chopped walnuts
3/4 c. diced celery
handful of red grapes, halved and pitted
pinch of salt

Prepare gelatin according to pkg. directions. Stir in all other ingredients. Pour into 2 qt. mold and chill 2 hr. or until set.

SALADS
for 8

COLESLAW

Preparation: 10 min.
Chilling: 2 hr.

1 c. mayonnaise
3 tbsp. tarragon vinegar
1 tbsp. sugar
1 tsp. celery seed
1/2 tsp. dry mustard
3 c. shredded cabbage
1/2 c. shredded carrots
1/2 c. shredded
　green pepper

Mix first 5 ingredients to make sauce. Chill. Just before serving toss vegetables with sauce.

GREEN BEAN SALAD

Preparation: 10 min.
Chilling: 2 hr.

3 cans (1-lb. size) cut green
　beans, drained
1 lrg. onion, thinly sliced
1/3 green pepper, minced
1/8 tsp. oregano
1/8 tsp. celery salt
1/8 tsp. garlic salt
1/3 c. red wine vinegar
1/3 c. olive oil
salt and pepper to taste

Place all ingredients in bowl and toss lightly. Cover and marinate in refrigerator for at least 2 hr. Toss occasionally. Serve very cold.

TOMATO ASPIC

Preparation: 5 min.
Chilling: 2 hr.

2 pkg. (3-oz. size) strawberry
　gelatin
4 c. tomato juice, heated
salt and pepper to taste
1/2 tsp. onion salt
4 tsp. horseradish

Mix all ingredients together and pour into 6-cup mold. Refrigerate for 2 hr.

DESSERTS
for 8

NOTE: A large selection of Cakes, Pies, Cookies and Squares appears in the Accompaniments Chapter.

APRICOT CHEESE DELIGHT

Preparation: 30 min.
Chilling: 4 hr.

2 pkg. (3-oz. size) orange gelatin
2 c. boiling water
3/4 c. sml. marshmallows
1 can (1-lb. 4-oz.) apricots, cut-up
1 can (1-lb. 4-oz.) crushed pineapple

Dissolve gelatin in water. Add marshmallows and stir until melted. Cool. Drain fruit, reserving juices. Add fruit to gelatin mixture and pour into a 9" x 9" or 11" x 7" dish and chill.

DRESSING:

1/2 c. sugar
3 tbsp. flour
1 egg, beaten
1/2 pt. cream, whipped
1/2 tsp. lemon extract
1 c. grated Cheddar cheese
1 c. apricot/pineapple juice

Combine sugar and flour. Add egg and fruit juices. Cook until slightly thickened and chill. Fold whipped cream into dressing mixture. Sprinkle with cheese.

BUTTERSCOTCH CRUNCH

Preparation: 20 min.
Baking: 15 min.
Freezing: 2 hr.

1 c. all-purpose flour
1/2 c. quick-cooking rolled oats
1/4 c. brown sugar
1/2 c. butter
1/2 c. chopped nuts
1 jar (12 oz.) butterscotch ice cream topping
1 qt. chocolate ice cream

Combine sifted flour, oats and sugar. Cut in butter until mixture resembles coarse crumbs. Stir in nuts. Pat mixture into 13" x 9" buttered pan. Bake at 400 degrees for 15 min. Stir. Crumble while still warm. Cool. Spread half the crumbs in buttered 9" x 9" baking pan. Drizzle about half ice cream topping over crumbs. Stir ice cream to soften and spoon carefully over crumbs. Drizzle remaining topping. Sprinkle with remaining crumbs. Freeze.

DESSERTS
for 8

CHOCOLATE DELIGHT

Preparation: 30 min.
Chilling: 3 hr.

1/2 angel food cake
1 pkg. (12 oz.) chocolate chips
2 egg yolks, slightly beaten
2 egg whites, stiffly beaten
2 c. heavy cream, whipped

Break cake into walnut sized pieces and put in 9" square pan. In top of a double boiler, melt chocolate chips. Remove from heat and add egg yolks very quickly. Fold in egg whites. Cool. Add half the whipped cream and stir gently. Pour over cake. Refrigerate 2-3 hr. Cut in squares and serve with dollop of whipped cream.

CHOCOLATE FONDUE

Preparation: 20 min.

1/2 c. heavy cream
1 lb. milk chocolate
3 tbsp. kirsch (opt.)
FOR DIPPING:
pound cake, cubed
pineapple chunks
bananas
marshmallows
strawberries

Warm cream in fondue pot, add chocolate pieces and stir until melted and well-blended. Add kirsch. Serve with any or all of listed foods used for dipping.

COFFEE CREAM

Preparation: 20 min.
Chilling: 4 hr.

1/2 lb. marshmallows
1/2 c. strong coffee, very hot
1/2 pt. heavy cream, whipped

Cut marshmallows into small pieces with wet scissors. Put in top of double boiler with coffee. When marshmallows are melted, put aside to cool. Add whipped cream and chill.

MRS. COOLIDGE'S COFFEE SOUFFLE

Preparation: 30 min.
Chilling: 4 hr.

1-1/4 c. strong coffee
2/3 c. sugar
1/2 c. milk
3 eggs, separated
1/4 tsp. salt
1 env. unflavored gelatin
1/4 c. cold water
1/2 tsp. vanilla
1/2 pt. heavy cream, whipped
grated bitter chocolate

Mix coffee with 1/3 c. sugar, add milk and heat in top of double boiler. Beat egg yolks with remaining sugar and add to coffee mixture. Add salt and cook over boiling water, stirring until mixture thickens. Remove from heat and add gelatin softened in cold water. Beat egg whites until very stiff and fold in. Add vanilla. Mold and chill. Serve with whipped cream. Garnish with chocolate.

DESSERTS
for 8

CRANBERRY DESSERT

Preparation: 20 min.
Baking: 1 hr.

1/4 lb. butter
1 c. brown sugar
1/2 c. flour
1 c. quick oatmeal
1 can (16 oz.) cranberry sauce
whipped cream or vanilla ice cream

Cream butter and add brown sugar. Sift and add flour. Add oatmeal to mixture and stir until just mixed. On an 8" x 8" greased pan, spread out a little more than half the mixture evenly over the bottom. Pour the cranberry sauce evenly over this. Sprinkle rest of oatmeal mixture on top. Bake at 350 degrees for 1 hr. Serve hot with whipped cream or ice cream.

CURRIED FRUIT

Preparation: 15 min.
Baking: 1 hr.

1 can (1 lb.) pineapple rings
1 can (1 lb.) pear halves
1 can (1 lb.) apricots or peaches (or both)
1/2 c. brown sugar, tightly packed
1/4 c. butter
1-2 tsp. curry powder
maraschino cherries
whipped cream

Drain juice from all fruit. In a shallow baking dish, arrange pineapple rings, topped with pears, apricots and/or peaches. In the center of each, add one cherry. Melt butter, sugar and curry powder and pour over fruit. Bake covered at 350 degrees about 1 hr. Top with whipped cream.

ICE CREAM MOLD

Preparation: 10 min.
Freezing: 6 hr.

1 box (10 oz.) peanut brittle
1/2 gal. softened vanilla or coffee ice cream

Butter a 2 qt. ring mold. Crush peanut brittle thoroughly and put in mold. Pack ice cream on top and freeze. Will keep in freezer for weeks.

DESSERTS
for 8

LEMON DESSERT

Preparation: 30 min.
Chilling: 6 hr.

4 eggs, separated
1 c. sugar
juice and grated rind of 2 lemons
4 tbsp. lemon gelatin
1/2 c. boiling water
1 lb. vanilla wafers
1/4 c. butter, melted
1/2 pt. heavy cream

In saucepan combine egg yolks, 1/2 cup sugar, juice and lemon rind. Stir over medium heat until thick. Add gelatin dissolved in boiling water. Stir to mix and let cool thoroughly. Crush vanilla wafers (reserve 1 cup for topping), and mix with melted butter, if desired. Press into greased 13" x 9" pan. Beat egg whites until thick, adding 1/2 cup sugar gradually continuing to beat. Beat cream until thick. Combine cream, egg whites and lemon mixture in large bowl beating slowly with electric mixer. Pour into cake pan. Top with reserved crumbs. Cover with foil and refrigerate 6 hr. Cut into squares.

LEMON MOUSSE

Preparation: 30 min.
Chilling: 2 hr.

4 eggs, separated
1 c. sugar
1/2 c. lemon juice
2 env. unflavored gelatin
1/2 c. cold water
3/4 c. boiling water
1/2 c. heavy cream

Beat together egg yolks and sugar. Soften gelatin in cold water. Add boiling water and stir to dissolve. Mix in lemon juice. Pour half of mixture into yolk/sugar mixture. Mix thoroughly and pour into remaining gelatin mixture. Stir and set aside. Whip cream and egg whites separately. Fold both into gelatin mixture. Turn into large mold. Chill until firm.

LEMON SOUFFLE WITH STRAWBERRIES

Preparation: 1-1/2 hr.
Chilling: 3-4 hr.

2 c. boiling water
2 pkg. (3-oz. size) lemon gelatin
2 bottles (7-oz. size) lemon-lime carbonated beverage
1/4 c. lemon juice
2 tsp. grated lemon rind
1 pt. heavy cream, whipped
few drops yellow food coloring
2 sml. pkg. frozen sliced strawberries

Pour boiling water over gelatin and stir until dissolved. Stir in lemon-lime beverage, lemon juice and rind. Chill until almost firm. Beat gelatin until foamy. Fold in whipped cream and food coloring. Pour into 1-1/2 qt. souffle dish until 1" from top. Place a 3" collar of waxed paper around inside of dish. Pour remaining mixture into dish and chill several hr. until firm. Remove paper and serve topped with strawberries.

DESSERTS
for 8

ORANGE MARSHMALLOW

Preparation: 15 min.
Chilling: 3 hr.

1 c. orange juice
26 marshmallows
1/2 pt. heavy cream, whipped

Heat orange juice to boiling point and pour it over the marshmallows. Fold in whipped cream. Pour into glass serving dish and refrigerate to set for about 3 hr.

BROILED PEACHES FLAMBE

Preparation: 5 min.
Broiling: 10 min.

12 canned peach halves
12 tbsp. dark brown sugar
12 dabs butter
1/3-1/2 c. bourbon or dark rum

Arrange peach halves in ovenproof dish. Place 1 tbsp. sugar and a dab of butter in center of each. Broil 3" from heat until sugar melts and peaches are heated through. Heat bourbon or rum and pour over peaches. Ignite. Serve at once.

PLUM PUDDING

Preparation: 15 min.
Cooking: 4 hr.

1 c. chopped suet
1 c. bread crumbs
1 c. sugar
1 c. raisins
1 c. currants
1 c. flour
1/2 c. chopped nuts
1 tsp. salt
1 tsp. cinnamon
1/2 c. lemon peel
4 eggs, beaten
1 c. milk

Mix all dry ingredients and fruits together. Add eggs and milk. Turn into a floured cloth and tie tightly with string. Drop into a large pot of boiling water to cover. Boil 4 hr. adding water to cover as it boils away. This makes a good-sized pudding.

HARD SAUCE:

1 lb. sweet butter
2 c. confectioners' sugar
4 tbsp. heavy cream
1 tsp. vanilla extract

Preparation: 20 min.
Chilling: 8 hr.

Cream butter until soft. Gradually blend in sugar and cream, beating constantly. Add vanilla and chill.

YIELD: 1-3/4 cups sauce

DESSERTS
for 8

LA PYRAMIDE DESSERT

Preparation: 20 min.
Baking: 5 min.

STEP I

- 6 egg yolks
- 1/4 c. granulated sugar
- 3/4 c. light cream
- 1 tbsp. cornstarch
- 2 oz. baking chocolate, grated

Beat yolks until lemon colored adding sugar gradually with electric beater in double boiler top. Add cream, cornstarch and chocolate. Place over hot water and cook, beating constantly, until heavy, creamy consistency. Remove from heat.

STEP II

- 2 doz. lady fingers
- 1/4-1/2 small jar currant jelly
- 1-1/3 c. heavy cream
- 6 egg whites
- 1/3 c. sugar

Spread jelly on lady fingers, then dip into cream. Place in baking dish. Pour custard (step 1) over. Beat whites until stiff, add sugar and beat until very stiff. Spread on lady finger/custard mixture. Bake at 400 degrees until hot and top is light brown, about 1-2 min. Serve with rum or kirsch syrup.

RUM OR KIRSCH SYRUP

- 1/2 c. water
- 1 c. sugar
- 2 lemon slices
- 2 orange slices
- a few dashes cinnamon
- 1" vanilla bean
- 1 clove
- 1/2 c. rum or kirsch

Boil all ingredients except liquor for 8-10 min. stirring frequently. Strain. Add liquor. Serve hot or cold. Can be frozen.

RASPBERRY MOUSSE

Preparation: 10 min.
Freezing: 2 hr.

- 1 pkg. (1 lb.) frozen raspberries
- 1/2 c. sugar
- 1/2 tbsp. lemon juice
- 1 pt. heavy cream, whipped

Thaw raspberries slightly and mix with sugar and lemon juice. Fold into whipped cream. Turn gently into 2 qt. mold or deep ice tray. Freeze 2 hr.

DESSERTS
for 8

SCANDINAVIAN APPLE DESSERT

Preparation: 15 min.
Baking: 40 min.

6 tbsp. butter
1/2 c. fine sugar
1/2 c. ground almonds
2 tsp. cornstarch
2 egg whites, stiffly beaten
6 c. sliced apples
3/4 c. brown sugar, tightly packed
juice of 1 lemon
1 generous tsp. cinnamon
1 c. heavy cream, whipped
   or 1 c. hard sauce (see index)
   or 1/2 pt. vanilla ice cream, sprinkled with 1 oz. rum

Mix first 4 ingredients together. Fold in egg whites. Pour into greased 2-3 qt. casserole. Place apples on top of mixture spreading evenly. Sprinkle on brown sugar, lemon and cinnamon. Bake at 350 degrees for 30-40 min. Serve with whipped cream, hard sauce or vanilla ice cream sprinkled with rum.

SWEDISH CREAM

Preparation: 15 min.
Chilling: 3-1/2 hr.

1 pt. med. cream
1 pt. sour cream
1 env. unflavored gelatin
1/2 c. sugar
1/2 tsp. vanilla
1/4 tsp. salt
fruit, canned or fresh
sprigs of mint

Heat cream just to boiling, but do not boil. Dissolve gelatin in a little cold water and add to cream. Add sugar and stir over medium heat to dissolve. Cool in refrigerator. Just before it gels, add vanilla and sour cream. Stir well. Pour into a mold that has been rinsed in cold water. Chill about 3 hr. Unmold onto platter and surround with fruit. Garnish with mint.

to serve 12

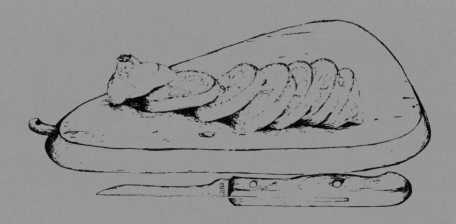

HORS D'OEUVRES
for 12

GUACAMOLE
Preparation: 20 min.

3 tbsp. minced onion
1 tomato
2 avocados, mashed
1 tsp. salt
2 tsp. chili powder
1 tbsp. lemon juice
tortillas

Peel and chop tomato. Mix with onion and avocado until smooth. Blend in salt, chili powder and lemon juice. Serve with tortillas.

BOUREKAKIA (Greek Cheese Puffs)
Preparation: 15 min.
Baking: 15 min.

1/2 lb. cottage cheese
3 oz. cream cheese, softened
2 eggs, beaten
1/2 lb. pkg. strudel leaves
1/4 lb. butter, melted

Combine cheeses and eggs. Cut strudel leaves in 4" x 8" strips and brush each with butter. Stack 4 strips. Place 1 tsp. of cheese mixture in the corner of stack and fold into a triangle. Repeat until cheese mixture is used. Brush each triangle with butter. Bake at 350 degrees for 15 min. or until golden.

CHEESE ALMOND BALLS
Marinating: 8 hr.
Preparation: 30 min.
Chilling: 3 hr.

8 oz. Camembert cheese
1 c. dry white wine
1/2 c. sweet butter, softened
1 c. ground salted almonds
toasted crackers

Pour wine over cheese in bowl and let stand at room temperature 8 hr. turning cheese once or twice. Discard liquid. Press cheese through a coarse sieve and blend in butter. Chill 3 hr. Shape into 24 small balls and roll in ground almonds. Serve with toasted crackers.

BAKED CLAMS ON THE HALF SHELL
Preparation: 15 min.
Baking: 30 min.

24 raw chowder clams
3 hard rolls
1 lrg. onion, minced
2 eggs
parsley flakes
pepper
poultry seasoning
bacon (opt.)
24 clam shells

Soak rolls in clam juice. Chop clams. Squeeze rolls nearly dry and mix with clams. Add onion and eggs. Mix. Coat with parsley flakes mixed with poultry seasoning. Put mixture on half shells. Bake at 375 degrees for 30 min.

NOTE: Strips of bacon may be put on top of mixture prior to baking.

HORS D'OEUVRES
for 12

CRABMEAT ALEXANDER

Preparation: 10 min.
Chilling: 2 hr.

18 oz. frozen crabmeat
2/3 c. olive oil
1/3 c. vinegar
2 tbsp. chopped chives
1 tbsp. chopped capers
4 anchovies, chopped
salt and pepper to taste
1/4 c. mayonnaise
1/4 c. chili sauce
36 sml. artichoke hearts
1/2 c. chopped parsley

Mix together oil, vinegar, chives, capers, anchovies, salt and pepper. Combine with crabmeat and chill at least 2 hr. Just before serving add mayonnaise and chili sauce. Spoon into chilled artichoke hearts. Sprinkle with chopped parsley and serve very, very cold.

CRABMEAT CANAPES

Preparation: 15 min.
Chilling: 2 hr.
Broiling: 5 min.

6 oz. crabmeat, flaked
1/2 c. celery, chopped fine
1 tbsp. mayonnaise
2 tbsp. ketchup
3 oz. cream cheese
1 tsp. Worcestershire
paprika
salt and pepper to taste
crackers
  or toast rounds
  or cucumber slices

Combine all ingredients and chill.
To serve cold: Spread on crackers, toast rounds or chilled 1/4" thick cucumber slices.
To serve hot: Spread on toast rounds and broil until bubbly.

DEVILED HAM PUFFS

Preparation: 20 min.
Baking: 12 min.

2 cans (2-1/4-oz. size)
  deviled ham
8 oz. cream cheese
1 tsp. onion juice
1/2 tsp. baking powder
1 tsp. dry mustard
1 egg yolk
salt to taste
24 bread rounds (2-1/2")

Blend together cheese, onion juice, baking powder, mustard, egg yolk and salt. Toast bread rounds on one side. Spread untoasted sides with deviled ham and cover each with mound of cheese mixture. Place on cookie sheet and bake at 375 degrees for 10-12 min. or until puffed up and brown. Serve hot.

HORS D'OEUVRES
for 12

EGG ROLL

Preparation: 1 hr.
Cooking: 30 min.

PASTRY:
6 eggs
1-1/2 c. water
1-1/2 tsp. salt
1-1/2 c. sifted flour
2 tbsp. oil

Beat together egg, water and salt. Beat in flour. Heat oil in 7" skillet and pour in a little batter to make a thin pancake. Brown on one side only. Continue until all batter is used.

FILLING:
3 c. chopped celery
1-1/2 c. sliced onion
3/4 c. chopped scallions
3 c. chopped Chinese or green cabbage
4 tbsp. oil
1-1/2 tsp. salt
3/4 tsp. pepper
1-1/2 c. cooked chicken
1 egg white, beaten

Cook celery, onions, scallions and cabbage in oil for 5 min. Add salt, pepper and chicken cut in strips. Cool. Place 1 heaping tbsp. cooled filling at one end of uncooked side of pancake and roll up, tucking ends in. Seal with a little beaten egg white and chill. Fry in deep fat until brown.
NOTE: Serve with hot mustard and duck sauce.

FROSTED PATE

Preparation: 30 min.
Chilling: 3 hr.

1 lb. liverwurst
1/2 tsp. basil
3 tbsp. minced onion
brandy to taste
8 oz. cream cheese
1 tsp. mayonnaise
1 clove garlic, minced
1-2 drops Tabasco
black caviar (sml. jar)

Blend liverwurst, basil, onion and brandy. Form into balls or mold in small loaf pan. Chill for 2 hr. Cover with mixture of cream cheese, mayonnaise, garlic and Tabasco. Chill for 1 hr. Just before serving spread thinly with caviar.

MUSHROOM PASTE

Preparation: 30 min.
Chilling: 2 hr.

1 lb. fresh mushrooms
3 tbsp. butter
salt and pepper to taste
1/4 c. flour
3/4 c. cream
1 tbsp. brandy
crackers

Grind mushrooms in meat grinder. Saute mushrooms in butter in large skillet 4-5 min. Season to taste. Add flour and blend. Add cream and brandy and stir constantly over medium heat, until smooth and hot, about 10 min. Chill covered about 2 hr. Serve with crackers.

HORS D'OEUVRES
for 12

STUFFED MUSHROOMS

Preparation: 15 min.
Broiling: 5 min.

40 mushrooms, med. size
8 oz. cream cheese
1 pkg. blue cheese
   salad dressing mix
2 tbsp. milk
1/4 c. minced onion
salt and pepper to taste

Destem mushrooms and chop enough stems, finely, to make 1 cup. Combine cream cheese, dressing mix and milk. Blend well. Stir in chopped mushroom pieces, onion, salt and pepper. Fill mushrooms caps. Broil 5 min. or until golden brown.

SWEET AND SOUR MEATBALLS

Preparation: 15 min.
Cooking: 1-1/2 hr.

2 lb. ground beef
1 med. onion, grated
1 egg, beaten
2 tbsp. bread crumbs
1 clove garlic, crushed
2 c. hot water
1/2 c. raisins
1/3 c. sugar
2 lemon slices
1 c. ketchup
1/2 c. chili sauce
1/2 tsp. Worcestershire
dash chili powder
dash nutmeg
salt and pepper to taste

Mix ground beef, onion, egg, bread crumbs and garlic. Form into 3/4" balls. Mix water, raisins, sugar and lemon slices in a saucepan and bring to a boil. Add ketchup, chili sauce, Worcestershire, chili powder and nutmeg. Stir to blend. Add meatballs and simmer covered for 1-1/2 hr. Season to taste.

EASY SHRIMP DIP

Preparation: 10 min.

2 cans (4-1/2-oz. size) shrimp
1 tbsp. lemon juice
1 c. mayonnaise
1 sml. onion, minced
dash Tabasco
pinch curry powder

Drain and mash shrimp. Combine with remaining ingredients.

STUFFED CHERRY TOMATOES

Preparation: 30 min.
Chilling: 1 hr.

1 box cherry tomatoes
1 tbsp. mayonnaise
1/3 c. walnuts, chopped
4 oz. cream cheese

Cut off tomato tops and scoop out insides with demitasse spoon. Mix remaining ingredients and fill tomatoes. Serve cold.

SOUPS
for 12

POTAGE CREME D'ARTICHAUTS

Preparation: 20 min.
Chilling: 2 hr.

3 pkg. froz. artichoke hearts
2 cans cream of
  chicken soup
1 c. heavy cream
2 c. chicken broth
1/2 c. dry white wine
onion salt to taste
salt and pepper to taste
chopped parsley
  or chopped chives

Cook artichoke hearts according to pkg. directions. Combine with soup, cream, broth, wine and onion salt. Blend in 2 or 3 batches in blender. Add salt and pepper and chill at least 2 hr. To serve, pour in cups and garnish with chopped parsley or chives.

CURRIED CHICKEN SOUP WITH AVOCADO

Preparation: 5 min.
Cooking: 10 min.

6 ripe avocados
2 c. chicken broth
  or 1 can cream of
    chicken soup
2/3 c. milk or half & half
1 tbsp. butter
1 tsp. curry powder
nutmeg or mace to taste
almonds
chives

Pare and slice avocados into soup bowls allowing 1/2 avocado per person. Heat rest of ingredients together until piping hot. Pour over avocado. Add almonds. Sprinkle liberally with chives.

CORN SOUP

Preparation: 15 min.
Heating: 10 min.

4 c. corn niblets
1/4 c. flour
2 qt. milk
1/4 c. butter
1 med. onion, thinly sliced
salt and pepper to taste
1 qt. half & half

Combine all ingredients except half and half and blend in 2 batches in blender. Pour into large double boiler top and add half and half. Heat until thickened, adding milk if necessary. Strain through fine sieve to remove husks. Serve hot.

NOTE: This can be frozen, but must be beaten well when reheating.

SOUPS
for 12

CRAB CHOWDER SUPREME

Preparation: 30 min.
Cooking: 17 min.

1 c. chopped onion
1 c. chopped celery
6 tbsp. butter
6 c. milk
2 cans potato soup
2 cans (7-1/2-oz. size) crabmeat
2 cans (8-oz. size) creamed corn
4 tbsp. chopped pimento
1/2 tsp. salt
1/2 tsp. dried thyme, crushed
2 bay leaves
1/2 c. dry vermouth
1/2 c. snipped parsley

In large saucepan cook onions and celery in butter until tender. Drain and flake crabmeat and add with remaining ingredients except vermouth and parsley. Cook and stir until heated through about 15 min. Stir in vermouth and heat 2 min. more. Remove bay leaves. Garnish with parsley.

CUCUMBER SOUP

Preparation: 40 min.
Chilling: 2 hr.

4 med. cucumbers, chopped
2 med. onions, chopped
8 tbsp. butter
4 chicken bouillon cubes
4 c. boiling water
salt and pepper to taste
2 c. sour cream
chopped chives

Dissolve bouillon cubes in water. In large skillet saute cucumbers and onions in butter until glistening. Add to bouillon and simmer 30 min. Add salt and pepper. Puree in blender until smooth. Strain. Chill for 2 hr. Top each serving with a dollop of sour cream and garnish with chives.

GAZPACHO

Preparation: 30 min.
Chilling: 2 hr.

1 cucumber, peeled
1 green pepper, chopped
1 lrg. onion, chopped
4 fresh tomatoes, peeled
1 lrg. can tomato juice
1 can (12 oz.) V-8 juice
4 tbsp. olive oil
4 tsp. vinegar
juice of 1 lemon
garlic salt to taste
salt to taste
1 c. each diced cucumber, onion, green pepper, tomatoes
1 c. croutons

Blend first 4 ingredients in blender. Combine with next 7 ingredients and chill at least 2 hr. Garnish with croutons and diced vegetables.

SOUPS
for 12

HAMBURG CHOWDER

Preparation: 30 min.
Chilling: 2 hr.

3 lb. chopped beef
2 med. onions, chopped
3-1/2 qt. boiling water
6 tsp. salt
4 c. chopped tomatoes
2 c. diced raw potatoes
2 c. diced celery
1 pt. cream
chopped parsley

In large saucepan brown beef and onions. Add other ingredients, except cream and parsley and simmer covered 2 hr. Just before serving add cream. Garnish with chopped parsley.

PORK BUTT SPECIAL SOUP

Preparation: 1-1/2 hr.
Heating: 15 min.

2 cans beef bouillon
2 cans chicken broth
6 soup-cans water
1 lrg. pork butt
4 carrots, sliced
4 onions, sliced
8 potatoes, sliced or quartered
2 bay leaves
garlic powder to taste
pepper to taste
4 tsp. chopped chives
4 tsp. chopped parsley

Combine all ingredients and cook in kettle for 1-1/4 hr. Remove bay leaves. Cut meat off bone, dice and add to soup. Correct seasonings and bring to serving temperature.

SPINACH SOUP

Preparation: 10 min.
Cooking: 10 min.

1 qt. chicken stock or broth
2 tsp. flour or corn starch
1 c. heavy cream
6 egg yolks
1 c. cooked, chopped spinach
salt and pepper to taste
2 tbsp. grated Parmesan cheese

Heat stock. Thicken with flour blended with a little cold water. Mix cream and egg yolks and add to stock mixture. Add spinach, salt and pepper. Reheat but do not boil. Garnish with cheese.

SOUPS
for 12

HEARTY TURKEY SOUP

Preparation: 3-1/2 hr.
Chilling: 8 hr.
Cooking: 1 hr.

carcass of roast turkey
water to cover
1/4 c. dried barley
1 c. coarsely chopped onion
1 c. diagonally sliced celery, 1/2" thick
1 pkg. frozen mixed vegetables
12 chicken bouillon cubes
1-2 c. stuffing
mixed dried herbs
salt and pepper to taste
Kitchen Bouquet

Start the day before soup is needed. Remove and reserve meat from carcass. Break up carcass and put in large kettle. Cover with water and simmer uncovered about 3 hr. Strain out solids. Remove remaining meat from bones and add to reserved meat. Discard bones, skin, etc. Bring broth to 3 qt. by adding water if necessary. Refrigerate 8 hr. Spoon congealed fat from top. In large saucepan cook barley in 4 cups broth for 45 min. Add reserved meat, onions, celery, mixed vegetables, bouillon cubes, stuffing, herbs, salt, pepper and remaining broth. Cook uncovered 15 min. Correct seasoning and color with Kitchen Bouquet.

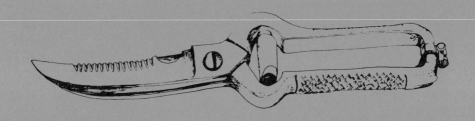

ZUCCHINI AND GREEN BEAN SOUP

Preparation: 30 min.
Chilling: 2 hr.

2 lb. zucchini, sliced
1/2 c. chopped onion
1 c. chopped celery
8 c. chicken broth
2 pkg. frozen green beans
1/2 tsp. pepper
1/4 tsp. salt
1 tsp. dried fines herbs

Cook zucchini, onions and celery in 4 cups broth until just done. Cook beans according to pkg. directions, using broth instead of water. Blend drained vegetables, herbs and seasonings and a little broth in blender. Mix puree in large saucepan with remaining broth. Heat, correct seasonings and serve hot or very cold.

MEATS
for 12

BAKED MANICOTTI

Preparation: 1 hr.
Cooking: 50 min.

SAUCE:

5 cans (8-oz. size) tomato sauce
1 c. minced onion
1 clove garlic, crushed
2 tbsp. chopped parsley
1-1/2 tsp. oregano
1/2 tsp. basil

SHELLS AND STUFFING:

24 manicotti shells
6 qt. boiling water
4 tbsp. oil
1 c. chopped onion
2 cloves garlic, crushed
1/2 lb. fresh mushrooms, chopped
2 lb. ground chuck
1 egg, slightly beaten
1 tbsp. salt
3/4 tsp. oregano
1/4 tsp. basil
1/4 tsp. pepper
8 oz. Mozzarella cheese, grated
1/2 c. grated Parmesan cheese

In a large saucepan bring all ingredients to a boil and simmer covered for 30 min.

Cook manicotti 8 min. in water and 1 tbsp. oil. Drain. Saute onion, garlic and mushrooms in remaining oil until onion is golden, about 5 min. Turn into large bowl. In same skillet, cook beef until it loses redness. Drain and add to vegetables with egg, salt, oregano, basil, pepper, 1-1/2 cups tomato sauce and Mozzarella. Stir to mix well. Rinse manicotti in cold water, drain and fill with about 2 heaping tbsp. of mixture per shell. Spread about 1 cup tomato sauce in 13" x 9" baking dish. Arrange 2 rows of manicotti lengthwise in dish. Cover with about 1 cup sauce and sprinkle with half the Parmesan. Place remaining manicotti in a row down center of dish. Cover with remaining sauce and sprinkle with remaining Parmesan and Mozzarella. Bake covered at 375 for 40 min. Remove cover and bake 10 min. longer.

BEEF STROGANOFF

Preparation: 15 min.
Baking: 40 min.

6 tbsp. butter
4-1/2 lb. round steak
1 can (16 oz.) sliced mushrooms, drained
3 pkg. onion soup mix
6 tbsp. flour
3 c. milk
1-1/2 c. water
salt to taste
1/2 tsp. pepper
3 c. sour cream
3 tbsp. minced parsley

Cut steak in narrow strips and brown in butter in large skillet. Stir in mushrooms. soup mix, flour, milk, water, salt and pepper. Mix well and simmer covered very gently, stirring occasionally, until meat is tender, 30 min. Stir in sour cream and heat slowly but do not boil. Garnish with parsley.

MEATS
for 12

BOEUF BOURGUIGNON

Preparation: 1 hr.
Cooking: 2-1/2 hr.

5 tbsp. oil or butter
6 lb. beef, 2" cubes
1/2 c. flour
1 tsp. salt
1/2 tsp. pepper
3 lrg. onions, sliced
4 c. red wine
2 cans beef bouillon
bouquet garni (sprigs
    of parsley, celery tops
    and thyme tied
    together)
16 carrots, 1" slices
1 lb. mushrooms, sliced
4 jars white onions, drained
4 tbsp. butter
salt and pepper to taste

Heat oil or butter in kettle. Shake meat in bag with flour, salt and pepper. Brown meat in oil on all sides. Add sliced onions and brown. Add wine, bouillon and bouquet garni. Cover and simmer 1 hr. Add carrots. Cover and simmer 1 hr. Saute mushrooms in butter and add with whole onions to kettle. Cover and simmer another 30 min. Correct seasonings and remove bouquet garni.

BEEF STUFFED CABBAGE

Preparation: 1 hr.
Cooking: 3 hr.

36 cabbage leaves
3 lb. ground beef
3 eggs
1 lrg. onion, grated
2 potatoes, grated
1 tsp. salt
1/2 tsp. pepper
2 tbsp. meat-herb mixture
3/4 c. instant rice
3 cans (20-oz. size)
    stewed tomatoes
2 cans (8-oz. size)
    tomato sauce
1/4 c. lemon juice
5 tbsp. sugar
1/8 tsp. baking soda

Put cabbage leaves in boiling water until soft enough to be folded, about 2 min. In large bowl mix beef, eggs, onion, potato, salt, pepper, herb mixture and rice. Form into 36 small balls and wrap each with cabbage leaf. Put into large kettle and just cover with water. Simmer uncovered about 30 min. Mix together remaining ingredients and add to cabbage rolls in water, stirring to mix sauce and water well. Simmer covered for 3 hr. Can be reheated.

MEATS
for 12

OVEN BEEF STEW

Preparation: 20 min.
Baking: 3 hr.

3 lb. beef, in 1" sq.
3 env. onion soup mix
3 cans cream of mushroom soup
15 carrots, cut-up
15 celery stalks, cut-up
4 green peppers, diced
1-1/2 lb. fresh mushrooms, sliced
1-1/2 c. beef broth
salt and pepper to taste

Mix all ingredients together in a large pot. Bake covered at 300 degrees for 3 hr.

CHILI BOWL

Preparation: 20 min.
Cooking: 1 hr.

1/4 c. butter
4 lb. ground beef
8 lrg. onions, chopped
2 green peppers, chopped
3 cloves garlic, minced
1/4 c. chili powder
1 tbsp. salt
1-1/2 tsp. oregano
1 lrg. bay leaf, crushed
2 cans beef bouillon
1 can (1 lb.) tomatoes
2 cans (8-oz. size) tomato sauce
2 heads iceberg lettuce, shredded
4 c. cooked rice
2 pkg. (8-oz. size) corn chips

Melt butter in large skillet and saute half of onions, all green pepper and garlic for 5 min. Stir occasionally. Add meat, cook and stir until brown. Add chili powder, salt, bay leaf, oregano, broth, tomatoes and tomato sauce. Bring to boil. Simmer covered 1 hr. Skim fat from surface occasionally. Serve with lettuce, rice, remaining chopped onions and corn chips in separate bowls.

DIFFERENT MEAT LOAF

Preparation: 15 min.
Baking: 1 hr.

2 green peppers, chopped
3 lb. chopped beef
2 pkg. cream of leek soup
2 c. crushed Ritz crackers
2 eggs
1/4 c. water
oregano
salt to taste

Semi-cook green peppers in boiling water. Mix all ingredients, except oregano, and place in loaf pan. Sprinkle with oregano. Bake uncovered at 350 degrees for 1 hr.

MEATS
for 12

DIVINE CASSEROLE

Preparation: 40 min.
Baking: 1 hr.

3 lb. ground chuck
6 cans (8-oz. size)
   tomato sauce
1-1/2 lb. cottage cheese
24 oz. cream cheese
3/4 c. sour cream
1 c. chopped onions
3 tbsp. minced green pepper
1-1/2 lb. noodles, cooked
6 tbsp. butter, melted
salt and pepper to taste

Saute meat in large skillet until cooked, stirring frequently. Drain off fat. Add tomato sauce. In large bowl, combine cheeses, sour cream, onions, green pepper and seasonings. Place half the noodles in 5-qt. buttered casserole. Spread cheese mixture on top. Add remaining noodles and pour melted butter over. Top with meat mixture. Bake uncovered at 375 degrees for 1 hr.

SWEDISH MEATBALLS

Preparation: 30 min.
Baking: 2 hr.

3 lb. ground beef
1-1/2 c. bread crumb stuffing
3/4 c. milk
3 eggs, beaten
salt and pepper to taste
1/2 tsp. basil
1/2 tsp. thyme
1/2 tsp. oregano
1/2-1 c. flour
bacon fat
3/4 c. water
3 cans (1-lb. size)
   Italian tomatoes
4 lrg. onions, sliced

Soften stuffing with milk and mix with meat. Add eggs and seasonings. Shape into 2'' balls. Roll in flour and brown in bacon fat. Remove to 4 qt. casserole. Add water to drippings in skillet. Stir and pour over meat. Add tomatoes (including juice) and onions. Cover and bake at 325 degrees for 2 hr.

UNCLE PETER'S MEAT SAUCE

Preparation: 30 min.
Heating: 10 min.

4 lb. ground beef
6 tbsp. oil
1/2 c. chopped parsley
salt and pepper to taste
3 tbsp. vinegar
1-1/2 tsp. garlic salt
2 cans (2-lb. 3-oz. size)
   Italian peeled tomatoes
2-4 tsp. sugar
8 cans (6-oz. size) tomato paste
1/2 tsp. oregano
1/2 tsp. basil

Brown beef in oil in large skillet. Transfer to large pot. Add remaining ingredients except half the tomato paste. Stir to mix. Simmer covered for 10-12 min. Add remaining tomato paste. Correct seasonings. Heat to serving temperature.

MEATS
for 12

BAKED HAM WITH MUSTARD GLAZE

Preparation: 5 min.
Baking: 2 hr.

1/2 c. mayonnaise
1/4 c. dark corn syrup
1 tbsp. horseradish
2 tbsp. prepared mustard
1 sml. smoked ham (4 lb.)

Mix first 4 ingredients and chill. Without removing fell, bake ham at 325 degrees at least 2 hr. 30 min. Before ham is done, spread with glaze mixture. Return to oven and finish baking.

SWISS HAM CASSEROLE

Preparation: 20 min.
Baking: 30 min.

12 med. heads endive
9 tbsp. butter
1/2 c. water
24 slices boiled ham
6 tbsp. flour
2 c. milk
1 c. light cream
1 c. grated Swiss cheese
1/2 tsp. salt
1/2 c. bread crumbs

In large skillet roll endives in 3 tbsp. melted butter. Add water, cover and simmer 10 min. Wrap each endive in 2 slices boiled ham. Arrange in single layer in shallow baking dish. Melt remaining butter in same skillet. Blend in flour, add milk and stir until boiling. Simmer 3 min. Add cream, remove from heat and stir in cheese and salt. Pour over casserole and sprinkle with bread crumbs. Bake uncovered at 350 degrees for 25-30 min.

BUTTERFLY BBQ LAMB

Preparation: 20 min.
Cooking: 20 min.
Sauce: 2-3 hr.

2 6—7-lb. legs of lamb
1/3 c. pepper
1/3 c. mixed herbs
   (or rosemary)

Have butcher remove bones from lamb and cut so it will lie flat. Do not remove fell. Use a mallet to pound to uniform thickness (about 1-1/2—2''). Rub fleshy side with pepper and herbs. Place meat, fell side down, on grill over charcoal. Leave until fell is charred. Turn over and grill for a few min. on other side. Remove when meat is still pink and juicy. Carve across the grain.

SAUCE:

cut up lamb bones
pepper
dried fines herbes
1/2 c. butter
5 beef bouillon cubes
salt to taste
Kitchen Bouquet

Cover bones with water. Simmer 2-3 hr. Add remaining ingredients to taste and color desired. Serve hot in separate dish.

MEATS
for 12

CAIRO CASSEROLE

Preparation: 20 min.
Chilling: 8 hr.
Baking: 30 min.

1/2 c. butter
1 lrg. eggplant
3 lrg. zucchini
2 cans Jerusalem artichokes, drained and sliced
2 lb. cooked lamb, chopped
salt and pepper to taste
nutmeg to taste

8 tbsp. butter, melted
8 tbsp. flour
1 qt. milk, heated
4 eggs, beaten
1 pt. Ricotta cheese

FIRST DAY:

Peel and thinly slice eggplant. Peel and slice zucchini lengthwise. Saute separately in butter. Set aside. In same pan saute lamb, seasoned with salt, pepper and nutmeg. Place meat and vegetables in alternate layers in buttered 5 qt. casserole. Cover and chill 8 hr.

SECOND DAY:

Blend flour and butter in large skillet. Add hot milk and stir until smooth. Add eggs slowly and stir in cheese. Drain liquid from casserole and cover with sauce. Bake at 375 degrees for 30 min. or until light brown.

KIDNEY STEW LOUISA

Preparation: 30 min.
Cooking: 20 min.

3 doz. lamb kidneys, sliced
1 c. butter
4 lrg. onions, minced
1 lb. fresh mushrooms
1 c. flour
4 cans beef bouillon
2 c. white wine
6 tbsp. chopped parsley
salt and pepper to taste
1/2 c. brandy (or to taste)

In large skillet saute onion in butter until golden brown. Add sliced mushrooms and kidneys. Simmer stirring for 15 min. Add flour and blend. Add bouillon and wine. Cook until thickened, stirring frequently. Add parsley, salt and pepper. Add brandy and simmer for about 10 min.

LAMB SCALLOP

Preparation: 30 min.
Baking: 1 hr.

6 c. chopped tomatoes
3 lrg. onions, chopped
6 c. cooked ground lamb
salt and pepper to taste
2 c. fine bread crumbs
6-8 tbsp. butter

Mix tomatoes and onion together. In a 5-6 qt. buttered baking dish arrange lamb and tomato/onion mixture in layers. Season with salt and pepper. Sprinkle with bread crumbs and dabs of butter. Bake uncovered at 350 degrees for 1 hr.

MEATS
for 12

MARINATED PORK

Preparation: 15 min.
Marinating: 48 hr.
Cooking: 3 hr.

5 lb. boned pork loin
2 tbsp. salt
2 c. dry white wine
1 c. wine vinegar
8 tbsp. olive oil
6 cloves garlic, halved
1 c. thinly sliced celery
1 c. thinly sliced carrots
1 c. thinly sliced onions
1 tsp. peppercorns
3 bay leaves
1 tsp. thyme
5 coriander seeds
3 tbsp. cornstarch
1/4 c. cold water

Remove as much fat as possible from pork. Rub salt into pork. Mix other ingredients except cornstarch and water in large bowl, add pork and baste. Cover. Turn and baste 3 or 4 times a day. Marinate in refrigerator for 2 full days. To cook, remove meat from marinade, roll and tie into a rolled roast. Sear in a large pot on top of stove, then cook in covered pot, surrounded by marinated vegetables and a little of the liquid about 3 hr. basting if necessary. Remove to warm platter. Dissolve cornstarch in water and add to marinade. Heat stirring constantly until thickened and hot.

TAHITIAN PORK CHOPS

Preparation: 15 min.
Baking: 1 hr.

2 doz. thin pork chops
2 c. sherry
3/4 c. soy sauce
3/4 c. salad oil
2 cloves garlic, crushed
2 tsp. ground ginger
3/4 tsp. oregano
1/2 c. maple syrup

Brown chops in a large ovenproof skillet. Put all other ingredients in blender and mix well. Pour over chops. Cover and bake at 350 degrees for 45 min. to 1 hr. Turn chops once during baking.

ITALIAN VEAL AND PEPPERS

Preparation: 30 min.
Baking: 45 min.

24 slices veal scallopine (3 lb.)
1 egg, beaten
1 c. water
2 c. bread crumbs
1/2 tsp. oregano
1/2 tsp. tarragon
salt and pepper to taste
1/2 c. olive oil
3 sml. jars fried peppers and onions
1 lb. Mozzarella cheese
2 lrg. jars marinara sauce

Soak veal in mixture of beaten egg and water. Cover completely with bread crumbs mixed with oregano, tarragon, salt and pepper. Brown over high heat in oil in large frying pan. Remove cutlets and drain. Place in large, ungreased casserole. Cover with undrained peppers, onions, and shredded Mozzarella. Pour marinara sauce over all. Bake uncovered at 350 degrees for 45 min. May be kept warm for a while at 300 degrees. Chicken cutlets may be substituted for veal.

MEATS
for 12

VEAL PALARMA

Preparation: 30 min.
Chilling: 8 hr. (opt.)
Baking: 30 min.

30 slices veal scallopine
4-6 tbsp. butter
4 c. thick cream sauce (see index)
2 cans (1-lb. size) tomatoes, drained
1 lb. cottage cheese
1 lb. Mozzarella cheese, cubed
4 tbsp. chopped chives
onion salt to taste
pepper to taste

In large skillet, melt butter and saute veal 3 min. per side. Remove to 4 qt. buttered casserole. In large saucepan, make cream sauce. Add tomatoes, cheeses, chives, onion salt and pepper. Stir to blend and pour over veal. Chill 8 hr. if desired. Return to room temperature, about 2 hr. and bake uncovered at 350 degrees for 30 min. or until sauce is bubbly and browned.

VEAL AND WATER CHESTNUT CASSEROLE

Preparation: 30 min.
Baking: 1-1/2 hr.
Finishing: 15 min.

1 c. butter
4 lb. boneless veal, cubed
2 onions, minced
2 cloves garlic, crushed
2 lb. fresh mushrooms, sliced
2 c. beef bouillon
1/4 tsp. nutmeg
1-1/2 bay leaves
3 tsp. salt
1 tsp. pepper
3 dashes cayenne
4 cans (5-oz. size) water chestnuts, drained and sliced
2 c. heavy cream
1/2 c. cognac
1/4 c. chopped parsley

In heavy skillet, melt half the butter. Brown meat on all sides, then onion and garlic. Place in large casserole. Saute mushrooms in remaining butter and add to meat. Deglaze skillet with bouillon. Add nutmeg, bay leaves, salt, pepper, cayenne and water chestnuts to cover meat two-thirds. Stir, cover and bake at 375 degrees for 1-1/2 hr. The casserole may be frozen at this point. When ready to serve, add cream and cook uncovered on top of stove for 15 min. stirring frequently. Add cognac and parsley. Stir well.

POULTRY & GAME
for 12

BAKED SHERRIED CHICKEN

Preparation: 15 min.
Baking: 1 hr. 15 min.

4 lb. chicken legs and thighs
3/4 c. flour
3 tsp. salt
1/4 tsp. pepper
4 tbsp. butter or fat
2 cans cream of mushroom soup
1 c. sherry
paprika

Shake chicken in bag with flour, salt, and pepper. Brown in fat in large skillet. Remove to 4 qt. baking dish. Combine soup and sherry with drippings in pan, blending well. Pour over chicken, cover and bake at 350 degrees for 45 min. Remove cover and continue baking until tender, 15-30 min. If sauce seems scant, add more sherry.

CHICKEN ASOPAO

Preparation: 45 min.
Cooking: 30 min.

6 c. uncooked rice
6 tbsp. sofrito
4 lb. chicken, cut-up
3 tbsp. shortening
2 cans (8-oz. size) tomato sauce
3 qt. boiling water
2 tbsp. salt
1 pkg. frozen peas
1 sml. jar stuffed olives
2 jars (4-oz. size) pimento

Soak rice in water about 30 min. Brown chicken in shortening in large skillet. Add sofrito and tomato sauce. Add drained rice and cook about 5 min. stirring constantly. Add boiling water and salt and let boil 10 min. Reduce heat to medium and let simmer covered until rice is tender and still moist, about 15 min. Add peas, olives and pimento and cook 5 min. longer. Serve immediately.

CHICKEN BROCCOLI CASSEROLE

Preparation: 40 min.
Baking: 30 min.

6 lb. chicken, cooked
4 pkg. froz. broccoli spears
2 cans cream of chicken soup
2 cans cream of mushroom soup
1 c. mayonnaise
1 c. shredded Cheddar cheese
2 tsp. ground thyme
2 tsp. lemon juice

Cut up chicken. Cook broccoli and drain. Heat soups, mayonnaise, cheese, thyme and lemon juice to boiling. In buttered 4 qt. casserole, arrange layer of half the chicken, then half the broccoli, and half the soup/cheese mixture. Repeat. Bake uncovered at 350 degrees for 30 min.

POULTRY & GAME
for 12

CHICKEN CASSEROLE

Preparation: 1 hr.
Baking: 1 hr.

12 whole chicken breasts, boned, skinned, and split
water to cover
1 onion, quartered
salt and pepper to taste
tops of 2-3 celery stalks
1 box (1 lb.) noodles
2 cans cream of mushroom soup
2 cans cream of celery soup
2 cans (3-oz. size) sliced mushrooms
3/4 c. grated Parmesan cheese

Cook chicken in water with onion, salt, pepper and celery tops. Simmer gently until tender about 30 min. Cool. Remove chicken and cut into large chunks. Strain broth and reserve. Cook noodles according to pkg. directions. Combine soups and 2 cups strained broth. Heat through. In 4 qt. buttered casserole, put alternate layer of noodles, mushrooms, chicken and sauce. Repeat. Cover generously with Parmesan cheese. Bake uncovered at 350 degrees for 1 hr.

CHICKEN LIVERS

Preparation: 45 min.
Cooking: 20 min.

8 lrg. onions, quartered
3/4 lb. butter
3 lb. fresh chicken livers, halved
3 lb. fresh mushrooms, quartered
3 tbsp. flour
2 c. sherry
3/4 c. dry vermouth
salt and pepper to taste

In a large skillet, lightly brown onions in butter. Add livers and sear. Add mushrooms and cook a few min. Sprinkle flour over all, stirring to coat evenly. Add sherry, vermouth, salt and pepper. Simmer covered 20 min.

CHICKEN MARICADO

Preparation: 5 min.
Baking: 1-1/2 hr.

12 whole chicken breasts, boned
1/2 tsp. salt
1/4 tsp. pepper
2 cans cream of mushroom soup
juice of 2 lemons
1 pt. sour cream
4 avocados, cubed
2 cloves garlic, crushed

Season chicken with salt and pepper. Place skin side down in baking dish. Bake covered at 350 degrees for 45 min. Combine remaining ingredients in blender until smooth. Turn chicken, cover with sauce and continue baking uncovered 30-45 min.

POULTRY & GAME
for 12

CHICKEN STUFFED AVOCADO

Preparation: 20 min.
Baking: 20 min.

6 avocados
3 c. diced cooked chicken
6 tbsp. lemon juice
3 c. white sauce (see index)
1 tbsp. minced onion
2 tbsp. grated Parmesan cheese

Halve avocados. Sprinkle all exposed meat with lemon juice. Prepare sauce. Add onion and chicken. Spoon into avocado halves, mounding slightly. Sprinkle with cheese and place in baking dish with 1/2" water. Bake at 350 degrees for about 20 min.

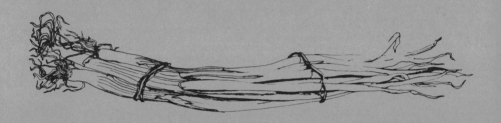

LADY ALEXANDRIA METCALF'S CHICKEN CASSEROLE

Preparation: 1-1/2 hr.
Baking: 1 hr.

1 lrg. or 2 sml. roasting chickens
1 bay leaf
1 onion
1 stalk celery, with greens
1 carrot
1 c. butter
1 lb. fresh mushrooms, sliced
1 c. flour
7 c. broth (from cooking chicken)
1/2 pt. heavy cream
1 tsp. Worcestershire
salt and pepper to taste
8 slices white bread, buttered, toasted, and cubed
1/2 lb. sliced ham, cubed

Cut chicken into serving pieces and boil in water with bay leaf, onion, celery and carrot for 45 min. or until tender. Cool chicken, remove meat from bones and dice. Reserve 7 cups strained broth. Melt 1/4 cup butter in skillet and saute mushrooms. Remove mushrooms. Melt remaining butter, add flour and cook until frothy. Add broth and whisk until smooth and thickened. Stir in cream. Add Worcestershire, salt and pepper. Butter a 5-6 qt. casserole and make alternate layers of bread, ham, chicken and mushrooms, ending with bread. Pour sauce over all. Bake at 350 degrees for 1 hr. If casserole gets too dry, add broth or milk.

POULTRY & GAME
for 12

VIVA LA CHICKEN

Preparation: 20 min.
Chilling: 24 hr.
Baking: 1-1/2 hr.

12 chicken breasts, boned
6 c. boiling salted water
2 cans cream of chicken soup
2 cans cream of mushroom soup
2 c. sour cream
2 onions, grated
2 cans (3-oz. size) green chili salsa
16 corn tortillas, in 1" strips
1/2 c. grated Cheddar cheese

Cut chicken into large pieces. Cook in boiling salted water. Add 6 tbsp. of strained stock from above to bottom of greased 4 qt. casserole. In large bowl mix soups, sour cream, onion and salsa. Place half the tortilla strips on top of stock. Add half the chicken and half the sauce. Repeat. Top with cheese. Chill 24 hr. Bake covered at 325 degrees for 1-1/4 hr. Remove cover and bake 15 min. longer.

PHEASANT FRANCKE

Preparation: 15 min.
Baking: 40 min.
Heating: 5 min.

6 pheasants
3 cans (6-oz. size) frozen orange juice
18 oz. cream cheese
18 strips bacon
2 cans (1-lb. size) mandarin orange sections
1 c. brandy (opt.)

Mix cream cheese with undiluted orange juice and stuff into cavities of birds. (Keep any extra stuffing for later use.) Cover the breast of each bird with 3 slices of bacon and wrap each bird tightly in foil. Bake at 350 degrees for 20 min. on each side (not upright). Carve. Put all juices from foil, all stuffing and brandy in casserole. Arrange carved pieces on top. Heat covered over low flame for 5 min. Garnish with orange sections.

SEAFOOD
for 12

CRABMEAT JOHNNY

Preparation: 30 min.
Baking: 20 min.

2 lb. lump crabmeat
dash fresh lemon juice
2 c. cream
1 lb. pimento cheese
1/2 lb. butter
1 lb. broad noodles
1 jar (4 oz.) pimento, drained and sliced
2 tbsp. sherry (opt.)
salt and pepper to taste

To crabmeat, add a few drops of lemon juice and toss. Melt cream and pimento cheese together in top of double boiler. Cook noodles in salted, boiling water 10 min. and drain. Add pimento and sherry to cream/cheese mixture. Correct seasonings. Stir and pour sauce over noodles in 6 qt. casserole. Add crabmeat and stir gently to mix. Bake covered at 350 degrees for 20 min.

FISH HASH

Preparation: 10 min.
Baking: 30 min.

1-1/2 lb. lobster meat, diced
1-1/2 lb. crabmeat, flaked
1-1/2 pt. half & half
6 tbsp. dry sherry
6 tbsp. butter
6 egg yolks, beaten
3 tbsp. flour
salt and pepper to taste
1 c. coarse bread crumbs
butter

Mix first 8 ingredients together in a buttered 6 qt. casserole. Sprinkle with bread crumbs and dot with butter. Bake uncovered at 350 degrees for 30 min. Do not overcook or eggs will curdle.

SEAFOOD
for 12

LENTEN TREAT

Preparation: 20 min.
Baking: 25 min.

8 tbsp. butter
8 tbsp. flour
2-1/2 c. light cream
1 c. chicken broth
2 c. grated American cheese
1/2 c. sherry
salt and pepper to taste
4 pkg. frozen broccoli spears cooked and drained
4 lb. fish fillets (sole, halibut, or any other)
paprika

In a saucepan melt butter and stir in flour. Add cream and chicken broth. Cook stirring constantly until mixture is smooth and thickened. Add cheese and stir over low heat until melted. Add sherry, salt and pepper. Arrange broccoli in greased shallow baking dish, 8" x 12". Arrange fillets over broccoli. Cover with sauce and dust with paprika. Bake at 375 degrees for 25 min. or until fish flakes when tested with fork.

LOBSTER PIE

Preparation: 10 min.
Baking: 40 min.

6 cans lobster bisque soup, undiluted
1 c. sherry
6 c. cut-up lobster meat
1/2 c. cracker meal
1 tbsp. paprika
1/2 c. crumbled potato chips
2 tbsp. grated Parmesan cheese
1/2 c. butter, melted

Mix soup and sherry. Add lobster and turn into buttered 6 qt. casserole. Sprinkle with mixture of cracker meal, paprika, potato chips, Parmesan cheese and butter. Bake uncovered at 350 degrees for 40 min. or until heated.

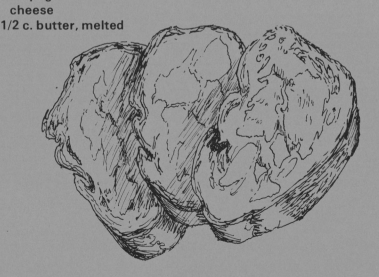

SEAFOOD
for 12

SALMON-RICE CASSEROLE

Preparation: 15 min.
Cooking: 30 min.

3 c. Minute Rice
1/4 c. butter
1/4 c. flour
2 tsp. salt
1/8 tsp. pepper
4 c. milk
2 cans (7-3/4-oz. size) salmon, drained and flaked
1/2 c. chopped stuffed olives
2 c. grated American cheese

Prepare rice according to pkg. directions. Melt butter in another saucepan. Add flour, salt and pepper and stir until blended. Add milk. Cook and stir until sauce is smooth and thickened. Arrange layers of rice, salmon, olives, cheese and sauce in greased 4 qt. casserole, ending with cheese. Bake covered at 350 degrees for 30 min. or until browned.

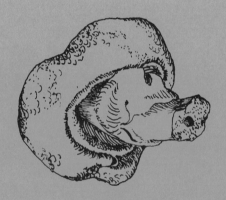

SCALLOPS SUPREME

Preparation: 20 min.
Broiling: 10 min.

3 lb. scallops, cut up
3 c. dry white wine
3 tbsp. lemon juice
3/4 lb. fresh mushrooms, sliced
12 shallots, finely chopped
1/4 c. chopped parsley
1/2 c. butter
3 tbsp. flour
2/3 c. heavy cream
salt and pepper to taste
1/3 c. buttered bread crumbs

Place scallops, wine and lemon juice in shallow pan. Bring to a boil, cover and simmer 5-10 min. or until tender. Drain and reserve liquid. Saute mushrooms, shallots and parsley in butter for 5 min. Stir in flour and blend in reserved liquid and cream. Bring to a boil stirring. Season to taste. Add scallops to sauce and pour into greased shallow casserole or individual scallop shells. Sprinkle with bread crumbs. Broil about 10 min. or until lightly browned.

SEAFOOD
for 12

MOLDED SHRIMP SALAD

Preparation: 20 min.
Chilling: 3 hr.

24 oz. cream cheese
1-1/2 cans cream of
 tomato soup
3 env. unflavored gelatin,
 softened in 1/2 c.
 cold water
1-1/2 c. chopped onion
1-1/2 c. chopped green
 pepper
3 c. chopped celery
3 cans (4-1/2-oz. size) shrimp
salt and pepper to taste
3 c. mayonnaise
horseradish to taste

In a large saucepan, stir together first 3 ingredients over low heat until gelatin is dissolved and mixture is thick and creamy. Remove from heat. Add remaining ingredients. Mix well. Pour into 4-5 qt. mold and chill until firm about 3 hr. Unmold and serve with mayonnaise mixed with a bit of horseradish.

SHRIMP DELIGHT

Preparation: 20 min.
Baking: 45 min.

4 med. onions, sliced
6 tbsp. butter
2 cans (16-oz. size)
 mushrooms, drained
4 cans cream of
 chicken soup
salt to taste
2 tsp. pepper
1/4 tsp. Tabasco
1 tbsp. Worcestershire
2 c. light cream
2 c. sliced ripe olives
4 lb. cooked shrimp
4 cans (7-oz. size) tuna,
 drained

In large saucepan, saute onion in butter. Add mushrooms, soup and seasonings. Simmer a few min. Add cream, olives, shrimp and tuna and mix. Pour into lightly greased 4 qt. casserole. Bake uncovered at 350 degrees for 45 min.

CHEESE & EGGS
for 12

ESCALLOPED HAM AND EGGS

Preparation: 20 min.
Baking: 25 min.

3/4 c. butter
1/2 c. flour
2 tsp. salt
1/8 tsp. pepper
4 c. milk
12 eggs, hard-boiled and sliced
1 can (4 oz.) chopped mushrooms, drained
4 c. cubed cooked ham
1/2 c. chopped green pepper
2/3 c. bread crumbs

In medium saucepan melt 1/2 cup butter. Blend in flour, salt, pepper and milk. Cook stirring constantly until sauce is smooth and thickened. Layer eggs, mushrooms, ham and green pepper in shallow baking dish 9" x 13". Pour sauce over all. Melt remaining butter, add crumbs and stir evenly until coated. Sprinkle crumbs on top. Bake at 350 degrees for 25 min. or until hot and bubbly around the edges.

GALETTES LAUSANNOISE

Preparation: 1 hr.
Baking: 30 min.

1/4 c. butter
4 tbsp. grated onion
3-1/2 c. Swiss cheese, diced
puff paste, or flaky pie crust dough for 12 tartlets
1 c. butter, melted
12 egg yolks
1/4 tsp. salt
1/4 tsp. cayenne
1/4 tsp. nutmeg
4 c. heavy cream
1/4 c. sweet butter

Saute onion in butter until light golden, stirring constantly. Cool and mix with cheese. Line individual tartlet pans with puff paste or flaky pie crust rolled very thin and brushed with melted butter. Beat egg yolks with salt, cayenne and nutmeg until light in color and texture. Gradually beat in cream. Beat briskly with wire whisk or rotary beater until thoroughly blended. Turn onion/cheese mixture into tartlet pans and cover with cream/egg mixture. Dot each with 1 tsp. sweet butter. Bake at 350 degrees for 25 min. or until custard is firm and a little blistered. Serve hot.

CHEESE & EGGS
for 12

OVERNIGHT CHEESE SOUFFLE

Preparation: 20 min.
Chilling: Overnight:
Baking: 1 hr.

- 16 slices bread, buttered and cubed
- 2 lb. mild Cheddar cheese, grated
- 10 eggs
- 2 lrg. onions, grated
- 5 c. milk
- 1-1/2 tsp. salt
- 1 tbsp. dry mustard
- 1 tsp. Worcestershire
- 1/8 tsp. cayenne

Layer half the bread in buttered 13" x 9" baking dish. Spread cheese on top, and add remaining bread cubes. Beat eggs until very light and add remaining ingredients. Pour over bread/cheese mixture. Cover loosely and refrigerate overnight. Bake uncovered at 350 degrees for 1 hr.

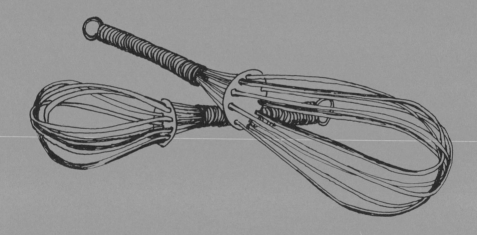

SWISS SOUFFLE

Preparation: 20 min.
Baking: 15 min.

- 1/2 c. butter
- 5 tbsp. flour
- 2 c. milk
- 4 eggs, separated
- 1-1/2 c. heavy cream
- 3 tbsp. grated Parmesan cheese
- 1 tbsp. grated Gruyere cheese
- 4 tbsp. grated Cheddar cheese
- salt and pepper to taste

In medium saucepan, blend butter and flour over medium heat. Add milk and bring to a boil. Add egg yolks and boil 2 min. whisking constantly. Remove from heat and allow to cool. Whip egg whites stiff and fold into sauce. Pour into 12 well-greased tartlet molds. Bake at 450 degrees for 4 min. Empty souffles gently into greased 15" x 18" ovenproof dish. Put cream on top and add cheeses. Return to oven for 7-10 min. (They will rise and absorb cream.)

119

POTATOES, RICE & PASTA
for 12

BROWN BRAISED POTATOES

Preparation: 15 min.
Cooking: 30 min.
Reheating: 10 min.

4 lb. new potatoes
6 tbsp. butter
2 tbsp. oil
1/2 tsp. salt
2-3 tbsp. minced parsley

Pare potatoes, cut into balls with ball cutter and dry. In large frying pan heat 1/16" melted butter and oil. Add potatoes and let them sit on heat uncovered for 2 min. Shake pan, return to heat to sear another side for 2 min. Continue until they are a pale, golden color all over. Sprinkle with salt, lower heat, cover and cook approx. 20 min. Cool with cover slightly askew. Reheat just before serving, about 10 min. Drain, and stir in remaining butter and parsley.

CHANTILLY POTATOES

Preparation: 20 min.
Baking: 20 min.

12 servings instant mashed potatoes
1 c. heavy cream, whipped
1 c. grated mild Cheddar cheese
salt and pepper to taste

Prepare potatoes according to pkg. directions. Mound in large greased baking dish. Fold cream into grated cheese and season with salt and pepper. Spread over potatoes. Bake uncovered at 350 degrees for 20 min. until delicately browned.

POTATOES, RICE & PASTA
for 12

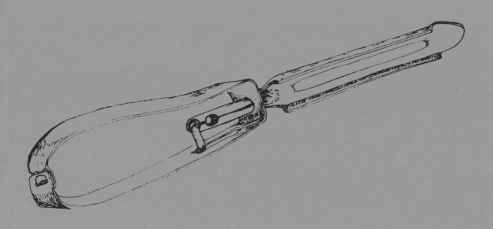

GOLDEN POTATO BAKE

Preparation: 15 min.
Baking: 30 min.

3 lb. potatoes (about 9 med.)
1-1/2 cans (16-oz. size) diced carrots, drained
3/4 c. hot milk
3 tbsp. butter, softened
salt and pepper to taste

Pare potatoes and cook in boiling salted water until tender about 20 min. Drain. Add carrots and mash with mixer at lowest speed. Add milk gradually until mixture is fluffy. Stir in butter, salt and pepper. Turn into buttered 3 qt. casserole. Dot with additional butter. Bake uncovered at 350 degrees for 30 min.

POTATO CHEESE PIE

Boiling: 40 min.
Mixing: 15 min.
Baking: 30 min.

4 lb. potatoes
1/2 c. butter
3/4 c. milk
3/4 c. grated Romano or Parmesan cheese
3 eggs, beaten
3 tbsp. chopped parsley
salt and pepper to taste
3/4 lb. Mozzarella cheese, cubed
3/4 c. bread crumbs

Boil potatoes in jackets. Peel and mash. Add 1/4 cup butter, milk, grated cheese, eggs, parsley, salt and pepper. Beat until creamy. Add Mozzarella and mix. In a large buttered baking dish sprinkle 1/4-1/2 cup of crumbs. Add potatoes. Sprinkle top with remaining bread crumbs and dot with remaining butter. Bake at 375 degrees for 20-30 min. or until golden brown.

POTATOES, RICE & PASTA
for 12

SWEET POTATOES WITH PECANS

Preparation: 40 min.
Baking: 30 min.

3-1/2 lb. sweet potatoes, cooked, peeled and mashed
3 eggs
1 c. brown sugar
3/4 c. butter, melted
1-1/2 tsp. salt
1-1/2 tsp. cinnamon
1 c. orange juice
1-1/2 c. pecan halves

Into mashed potatoes, beat eggs, 1/3 cup sugar, 1/4 cup butter, salt and cinnamon. Add enough orange juice to make potatoes moist and fluffy. Put in 4 qt. casserole. Arrange pecan halves on top and sprinkle with remaining brown sugar and drizzle with remaining butter. Bake at 375 degrees for 30 min.

WALNUT RICE

Preparation: 10 min.
Cooking: 25 min.

5 chicken bouillon cubes
4 c. boiling water
2 c. long-grain rice
salt to taste
1/2 tsp. pepper
1/2 c. butter
1-1/3 c. chopped walnuts
1/4 tsp. nutmeg or mace
3 tbsp. chopped parsley

Dissolve bouillon cubes in water in a heavy saucepan. Add rice, salt and pepper and simmer covered for 20 min. or until liquid is absorbed and rice is tender. Heat butter in small frying pan until lightly browned, but not burned. Add nuts and nutmeg or mace and mix. Stir into rice and toss to mix thoroughly. Serve garnished with parsley.

POTATOES, RICE & PASTA
for 12

WILD RICE CROQUETTES

Soaking: Overnight
Preparation: 45 min.
Chilling: 2 hr.
Cooking: 15 min.

1-1/2 c. uncooked wild rice
6 c. salted water
1 lrg. onion, finely chopped
10 mushrooms, finely chopped
3 tbsp. butter
1-1/2 c. thick cream sauce (see index)
2 eggs, slightly beaten
1/2 c. flour
1 egg
1/2 c. milk
1/2 c. bread crumbs or crushed shredded wheat
oil

Soak wild rice overnight in salted water. Boil for 30 min. or until tender but not mushy. Drain if necessary. Simmer onions and mushrooms in butter until golden. Mix rice, onions, mushrooms and cream sauce together. Stir in beaten eggs and chill. Shape into croquettes. Roll in flour then in egg mixed with milk, then in bread crumbs or shredded wheat. Deep fry in hot oil at 375 degrees for 5-8 min. or until browned.

YAM STUFFED APPLES

Preparation: 15 min.
Baking: 45 min.
Broiling: 2 min.

12 lrg. baking apples
4 tbsp. sugar
2 cans (1-lb. size) yams or sweet potatoes
1 tbsp. butter
cinnamon
salt and pepper to taste
1 pkg. (1 lb.) marshmallows

Core apples and hollow out slightly. Sprinkle 1/2 tsp. sugar inside each. Mash sweet potatoes with 1 tbsp. butter and apple meat from cores, just enough to keep mixture moist. Season to taste with salt, pepper, remaining sugar and cinnamon. Mound potato mixture into apple shells. Bake uncovered at 325 degrees for 45 min. or until apples feel soft, but remain intact. Just before serving, place a large marshmallow on top of each apple and broil about 2 min. until marshmallows are slightly browned.

VEGETABLES
for 12

ASPARAGUS AU FROMAGE

Preparation: 20 min.
Baking: 10 min.

3/4 c. butter
1/4 c. minced onion
1/2 tsp. seasoned salt
1/4 tsp. pepper
4 pkg. froz. asparagus spears
1 lb. Mozzarella cheese
4-5 tbsp. grated Parmesan cheese
paprika

Cream together butter, onions, salt and pepper. Cook asparagus and drain. Arrange in 9" x 13" baking dish or in individual au gratin dishes. Spread butter mixture on top and cover with thinly sliced Mozzarella. Sprinkle with Parmesan. Bake at 450 degrees for 10 min. or until cheese is melted and golden brown. Dust with paprika.

PRESSURE COOKER BAKED BEANS

Soaking: 2 hr.
Preparation: 20 min.
Cooking: 30 min.

1 pkg. soldier or navy beans
1-1/2 qts. water
1/2 lb. lean salt pork, skinned and diced
1 sml. red onion, diced
1/3 c. dark molasses
3 tbsp. sugar
1 tsp. dry mustard
2 tsp. salt
1/4 tsp. black pepper
1 tbsp. vinegar
1 c. boiling water

Soak beans 2 hr. in warm water, well-covered. Drain and cook in pressure cooker 20 min. with 1-1/2 qts. water. Let cool normally 5 min. and finish cooling under cold running water. Drain. Saute salt pork in skillet with onion until brown. Add molasses, sugar, mustard, salt, pepper and vinegar. Stir until well-blended and add to beans with 1 cup boiling water. Cook 10 min. longer in pressure cooker. Cool under running water and cover loosely. Reheat uncovered to serving temperature.

GREEN BEANS IN MUSTARD SAUCE

Preparation: 20 min.
Cooking: 5 min.

4 pkg. frozen string beans
1 tbsp. butter
1 tbsp. flour
1 tsp. dry mustard
1-1/2 c. milk
3 egg yolks, beaten
1/2 tsp. salt
2-3 tbsp. lemon juice
paprika

Cook beans according to pkg. directions. In saucepan melt butter. Add flour and mustard and cook until frothy. Add milk and whisk until smooth. It will not be very thick. Add egg yolks and continue to whisk. Cook a few min. or until sauce thickens a bit. Add salt and lemon juice to taste and stir well. Pour over beans and garnish with paprika.

VEGETABLES
for 12

CURRIED LIMA BEANS AU FROMAGE

Preparation: 20 min.

3 pkg. frozen baby lima beans
1-1/2 c. med. white sauce (see index)
1 c. shredded Swiss cheese
1/2 tsp. curry powder
paprika

Cook beans according to pkg. directions. Make white sauce and add cheese, curry, and beans. Garnish with paprika.

TEXAS BEANS

Preparation: 10 min.
Cooking: 1 hr.

3 cans (28-oz. size) pork and beans
2 cans cream of tomato soup
2 tbsp. dry mustard
2 c. brown sugar
3 onions, chopped
2 green peppers, chopped
3 tbsp. Worcestershire
10 drops Tabasco
salt and pepper to taste
6 slices bacon, halved

Place all ingredients in large casserole and top with bacon. Bake uncovered at 350 degrees for 1 hr.

BUTTERED SPICED BEETS

Preparation: 10 min.
Cooking: 15 min.

6 c. cooked sliced beets
1/2 c. sugar
1 tbsp. cinnamon
1/2 tsp. salt
1/4 tsp. ground cloves
1/4 tsp. pepper
1/4 c. butter
1/3 c. vinegar
1/4 c. water

Mix ingredients in large sauce pan. Simmer covered for 15 min.

VEGETABLES
for 12

PARTY BRUSSELS SPROUTS

Preparation: 25 min.

1-1/2 c. butter
3 med. onions, chopped
3 med. cucumbers, pared
3 pkg. froz. Brussels sprouts
6 tbsp. lime juice
3 tsp. sugar
3 tsp. salt
3/4 tsp. dried dillweed
1/2 tsp. pepper

Melt butter in large skillet over moderate heat. Add onion and cook until crisp-tender. Add thinly sliced cucumber and thawed brussels sprouts with remaining ingredients. Cook uncovered stirring frequently, until sprouts are tender and juices are cooked down.

DEVILED CARROTS

Preparation: 10 min.
Cooking: 15 min.

12 lrg. carrots, quartered lengthwise
1/2 c. butter
4 tbsp. brown sugar
1 tbsp. dry mustard
2 dashes Tabasco
3/4 tsp. salt
pepper to taste

Saute carrots in butter in large skillet for 5 min. Stir in remaining ingredients. Simmer uncovered for 10 min. or until tender.

CHINESE CELERY

Preparation: 30 min.

2 lrg. bunches celery
3 tbsp. oil
1/2 tsp. salt
1/2 tsp. MSG
1/2-1 tsp. pepper

Cut celery diagonally, making slices very thin. Heat oil in heavy skillet over high heat. When extremely hot, add celery, stirring to mix with oil. Add salt, MSG, and pepper. Cook covered for a few min. making sure it doesn't burn. Color should be clear and texture crisp and tender.

SEATTLE CORN

Preparation: 15 min.
Baking: 45 min.

2 cans (1-lb. size) cream corn
2 med. onions, chopped
2 heaping tsp. celery seed
salt and pepper to taste
2 "stack" packs Ritz crackers, crumbled
1/2 c. butter
paprika

Mix all ingredients in a 12" buttered pie plate. Flatten mixture leaving space around edges. Dot generously with butter and sprinkle with paprika. Bake at 350 degrees for about 45 min. or until crisp on bottom.

VEGETABLES
for 12

BAKED EGGPLANT

Preparation: 30 min.
Baking: 45 min.

2 med. eggplants
1 c. water
juice of 1 lemon
5 med. tomatoes, sliced
3 med. onions, thinly sliced
1/4 c. flour
1 tbsp. salt
1/2 tsp. pepper
1-1/2 c. sour cream

Peel and cut eggplant into 1/3" slices. Combine water and lemon juice and dip eggplant slices into mixture. Rinse briefly in cold water. Cook in 1/2" boiling water in saucepan for 8 min. or until just tender. Drain. In 3-4 qt. baking dish, arrange eggplant in alternate layers with tomatoes and onions. Combine flour, salt and pepper. Sprinkle over casserole. Top with sour cream and bake covered at 350 degrees for 45 min.

BAKED PEAS AND CELERY

Preparation: 15 min.
Baking: 30 min.

3 pkg. frozen peas
2 c. diced celery
2 cans (3-oz. size) chopped mushrooms, drained
2 tbsp. minced onions
1/4 c. diced pimento
salt and pepper to taste

In buttered 3 qt. casserole, put first 4 ingredients. Cover tightly and bake at 375 degrees for 15 min. Stir and add remaining ingredients. Cover and bake 15 min. longer.

GOURMET SPINACH

Preparation: 30 min.
Baking: 30 min.

4 pkg. frozen chopped spinach
1/4 c. minced onion
6 tbsp. butter
6 tbsp. flour
4 c. milk
3/4 tsp. nutmeg or ground mace
6 eggs, hard-boiled and chopped
salt and pepper to taste
1 c. grated American cheese
1 c. buttered bread crumbs
paprika

Cook spinach according to pkg. directions and drain thoroughly. Saute onion in butter until clear. Add flour, blend in milk and cook until smooth and thickened. Stir in spinach, nutmeg, eggs, salt and pepper. Turn into large buttered shallow dish. Top with cheese and bread crumbs. Sprinkle with paprika. Bake uncovered at 375 degrees for 30 min.

VEGETABLES
for 12

SPINACH SOUFFLE WITH GLAZED CARROTS

Preparation: 45 min.
Baking: 55 min.
Assembling: 10 min.

2 pkg. frozen chopped spinach
2 tbsp. butter
3 tbsp. flour
1 c. milk
3 eggs, separated
2 tbsp. grated onion
1 tsp. salt
1/8 tsp. pepper
1/4 tsp. nutmeg

Cook spinach according to pkg. directions and drain. Make cream sauce by melting butter, adding flour and milk and stirring until thickened. Stir in egg yolks, spinach, onion, salt, pepper and nutmeg. Remove from heat. Beat egg whites until stiff but not dry and fold into spinach mixture. Pour into greased 5-1/2 cup ring mold. Set mold in pan of hot water and bake at 350 degrees for about 55 min. Let stand 10 min. Unmold onto serving platter.

1 tbsp. ginger
6 tbsp. sugar
2 cans (15-oz. size) whole, baby carrots
4 tbsp. butter
1 tbsp. concentrated orange juice or orange liqueur (Curacao)

Mix sugar and ginger together. Roll carrots in mixture. Melt butter in skillet and add carrots. Turn slowly and often over low heat until carrots are glazed. Add orange concentrate or Curacao just before removing from heat. Pour into center of spinach ring.

ACORN SQUASH BAKED WITH PINEAPPLE

Preparation: 50 min.
Baking: 15 min.

6 acorn squash, halved
4 tbsp. sherry
4 tbsp. brown sugar
3/4 c. butter
1 c. crushed pineapple, drained
1/2 tsp. ground nutmeg
1-1/2 tsp. salt

Scoop out seeds and fibers, and place squash halves in baking dish. Put 1 tsp. each of sherry, brown sugar and butter in each half. Cover and bake at 400 degrees for 30 min. Scoop cooked squash out of shells, leaving wall about 1/2" thick. Mash squash and combine with pineapple, remaining butter, nutmeg and salt. Beat until well-blended. Spoon back into shells and return to oven. Bake uncovered at 425 degrees for 15 min.

VEGETABLES
for 12

TOMATOES GEORGE, JR.

Preparation: 15 min.
Baking: 30 min.

1/2 c. butter
6 onions, sliced
4 cans (1-lb. size)
   stewed tomatoes, undrained
3 slices bread, broken-up
salt and pepper to taste
6 slices American cheese,
   cut in 1" sq.
3/4 c. croutons
1/2 c. chopped parsley

In large casserole, slowly saute onions in butter until transparent. Add tomatoes, bread, salt, pepper and cheese and stir well. Bake covered at 325 degrees for 20 min. Top with croutons. Replace lid and bake another 10 min. Garnish with parsley.

BAKED ZUCCHINI

Preparation: 15 min.
Baking: 30 min.

12 med. zucchini,
   1/2" slices
1/2 c. chopped onion
8 tbsp. olive oil
4 tbsp. chopped parsley
4 ripe tomatoes, peeled
   and thinly sliced
salt and pepper to taste
Parmesan cheese

Cook zucchini in salted boiling water until tender about 10 min. Drain. Saute onion in olive oil until transparent. Add parsley and remove from heat. In casserole arrange in layers zucchini, sliced tomatoes, and onion mixture. Sprinkle with salt, pepper and grated Parmesan. Bake uncovered at 375 degrees for 30 min.

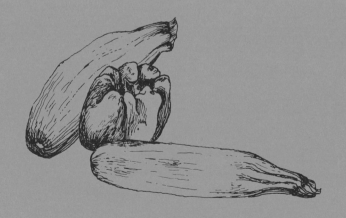

SALADS
for 12

NOTE: A selection of Salad Dressings for tossed green or mixed salads appears in the Accompaniments Chapter.

ASPARAGUS AND CARROT SALAD

Preparation: 10 min.
Chilling: 2 hr.

2 cans (1-lb. size) carrot strips, drained
2 cans (1-lb. size) asparagus, drained
1 c. Crowell's salad dressing (see index)
Boston lettuce
sprigs of parsley

Place asparagus in flattish bowl with 1/2 cup salad dressing. Refrigerate for at least 2 hr. Repeat in separate bowl with carrots. Arrange lettuce on serving platter and with slotted spoon place vegetables. Garnish with sprigs of parsley.

AVOCADO MOLD

Preparation: 20 min.
Chilling: 2-1/2 hr.

9 chicken bouillon cubes
6 c. cold water
4 env. unflavored gelatin
1 tbsp. lemon juice
1/4 tsp. Tabasco
1-1/2 tsp. salt
1/4 tsp. white pepper
1 grapefruit
3 avocados
4 tbsp. chopped chives
2 tbsp. chopped basil
lettuce

In large saucepan mix bouillon cubes, water, gelatin, lemon juice, Tabasco, salt and pepper. Heat stirring until gelatin is dissolved. Chill until slightly thickened about 30 min. Halve grapefruit and remove sections. Peel and dice avocados. Gently fold grapefruit, avocado and herbs into gelatin. Spoon into large ring mold and chill at least 2 hr. Unmold onto bed of lettuce.

BROCCOLI RING

Preparation: 30 min.
Chilling: 3 hr.

2 pkg. frozen chopped broccoli
1 c. mayonnaise
1 can beef consomme
6 eggs, hard-boiled and finely chopped
1 env. unflavored gelatin
salt and pepper to taste
juice of 1 lemon

Cook broccoli according to pkg. directions and drain. Add mayonnaise and eggs. In a separate pan add gelatin to consomme and heat to dissolve and add to broccoli mixture with salt, pepper and lemon juice. Pour into 2 qt. mold and refrigerate at least 3 hr. Serve garnished as desired. Can be made a day ahead.

SALADS
for 12

SOUNDS AWFUL SALAD

Preparation: 10 min.
Chilling: 2 hr.

3 pkg. (3-oz. size) raspberry gelatin
1-1/2 c. boiling water
2 cans (20-oz. size) stewed tomatoes
6 dashes Tabasco
1 tbsp. horseradish
salt and pepper to taste
1 avocado, sliced
1/2 lb. cottage cheese

Pour boiling water over gelatin and stir until dissolved. Mix in remaining ingredients except avocado and cottage cheese. Pour into 2 qt. ring mold and chill until firm. Unmold on platter. Garnish with avocado slices around outside of ring and cottage cheese in center.

WILTED SPINACH SALAD

Preparation: 20 min.

8 tbsp. vinegar
2/3 c. water
1 tbsp. sugar
1 tsp. salt
1/4 tsp. pepper
2 lb. spinach, washed and destemmed
6 slices bacon, cooked and crumbled
4 scallions, chopped
4 eggs, hard-boiled and chopped

In saucepan, mix vinegar, water, sugar, salt and pepper, and heat but do not boil. Place spinach, bacon, scallions, and eggs in china or glass bowl. Pour hot dressing over and toss.

TOMATOES STUFFED WITH ASPARAGUS

Preparation: 15 min.
Chilling: 2 hr.
Assembling: 15 min.

2 lb. fresh asparagus spears (or 2 pkg. frozen)
1/2 lb. fresh mushrooms, thinly sliced, or 2 cans (3-oz. size)
1/2 bunch scallions, chopped (bulbs with greens)
1/2 c. oil and vinegar salad dressing
2 tsp. chopped basil
12 med. tomatoes
1 tsp. salt (approx.)
1 tsp. chopped parsley
dash onion salt

Cook asparagus, drain and cut into 1-1/2" pieces. Combine asparagus, mushrooms, scallions, salad dressing and half the basil. Toss and chill for at least 2 hr. Toss occasionally during chilling. Cut thin slice from top of each tomato and scoop out meat, leaving thick shell. Sprinkle inside with salt and chill. Just before serving, spoon asparagus mixture into shells. Top with blend of remaining basil, parsley and onion salt. Pour marinating liquid over all.

DESSERTS
for 12

NOTE: A large selection of Cakes, Pies, Cookies and Squares appears in the Accompaniments Chapter.

APPLE CRUMBLE

Preparation: 20 min.
Baking: 45 min.

4 c. self-rising flour
1 c. sweet butter
1 c. extra fine granulated sugar
3 lb. sharp cooking apples
pinch of ground cloves or cinnamon

SAUCE:

heavy cream
  or 1 can (1 lb.) apricots
1/2 tsp. cornstarch

Peel, core and slice apples. Place in a 13" x 9" fireproof dish with 1/2 cup sugar, spice and small knob of butter. Place in bottom of 375 degree oven uncovered for 20-25 min. Mix flour and remaining sugar together. Rub in butter lightly until heavy sandy texture is reached. Smooth this mixture on top of cooked apples. Move to center of oven. Bake 20 min. or until nicely browned. Serve with cream or apricot sauce.

Bring apricots and juice to a boil and thicken with cornstarch.

EASY BANANA DESSERT

Preparation: 10 min.
Chilling: 2 hr.

12 ripe bananas
1-1/2 c. dry cocoa
1-1/2 c. sifted sugar

Combine cocoa and sugar in shallow bowl. Peel bananas and roll in sugar/cocoa mixture, patting on with fingers, until bananas are thoroughly coated. Slice bananas into a separate bowl. Cover with remaining sugar/cocoa mixture and refrigerate at least 2 hr.

BREAD PUDDING

Preparation: 10 min.
Baking: 40 min.

8 slices bread, buttered
2 c. brown sugar, tightly packed
4 eggs
1 qt. milk
1/2 tsp. vanilla
1 tsp. nutmeg
1 tsp. cinnamon
1 qt. vanilla ice cream
  or 1-1/2 c. heavy cream
    1/4 c. fine sugar

Put brown sugar in bottom of greased 3 qt. casserole. Break bread into it. Beat eggs with milk and vanilla and pour over bread. Combine nutmeg and cinnamon and sprinkle on top. Bake uncovered at 350 degrees for about 40 min. or until moderately brown and puffed up. Serve warm topped with ice cream or cream whipped with sugar.

DESSERTS
for 12

COFFEE ICEBOX DELIGHT

Follow directions for Coffee Cream page 87.

2 doz. lady fingers
1/2 pt. heavy cream
1/2 tsp. vanilla
1/4 c. sugar
sprinkles
  or shaved semi-sweet chocolate

Preparation: 30 min.
Assembling: 15 min.
Chilling: 2-1/2 hr.

Line large glass bowl with lady fingers. Add half the coffee cream and spread evenly, without disturbing lady fingers. Put another layer of lady fingers on top. Add remaining coffee cream, spreading evenly and gently. Refrigerate at least 1 hr. Just before serving, whip cream, adding sugar gradually at the end of beating. Fold in vanilla. Spread on top of refrigerated dessert. Garnish with sprinkles or chocolate.

ENGLISH TRIFLE

1/3 of a pound cake
1/2 c. sherry (approx.)
1 can (1 lb.) fruit cocktail
1 pkg. (3 oz.) fruit flavored gelatin
1 pkg. (4-1/2 oz.) vanilla pudding mix
1 c. heavy cream, whipped
chopped almonds

Preparation: 20 min.
Chilling: 4 hr.

Cut cake into 2" cubes and soak in sherry. Place in glass bowl and add fruit from fruit cocktail. Reserve juice. Prepare gelatin according to pkg. directions, except substitute juice from fruit for cold water. Pour immediately over cake and fruit. Refrigerate until set. Prepare vanilla pudding according to pkg. directions. Cool slightly and pour over set gelatin. Refrigerate until set. Top with whipped cream. Decorate with chopped almonds.

FRUIT MERINGUE

4 egg whites
2 c. confectioners' sugar
2 pkg. frozen peaches, thawed and drained
2 pkg. frozen strawberries, thawed and drained
3 c. heavy cream, whipped

Preparation: 20 min.
Baking: 4 hr.

Beat egg whites until very stiff. Beat in half the sugar and fold in the rest. Place in forcing bag fitted with star pipe. Pipe into a round base 15" in diameter and around the edge to make a 2" to 3" wall. Bake on ungreased cookie sheet at 250 degrees for 3-4 hr. or until crisp and dry. Keep dry until ready to use. Into whipped cream fold all fruit except a few pieces of each. Spoon into center of meringue. Decorate with reserved fruit.

DESSERTS
for 12

FANCY JELL-O

Preparation: 25 min.
Chilling: 8 hr.

2 pkg. (3-oz. size) lemon gelatin
2 pkg. (3-oz. size) orange gelatin
3-1/2 c. hot water
2 cans (8-oz. size) seedless grapes, drained
1 c. white wine
2 c. orange juice

Boil water and add to gelatin. Add wine and orange juice. Cool and add grapes. Pour into 2 qt. mold and chill 8 hr.

SAUCE:
4 egg yolks
4 tbsp. sugar
1 c. milk
1/2 c. Grand Marnier
1 c. heavy cream, whipped
strawberries

Beat egg yolks in double boiler. Add sugar, milk and Grand Marnier. Cook and stir over simmering water until mixture thickens slightly. Cool. Fold in whipped cream. Pour over unmolded dessert. Garnish with strawberries.

LEMON SOUFFLE

Preparation: 40 min.
Chilling: 8 hr.

2 env. unflavored gelatin
1-1/2 c. cold water
6 eggs, separated
2 c. sugar
grated rind and juice of 4 lemons
2 c. heavy cream, whipped

Soften gelatin in water in GLASS measuring cup. Beat egg yolks and sugar until thick and light colored. Beat in juice and grated lemon rinds. In a separate bowl beat egg whites until stiff but not dry. Dissolve gelatin by putting cup into pan of simmering water. Fold into lemon mixture, then fold in beaten whites and whipped cream. Place in large souffle dish. Chill 8 hr.

LEMON SPONGE

Preparation: 25 min.
Baking: 35 min.

6 tbsp. flour
2 c. sugar
1/4 tsp. salt
4 eggs, separated
4 tsp. grated lemon peel
1/4 c. lemon juice
2 tbsp. butter, melted
2 c. milk

Have boiling water ready. Mix flour, sugar and salt. Beat egg yolks slightly and mix with lemon peel, lemon juice and butter. Stir in milk and flour mixture. Beat egg whites until stiff but not dry. Fold into lemon mixture. Pour into 12 custard cups. Set in pan with boiling water to same level as mixture in cups. Bake at 350 degrees for 35 min. or until browned.

DESSERTS
for 12

MOCHA DESSERT

Preparation: 25 min.
Chilling: 2 hr.

4 env. unflavored gelatin
1 c. cold water
7 c. coffee
3 tbsp. sugar
2 c. heavy cream, whipped
4 tbsp. unsweetened cocoa

Soften gelatin in water and heat with coffee and sugar over moderate heat, stirring until dissolved. Pour into 2 qt. ring mold and chill at least 2 hr. Stir cocoa into whipped cream and place in center of unmolded dessert.

ORANGE MOLD

Preparation: 20 min.
Chilling: 2-1/2 hr.

2 cans (11-oz. size) mandarin orange sections
1/2 tsp. salt
6" cinnamon stick
1/2 tsp. whole cloves
4 pkg. (3-oz. size) orange gelatin
4 c. cold water
6 tbsp. lemon juice
3/4 c. chopped walnuts

Drain orange sections, putting liquid in saucepan. Add enough water to make 2-2/3 cups. Add salt, cinnamon and cloves. Cover and simmer 10 min. Remove from heat and let stand 10 min. Strain into large bowl. Dissolve gelatin in hot mixture. Add water and lemon juice and stir to mix well. Chill until partially set. Carefully fold in orange sections and walnuts. Turn into 2 qt. mold and chill about 2 hr.

PEACHES IN BRANDY SAUCE

Preparation: 10 min.
Chilling: 1 hr.
Baking: 15 min.

SAUCE:
3 eggs, separated
2 c. confectioners' sugar
scant 1/4 tsp. salt
1-1/2 c. heavy cream, whipped
1/2 c. brandy

Beat egg whites, stir in sugar, salt and slightly beaten egg yolks. Fold in whipped cream and brandy. Chill 1 hr.

3 cans (1-lb. 1-oz. size) peach halves, drained
3/4 c. maple syrup
1/2 c. brandy

Place peaches in ovenproof dish and cover with maple syrup. Bake uncovered at 350 degrees for 10-15 min. or until fruit and dish are hot. Bring to table, pour on brandy, ignite and baste. Serve with brandy sauce.

DESSERTS
for 12

STRAWBERRY-ALMOND MOLD

Preparation: 45 min.
Chilling: 2-3 hr.

4 pt. strawberries
1-1/2 c. sugar
4-1/2 env. unflavored gelatin
3/4 c. cold water
1-1/2 tbsp. lemon juice
1-1/2 tsp. almond flavoring
3/4 c. toasted, chopped, blanched almonds
3 c. heavy cream, whipped

Reserve 1 doz. strawberries, and blend remainder in blender. Pour into bowl, add sugar and let stand 30 min. In large saucepan soften gelatin in water and heat to dissolve. Stir in strawberry puree, lemon juice, almond flavoring and almonds. Chill until mixture begins to thicken, then fold in whipped cream. Pour into large ring mold and chill until firm.

SAUCE:

2 pts. strawberries
1 c. extra fine sugar
3 tbsp. kirsch
water or juice from strawberries

Puree strawberries in blender. Add sugar and kirsch. Thin to proper consistency with water or juice. Pour over unmolded dessert and garnish with reserved berries.

STRAWBERRY ICE CREAM

Preparation: 10 min.
Freezing: 2 hr. 45 min.

2 lrg. or 4 sml. pkg. frozen strawberries
2 pt. sour cream
1 c. sugar
2 tbsp. lemon juice

Thaw strawberries slightly. Combine with other ingredients and soft-freeze in ice tray(s), about 45 min. Beat to break ice crystals. Refreeze in 2 qt. mold or in individual serving cups for 2 hr. Remove from freezer 10 min. before serving.

ZWIEBACK TORTE

Preparation: 10 min.
Baking: 50 min.

6 eggs, separated
1 c. sugar
1 c. ground walnuts
12 zwieback, ground
1 tsp. baking powder

Beat egg yolks with sugar and mix with walnuts, zwieback and baking powder. In separate bowl beat whites until stiff and fold into yolk mixture. Pour into buttered 3 qt. souffle dish. Bake uncovered at 350 degrees for 45-50 min.

to serve 16 or more

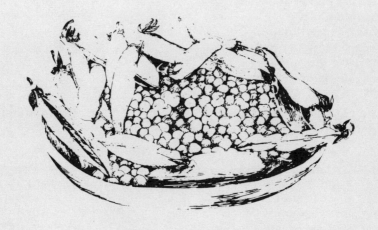

HORS D'OEUVRES
for 16

ASPARAGUS ROLL UPS

Preparation: 25 min.

12 slices white bread
8 oz. cream cheese
4 tbsp. sour cream
1 tbsp. blue cheese
1/4 tsp. dill seed
1/4 tsp. pepper
2 cans (10-oz. size) thin asparagus, drained
4 tbsp. butter, melted

Remove bread crusts. Roll each slice thin with a rolling pin. Mix cheeses, seasonings and sour cream and spread on slices. Roll one asparagus spear in each, jelly-roll style. Put seam side down on cookie sheet and brush with butter. Brown lightly on both sides under broiler. Slice each roll into bite-size pieces. Can be frozen.

CHEESE ROLL

Preparation: 15 min.

2 lb. cream cheese
1 lb. blue cheese
1/4 lb. butter
1/2 c. chopped ripe olives
2 tbsp. chopped chives
1 tbsp. brandy
1 can (6 oz.) pecans, crushed

Mix all ingredients except nuts together to form smooth paste. Shape into 1 long roll or 2 to 3 smaller ones. Roll in crushed nuts until completely coated. Refrigerate until ready to use.

LIPTAUER CHEESE A LA BARTLETT

Preparation: 20 min.

16 oz. cream cheese
2 tbsp. capers
2 tbsp. grated onion
2 oz. anchovy paste
2 tsp. dry mustard
2 tsp. paprika
1 tbsp. Worcestershire
4 tbsp. sour cream
1/4 tsp. garlic powder
1 oz. brandy or beer

Put all ingredients in a large bowl. Beat with electric mixer until smooth. Refrigerate in tightly covered jars or crocks.

YIELD: Approximately 3 cups

CLAMS ALEXANDRE

Preparation: 15 min.
Baking: 15 min.

6 doz. cherrystone clams
6-8 slices bacon, minced
1 green pepper, minced
1/2 c. minced shallots
1 jar pimentos, minced
Worcestershire sauce
rock salt

Open clams and loosen meat, leaving it on bottom shell. Mix bacon, green pepper, shallots and pimentos. Mound 1/2 tsp. of mixture on each clam and add dash of Worcestershire. Place on bed of rock salt on cookie sheets. Bake at 400 degrees for 15 min. or until bacon is crisp.

HORS D'OEUVRES
for 16

STEAMED CLAMS

Preparation: 30 min.
Steaming: 15 min.

12 doz. clams (about 5 measures)
1/2 c. corn meal
6 c. boiling water
1 lb. butter, melted
1/4 c. lemon juice
1 tsp. pepper

Scrub clams with stiff brush. Let stand in cold water and cornmeal for at least 2-3 hr. Drain, rinse and drain again. Place in 2 batches in large kettle with boiling water, and cover tightly. Steam until shells just open about 10-15 min. Heap clams into large bowl. In a smaller bowl, serve butter with lemon juice and pepper. Also in another small bowl serve hot clam broth from kettle.

CRAB BALL

Preparation: 15 min.
Chilling: 2 hr.

1 lb. crabmeat
4 tbsp. celery, chopped
2 tbsp. chopped green pepper
4 eggs, hard-boiled
4 tsp. horseradish
1/4-1/2 tsp. onion salt
1/4-1/2 tsp. garlic salt
1/2 tsp. salt
2 tsp. cooking sherry
8 oz. cream cheese

Chop eggs and combine all ingredients, adding crabmeat last. Chill. Form into 2 large balls and serve with assorted crackers or Melba rounds.

HAM APPETIZER

Preparation: 30 min.
Chilling: 3 hr.

2 env. unflavored gelatin
1-1/2 c. cold stock
1/2 lb. lean ham, minced
1 tbsp. sherry
pepper to taste
dash cayenne
juice of 1/2 lemon
1/4 lb. beef tongue, cooked and minced
1/2 c. heavy cream, whipped
4 egg whites, stiffly beaten
crackers
  or Melba rounds

Soften gelatin in broth. Place first ingredients in blender and mix at high speed. Add tongue and blend again. Remove to bowl and fold in whipped cream. Chill 1 hr. until just about to set. Fold in egg whites and pour into 2 qt. mold. Chill 2 hr. Unmold and serve with crackers or Melba rounds.

HORS D'OEUVRES
for 16

FROSTED LIVER PATE

Preparation: 15 min.
Chilling: 8 hr.
Frosting: 20 min.

3 cans (4-1/2-oz. size) liver pate
1-1/2 oz. cream cheese
1 tbsp. grated onion
2 tbsp. minced walnuts
2 tbsp. lemon juice

FROSTING:
4-1/2 oz. cream cheese
1 tbsp. milk
pimento, parsley, chives or decorating icing

In medium bowl, mix pate with cream cheese, onion, nuts and lemon juice. Line 3-cup bowl with wax paper strips to extend over bowl. Turn pate into bowl and press down firmly. Refrigerate.

Beat cream cheese with milk until smooth and fluffy. Invert pate on platter and frost surface with cheese mixture. Decorate with pimento, parsley, chives or designs made with icing.

MOLDED PATE

Preparation: 45 min.
Chilling: 3 hr.

1/2 lb. liverwurst
8 oz. cream cheese
1/2 med. onion, grated
1 tsp. parsley flakes
1/4 tsp. sage
1/2 tsp. Worcestershire
1/2 tsp. mustard
salt and pepper to taste
1 can beef consomme
1/2 env. unflavored gelatin
olive slices or pimento

Mix first 8 ingredients. Blend well. Put consomme and gelatin in saucepan and heat over very low flame until dissolved. Pour enough consomme into small mold to coat bottom 1/4". Arrange olive slices or pimento in pattern on consomme. Refrigerate 1 hr. Put pate into mold, leaving about 1/8" between pate and sides of mold. Pour remaining consomme around edge and refrigerate at least 2 hr.

STUFFED MUSHROOMS

Preparation: 20 min.
Baking: 10 min.

32 med. mushrooms
4 tbsp. butter
8 tbsp. chopped onion
8 tbsp. bread crumbs
6 slices bacon
2 tbsp. chopped parsley
2 tsp. salt
1/2 tsp. pepper
1/4 tsp. marjoram

Fry bacon, drain and crumble. Remove and chop stems from mushrooms. Saute onion and mushroom stems in butter for 5 min. Add bread crumbs, bacon, parsley, salt, pepper and marjoram. Stuff mushroom caps with mixture. Bake on buttered baking sheet at 350 degrees for 10 min.

HORS D'OEUVRES
for 16

PHEASANT PATE

Preparation: 30 min.
Chilling: 30 min.

2 c. ground cooked pheasant
1/2 c. butter
2 generous tbsp. French brandy
salt and pepper to taste
2 pinches ground thyme

With electric mixer, cream butter until fluffy. Add ground meat gradually, alternating with brandy. Mix on slow setting until well-blended. Add salt, pepper, and thyme. Refrigerate 30 min.

SPANACOPITA

Preparation: 20 min.
Baking: 25 min.

2 pkg. frozen chopped spinach
1 bunch scallions, minced
1 tbsp. minced dill
1/2 lb. feta or cottage cheese
4 eggs
12 strudel leaves
3 tbsp. olive oil
6 tbsp. butter

Cook spinach and drain thoroughly. Saute in olive oil with scallions and dill. Remove from heat. Add cheese and eggs. Stack 6 buttered strudel leaves in buttered 13" x 9" pan. Add spinach/cheese mixture, spreading evenly. Cover with stack of 6 buttered strudel leaves. Bake at 350 degrees for 25 min. or until golden brown. Cut into serving pieces while hot.

STEAK TARTARE

Preparation: 20 min.

2 lb. ground round beef
1/2 c. minced onion
1/2 c. capers
8 anchovy fillets, minced
2 eggs, slightly beaten
salt and pepper to taste
1 tsp. paprika
2 tsp. chopped parsley
1 tsp. Worcestershire
3 dashes Tabasco

Blend all ingredients well. Form into 3/4" balls or a large mound.

SWEET AND SOUR MEAT BALLS

Preparation: 20 min.
Cooking: 30 min.

2 bottles chili sauce
1 jar (10 oz.) grape jelly
2 lb. ground beef
1 tsp. salt
1 tsp. garlic salt
2 eggs
1/2 raw potato, grated
4 saltines, crushed

Heat chili sauce and grape jelly to boiling. Mix meat, seasonings, egg, potato and crackers. Blend well. Form 3/4" balls and drop into boiling sauce. Simmer covered for 30 min.

SOUPS
for 16

BEEF VEGETABLE SOUP WITH BARLEY

Preparation: 20 min.
Cooking: 2 hr. 45 min.

- 1 can (1-lb. 12-oz.) tomatoes
- 1 qt. water
- 2 lb. boneless chuck, in 1" cubes
- 2 tbsp. salt
- 1 tsp. pepper
- 1 c. sliced celery including greens
- 1/4 c. chopped parsley
- 2 c. coarsely chopped cabbage
- 1 bay leaf
- 1/2 c. barley
- 2 cans (18-oz. size) V-8 juice
- 1 pkg. frozen cut green beans
- 2 c. sliced carrots
- 1-1/2 c. thinly sliced onion
- 1-2 tsp. mixed dried herbs
- 1 tsp. Worcestershire
- 2 beef bouillon cubes
- 1 c. grated Parmesan cheese

Drain tomatoes, reserving liquid. Add water to liquid and place with meat, salt, pepper, celery, parsley, cabbage and bay leaf in large kettle. Cover and simmer 1 hr. Discard bay leaf, celery leaves and parsley. Add 1 cup water and barley and cook uncovered 30 min. to 1 hr. longer, stirring occasionally. Add juice, tomatoes, beans, carrots, onion, herbs, Worcestershire, bouillon cubes and 1 cup water. Simmer uncovered about 45 min. Correct seasoning and serve in bowls. Sprinkle each serving with Parmesan cheese. Can be frozen.

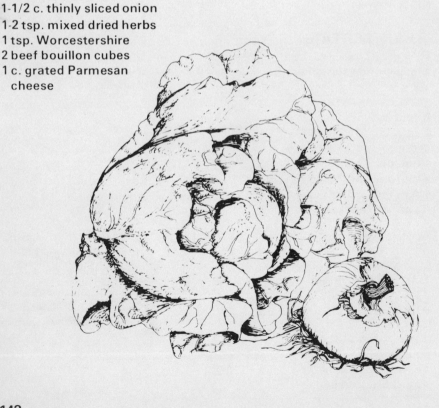

SOUPS
for 16

ZARAGOZANA BLACK BEAN SOUP

Soaking: 8 hr.
Preparation: 35 min.
Cooking: 3 hr. 10 min.

- 1 lb. black beans
- 2-1/2 qt. + 1 tbsp. water
- 5 cloves garlic
- 4 tbsp. salt
- 1 tbsp. pepper
- 1-1/2 tsp. cumin
- 1-1/2 tsp. oregano
- 6 tbsp. olive oil
- 1 tsp. vinegar
- 5 med. onions, finely chopped
- 2 green peppers, chopped
- 4 c. cooked rice

Soak beans 8 hr. in cold water to cover. Drain and put in kettle with 2-1/2 qt. water. Simmer covered about 3 hr. or until beans are mushy. Marinate half the onions in vinegar and 1 tbsp. oil Crush together garlic, salt, pepper, cumin and oregano. Heat remaining oil in saucepan and saute green pepper, remaining onions and herb mixture for 2-3 min. Stir in 1 tbsp. water and simmer uncovered 5-10 min. Add to cooked beans and simmer uncovered 5-10 min. Place 1/4 cup rice in each bowl and add soup. Garnish with marinated onions.

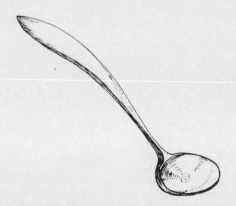

CHEESE SOUP

Preparation: 30 min.

- 8 c. shredded Cheddar cheese (mild)
- 1 c. shredded carrot
- 1/2 c. chopped onion
- 1 c. butter
- 1 c. flour
- 1 tbsp. salt
- 1 tsp. pepper
- 4 qt. milk
- 1/2 c. chopped chives

In large kettle, saute carrot and onion in butter. Stir in flour, salt, pepper, add milk. Whisk until smooth and thickened. Add cheese a little at a time, stirring after each addition. Continue stirring until well blended. Correct seasonings. Bring to serving temperature. Garnish with chives.

SOUPS
for 16

CHESTNUT SOUP

Preparation: 20 min.
Cooking: 35 min.

3 cans (10-oz. size) fresh whole chestnuts, drained
8 c. clear mushroom soup (see index) or 8 c. chicken broth
3 tsp. salt
6 tbsp. butter
1-1/2 qt. milk, heated
3/4 tsp. pepper
1 c. sherry
1 c. heavy cream, whipped

Puree half of chestnuts in blender with 1 cup mushroom soup or broth. Remove to large bowl over kettle of simmering water. Repeat with second half of chestnuts and another cup of soup. Add remaining soup, salt and butter and stir until heated through and butter is melted. Heat milk and pepper and add to soup. Cover and increase heat so water under bowl is boiling. Cook for 30 min. Add sherry and heat for 5 min. Garnish with whipped cream.

CRABMEAT SOUP

Preparation: 5 min.
Cooking: 20 min.

4 cans cream of tomato soup
4 cans pea soup
6 soup-cans milk
1 pt. heavy cream, slightly beaten
2 cans (7-1/2-oz. size) crabmeat, drained and flaked
salt and pepper to taste
sherry (opt.)

Heat all ingredients except sherry in large saucepan just to boiling point. Do not boil. Add sherry to taste.

SOUPS
for 16

CREAM OF ONION SOUP

Preparation: 40 min.
Cooking: 1-1/2 hr.

16 med. onions, finely chopped
4 med. potatoes, diced
12 c. water
1 gal. milk
1 tsp. pepper
1 tsp. paprika
2 tsp. salt
4 chicken bouillon cubes
1/4 c. butter
16 sprigs parsley

In large kettle combine onions and potatoes. Cover with water and simmer 1 hr. or until the consistency of puree. Add milk, seasonings and bouillon cubes. Heat to serving point and add butter. Swirl until butter is melted. Garnish with parsley.

HEARTY OYSTER STEW

Preparation: 10 min.
Heating: 30 min.

4 cans (7-1/2-oz. size) minced clams
2 qt. shucked oysters and liquor
1 qt. clam broth
3 pt. heavy cream
1 tsp. white pepper
salt to taste
Worcestershire sauce
1/2 lb. butter
paprika

Puree clams with liquor from oysters in 2 batches in blender Put in large bowl over large pot of boiling water. Add broth, cream, pepper and oysters. Heat until oysters rise to surface, but do not boil. Correct seasonings. Add salt and Worcestershire if desired. Garnish with butter pats and paprika.

SPINACH SOUP

Preparation: 30 min.
Chilling: 8 hr.

4 pkg. frozen chopped spinach
8 c. heavy cream
8 c. milk
16 chicken bouillon cubes
1 c. dry vermouth
4 tsp. grated lemon rind
2 tsp. ground mace
salt and pepper to taste
6 eggs, hard-boiled and finely chopped

Cook spinach according to pkg. directions and drain. Put in blender and reduce to pulp. Put bouillon cubes in milk and cream and scald, stirring until dissolved. Add part of mixture to spinach in blender. Blend briefly and pour into milk/cream mixture. Stir in vermouth, lemon rind, mace, salt and pepper. Chill. Stir vigorously before serving. Garnish with egg.

MEATS
for 16

BAKED MEATBALLS

Preparation: 30 min.
Marinating: 1 hr.
Baking: 30 min.

5 lb. ground beef
1/2 tsp. garlic salt
1/2 tsp. pepper
3/4 c. minced onion
1 lb. chow mein noodles, finely crushed
2 c. milk
2 c. soy sauce
1 c. water
8 tbsp. salad oil
2 garlic cloves, crushed
2 tsp. ground ginger
4 tbsp. sugar

Mix beef, garlic salt, pepper, onion, noodles and milk. Shape into 3/4" balls and place in shallow baking pan. Combine soy sauce, water, salad oil, garlic, ginger and sugar. Mix well. Pour over meatballs. Marinate at least 1 hr. turning occasionally. Bake uncovered in marinade at 350 degrees for 30 min. Serve hot. Can be frozen.

BLUE CHEESE STUFFED MEAT LOAF

Preparation: 20 min.
Baking: 1 hr.

16 slices bread, diced
1 c. milk, scalded
1 c. crumbled blue cheese
5 eggs
4 lb. ground beef
1/2 lb. ground pork
2 c. soft bread crumbs
2 med. onions, minced
3 tbsp. salt
1 tsp. pepper
5 tbsp. chopped parsley
1 c. ketchup

In bowl, pour milk over diced bread and mix well. Add cheese and 2 beaten eggs. Mix well. In separate bowl, combine remaining ingredients. Mix well. Spread meat mixture evenly on 12" x 15" wax paper. Spread cheese mixture on meat, leaving 1" perimeter uncovered. Roll up lengthwise (so that roll will be 12" long). Press firmly. Place seam side down in loaf pan, or shallow baking pan. Bake at 375 degrees for 1 hr.

CALIFORNIA MEATBALLS

Preparation: 55 min.
Cooking: 20 min.

3 cans (1-lb. size) whole cranberry sauce
2 bottles (12-oz. size) chili sauce
6-3/4 c. water
3 lrg. onions, minced
6 lb. lean ground beef
salt and pepper to taste
3 eggs, beaten

Mix together cranberry sauce, chili sauce, 6 cups water and onions. Simmer 45 min. stirring frequently. To ground beef, add salt, pepper, eggs and 3/4 cup water. Form into small balls and add to sauce. Cook about 20 min. or until done.

MEATS
for 16

HAMBURGER STROGANOFF

Preparation: 1 hr.
Baking: 1 hr.

2 lb. noodles
4 lb. chopped beef
2 med. onions, thinly sliced
2 cans cream of celery soup
2 cans cream of mushroom soup
2 cans (3-oz. size) chopped mushrooms
1 pt. sour cream
1 c. red wine
2 tbsp. dill seed
1 c. fresh chopped parsley
salt and pepper to taste
Worcestershire to taste
paprika
sprigs or parsley

Cook noodles according to pkg. directions. Drain and put in 5-6 qt. casserole. Brown meat in large skillet. Remove to casserole with slotted spoon. Simmer onion in fat until golden. Add soups, mushrooms, sour cream, wine, dill seeds and chopped parsley to skillet. Season to taste. Pour over casserole and stir to blend. Bake covered at 300 degrees for 1 hr. Garnish with paprika and parsley sprigs.

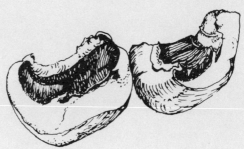

ORIENTAL HAMBURGER CASSEROLE

Preparation: 30 min.
Baking: 30 min.

4 lb. ground chuck
2 cans (8-oz. size) chopped mushrooms
4 cans (16-oz. size) green beans
6 med. onions, thickly sliced
6 tbsp. oil
2 tbsp. ground ginger
3/4 c. cornstarch
salt and pepper to taste

Brown onions lightly in large skillet in 3 tbsp. oil. Set aside. Add remaining oil and beef. Brown and add drained mushrooms (reserving liquid), and ginger and stir well. Cook slowly until meat is cooked through. To reserved mushroom juice, add enough water to make 4 cups. Add cornstarch and blend. Stir into meat mixture, adding onions and drained beans. Season to taste. Bake covered at 350 degrees for 30 min.

MEATS
for 16

HEARTY ITALIAN MEAT SAUCE

Preparation: 30 min.
Cooking: 2 hr.

3 lb. ground beef
1/2 lb. bulk Italian sweet sausage
2 cans (28-oz. size) tomatoes, chopped
3 c. Chianti
3 c. water
2 cans (12-oz. size) tomato paste
2 c. chopped onion
1-1/2 c. chopped green pepper
1 tbsp. Worcestershire
2 tsp. salt
2 tsp. sugar
1 tsp. chili powder
1/4 tsp. pepper
2 cloves garlic, minced
4 bay leaves, crumbled
3 cans (6-oz. size) sliced mushrooms, drained or 1/2 lb. fresh mushrooms, sliced and sauteed

In Dutch oven or large frying pan, brown beef and sausage. Drain off fat. Stir in remaining ingredients except mushrooms. Bring to boil. Reduce heat and simmer uncovered for 1-1/2 hr. stirring occasionally. Add mushrooms and stir. Can be frozen.

COCKTAIL PARTY ROAST BEEF

Baking: 2 hr. 50 min.

10 lb. roast beef
salt and pepper to taste

Preheat oven to 500 degrees. Roast beef for 5 min. per pound. Turn off oven. KEEP OVEN DOOR CLOSED and heat off for 2 hr. Serve immediately.

NOTE: This timing is for rare. Add 1 min. per pound for medium; 2 min. per pound for well done.

MEATS
for 16

DRIED BEEF DELUXE

Preparation: 15 min.
Heating: 30 min.

4 jars dried beef, diced
6 tbsp. butter
4 pts. sour cream
4 lrg. cans artichoke hearts
1/2 c. sherry
16 English muffins

Melt butter in top of double boiler. Add beef, and cook for a few min. Strain. Add sour cream, artichoke hearts and sherry. Heat, but do not boil. Pour over muffins, which have been split, toasted and buttered.

GOOD GOULASH

Preparation: 40 min.
Cooking: 3-1/4 hr.

1 c. chopped onion
1 c. chopped green pepper
2 tbsp. butter
3 tbsp. paprika
3 lrg. cans whole tomatoes
salt to taste
1 tbsp. sugar
celery salt to taste
garlic salt to taste
2 lb. lamb, cubed
2 lb. pork, cubed
2 lb. beef, cubed
2 qt. sauerkraut
2 pt. sour cream

Saute onion and pepper in butter and paprika. Add tomatoes, salt, sugar, celery salt and garlic salt. Heat and put in large casserole. Brown meat, add salt and pepper and add to casserole. Simmer uncovered on very low flame about 2-3 hr. Wash, drain and add sauerkraut. Simmer 15 min. longer. Just before serving, add 1 pt. sour cream and serve remainder in separate bowl.

IMPERIAL GOULASH

Preparation: 1 hr.
Cooking: 3 hr.

8 lb. round steak, cubed
1-1/2 c. flour
2 tbsp. salt
2 tsp. pepper
1 tsp. savory
2/3 c. butter
2 lb. onions, sliced
2 lb. fresh mushrooms, sliced
2 cloves garlic, crushed
1/4 tsp. oregano
2-3 tsp. paprika
2 c. Burgundy wine
1 c. sour cream

Lightly dredge beef cubes in mixture of flour, 1 tbsp. salt, 1 tsp. pepper and 1/2 tsp. savory. In 1/2 cup butter in large heavy pan brown meat on all sides, adding butter as needed. Set aside. Saute onions, mushrooms and garlic in butter until tender. Return meat to pan. Season with remaining salt, pepper, savory, oregano and paprika. Stir and add Burgundy. Cover and simmer slowly, stirring occasionally, about 3 hr. or until meat is fork-tender. Add more wine if needed to keep mixture from getting too thick. Just before serving, stir in room temperature sour cream. Can be frozen.

MEATS
for 16

TEXAS HASH

Preparation: 25 min.
Baking: 50 min.

4 lrg. onions, sliced
3 green peppers, minced
4 tbsp. oil
4 lb. chopped beef
2 cans (1-lb. size) tomatoes
1 c. uncooked rice
1 tsp. chili powder
2 tsp. salt
1/2 tsp. pepper
2 cans (4-1/2-oz. size) black olives, sliced
1/2 lb. peperoni thinly sliced

Cook onion and green pepper slowly in oil until onion is transparent. Add meat and cook until it falls apart. Add remaining ingredients. Place in 5-qt. greased casserole and bake covered at 375 degrees for at least 50 min. Test rice to see if done. Can be frozen.

FLANK STEAK WITH HOWARD'S SAUCE

Preparation: 15 min.
Broiling: 8 min.

6 tbsp. butter
3 c. ketchup
1-1/3 c. prepared mustard
1/4 c. Worcestershire
2 tsp. onion salt
4-5 flank steaks

Melt butter in saucepan and add remaining ingredients. Heat and stir. Do not boil and do not reheat, as this causes sauce to curdle. Broil flank steak 3-4 min. per side on charcoal grill or in broiler. Slice diagonally, against the grain, very thin. Cover with sauce.

BURGUNDY BEEF STEW

Preparation: 5 min.
Baking: 3 hr.

3/4 c. instant flour
1 c. cold water
8 lb. beef, cubed
3 c. Burgundy wine
6 c. beef consomme
1 tbsp. salt
2 tsp. pepper
1 lrg. onion, sliced
2 c. bread crumbs

Dissolve flour in water and combine with remaining ingredients in 5 qt. casserole. Bake covered at 300 degrees for 3 hr.

MEATS
for 16

MONTE'S STEW

Preparation: 45 min.
Baking: 2-1/2 hr.

6 lb. stew meat, cubed
1-1/2 c. flour, seasoned with salt and pepper
4 cans (16-oz. size) small, white potatoes
2 jars (16-oz. size) whole peeled onions
3 jars (16-oz. size) whole baby carrots
1/5 gal. hearty Burgundy
3 or 4 pkg. beef stew seasoning mix
water
1/4-1/2 c. oil or bacon fat
salt to taste

Roll meat in flour and brown well in oil or fat. Add a cup of water to skillet. Empty liquid to large stew pot. Add seasoning mix, water and wine according to instructions on seasoning pkg. Test and correct seasonings. Add meat, cover and bake at 300 degrees for 2-1/2 hr. Half an hour before eating, add drained vegetables. Stir gently occasionally. Add wine for liquid if necessary.

HAM AND NOODLE CASSEROLE

Preparation: 30 min.
Baking: 1 hr.

1 lb. noodles
6 c. cooked and diced ham
8 c. med. white sauce (see index)
1-1/2 c. grated Parmesan cheese
1 c. chopped parsley
1 c. finely chopped onion
1 c. bread crumbs
5-6 tbsp. butter
salt and pepper to taste

Cook noodles minimum amount of time suggested on pkg. and drain. Layer buttered casserole with 1/3 of the noodles, 1/2 of the meat, onion, parsley and white sauce to which cheese has been added. Repeat layers except for sauce. Final layer should be noodles covered with remaining sauce. Sprinkle with bread crumbs and small dabs of butter. Bake uncovered at 350 degrees for about 1 hr.

HAM WITH ENDIVE

Preparation: 30 min.
Baking: 30 min.

16 lrg. heads endive
6-8 c. beef bouillon
16 thin slices cooked ham
6 c. Mornay sauce (see index)
bread crumbs (opt.)
butter (opt.)

Simmer endive in bouillon about 15 min. and drain. Roll each head in a thin slice of ham. Arrange in ungreased 13" x 9" baking dish. Cover with Mornay sauce. If desired top with bread crumbs and dot with butter. Bake at 375 degrees for 30 min.

MEATS
for 16

LAMB AND ARTICHOKE STEW

Preparation: 1-1/2 hr.
Cooking: 1-1/2 hr.

6 lb. lamb, cubed
4 tbsp. oil
2 lrg. onions, sliced
1-1/2 c. dry white wine
4 c. water
4 tsp. salt
1/4 tsp. pepper
2 bay leaves
2 tbsp. chopped fresh dill or 1 tbsp. dried dill
3 cans (14-oz. size) artichoke hearts
4 tbsp. flour
3 eggs
1/4 c. lemon juice
1 lemon, very thinly sliced
sprigs of fresh dill

Brown lamb in oil in large kettle. Remove. Saute onion until golden 5-10 min. Return meat. Add 1 cup wine. Cover and simmer about 15 min. Stir in water, salt, pepper and bay leaves. Cover and simmer 1-1/2 hr. Discard bay leaves. Place meat in large casserole, add artichokes to meat and toss gently. Cover and keep warm. Bring cooking liquid to 6 cups by adding wine. Blend flour and 1/2 cup wine in small bowl and stir into liquid. Cook and stir until thick. Beat eggs until light and fluffy. Add lemon juice gradually continuing to beat. Add some boiling liquid to egg mixture beating constantly. Return to pot. Stir constantly over low heat for 1-2 min. Add dill and correct seasonings. Pour sauce over meat and artichokes. Garnish with sliced lemon and sprigs of fresh dill.

PORK CHOPS IN PLUM SAUCE

Preparation: 15 min.
Baking: 1 hr.

16 pork chops, med. thick
1 c. flour
salt and pepper to taste
4 jars (4-3/4-oz. size) strained plums
1 tbsp. grated lemon peel
2 tsp. cinnamon
1 tsp. ground cloves
2 c. port

Trim fat and coat chops lightly with mixture of flour, salt and pepper. Brown both sides in large ovenproof skillet. Mix remaining ingredients and pour over chops. Cover and bake at 325 degrees for 1 hr.

VEAL AND MUSHROOMS

Preparation: 15 min.
Baking: 2 hr.

8 lb. veal, cut in lrg. cubes
1-1/2 c. seasoned flour
5 lb. mushrooms, sliced
1-1/2 c. butter

Melt butter in skillet. Roll veal cubes in flour and sear on all sides. In a 6 qt. casserole place meat and raw mushrooms alternately with melted butter from skillet. Cover tightly and bake at 350 degrees for 2 hr.

MEATS
for 16

VEAL PARMIGIANA

Preparation: 15 min.
Baking: 50 min.

3/4 c. butter
2-2/3 c. cornflake crumbs
1-1/3 c. grated Parmesan cheese
2 tsp. salt
1/4 tsp. pepper
4 lb. veal cutlets, 1/4" thick
3 eggs, slightly beaten
4 cans (6-oz. size) tomato paste, or to taste
4 cans (8-oz. size) tomato sauce
1 tsp. crushed oregano
1 tsp. sugar
1/4 tsp. onion salt
1/2 lb. Mozzarella cheese, sliced

Melt butter in 17" x 13" baking dish. Combine cornflake crumbs, Parmesan cheese, salt and pepper. Cut veal into serving pieces and dip in egg, then in crumb mixture. Arrange in baking dish and bake uncovered at 400 degrees for 20 min. Turn meat and continue baking 15-20 min. or until tender. Meanwhile, combine tomato sauce, tomato paste, oregano, sugar and onion salt in large saucepan. Heat just to boiling, stirring frequently. Pour sauce over meat. Top with Mozzarella. Sprinkle with oregano and return to oven to melt cheese (about 3 min.).

VEAL CUTLETS ZINN ARTURO

Preparation: 40 min.
Baking: 20 min.

16 veal cutlets, pounded very thin
1-1/2 c. flour, seasoned with salt and pepper
1/2 c. butter
16 leeks, chopped
2-1/2 heads cauliflower, in flowerets
10 carrots
2-1/2 lb. green beans
5 onions, chopped
1/4 tsp. chopped chives
1/4 tsp. chopped parsley
1/4 tsp. chopped thyme
1/4 tsp. chopped basil
1/4 tsp. chopped tarragon
16 paper-thin slices Swiss cheese

Dip cutlets in seasoned flour and saute in butter about 2 min. per side. Arrange on ovenproof serving platter. Prepare carrots and beans julienne style (narrow, long strips) and cook with other vegetables for 3 min. in butter adding herbs. Top cutlets with vegetable mixture and cover with cheese slices. Bake at 375 degrees for 15-20 min. or until cheese is glazed.

MEATS
for 20

TRITTINI

Preparation: 1 hr.
Baking: 30 min.

4 lb. ground beef
1 c. minced onion
4 cans (6-oz. size) tomato paste
4 cans (8-oz. size) tomato sauce
4 tsp. dried basil
4 tsp. dried parsley flakes
salt to taste
4 tsp. sugar
2 tsp. oregano
dash garlic salt
1/2 tsp. pepper
4 cans (3-oz. size) sliced mushrooms, drained
4 pkg. frozen chopped spinach, thawed
2 lb. cottage cheese
1/2 lb. Mozzarella cheese

Saute beef and onion in large skillet until beef loses its color and onion is transparent. Add next 9 ingredients. Set aside 15 mushroom slices. Mix the rest into meat and simmer for 10 min. or until thick. Separate into 5 equal portions. Drain spinach thoroughly and combine with cottage cheese and salt. Divide into 5 equal portions. Slice 12 strips of Mozzarella 2-1/2" x 1/2" x 1/2" and dice the rest. In 13" x 9" baking dish arrange alternately in lengthwise strips, 3 portions of spinach mixture and 2 portions of meat mixture. Sprinkle with diced Mozzarella. On top of diced cheese, arrange alternately in lengthwise strips, 3 portions of meat mixture and 2 of spinach mixture. With Mozzarella strips, make 4 crosswise rows over mixture, using 3 strips end-to-end in each row. Garnish with the 15 mushroom slices. Bake at 375 degrees for 25-30 min. until bubbling.

COMPANY BEEF CASSEROLE

Preparation: 5 min.
Cooking: 5 hr.

10 lb. chuck, 1" cubes
2 jars (16-oz. size) onions
2 cans onion soup
2 cans cream of tomato soup
2 cans beef bouillon
4 c. claret
4 cans (3-oz. size) mushrooms
1/2 c. instant flour
  or 1/4 c. cornstarch
1/4-1/2 c. water
1/4 c. cognac

Mix first 7 ingredients in large casserole and bake covered at 325 degrees for 5 hr. Just before serving, dissolve flour or cornstarch smoothly in water and add to gravy, stirring to thicken. Stir in cognac.

MEATS
for 30

LASAGNE

Preparation: 2-1/2 hr.
Baking: 1 hr.

6 tbsp. olive oil
6 med. onions, chopped
6 cloves garlic, crushed
4 lb. ground meat (combined beef and pork)
1 lb. hot Italian sausage, cut-up
3 cans (1-lb. 12-oz. size) whole tomatoes
3 cans (1-lb. 12-oz. size) tomato puree
3 cans (6-oz. size) tomato paste
3 c. beef broth
6 tsp. salt
3/4 tsp. pepper
3 tsp. sugar
3 lb. lasagne noodles
6 eggs
3 lb. Ricotta or cottage cheese
1-1/2 c. grated Parmesan cheese
3 tbsp. basil
6 tbsp. oregano
3 lb. Mozzarella cheese, sliced

Cook onions in oil in large Dutch oven until soft. Add garlic, meat and sausage and saute 15 min. Add tomatoes, puree, tomato paste, broth, salt, pepper and sugar. Simmer for 2 hr. Boil noodles 15 min. Drain and rinse. Beat eggs until foamy. Mix with cottage cheese or Ricotta. Spoon sauce over bottom of baking dish(es). Cover with noodles, dot with cheese mixture and sprinkle with Parmesan. Cover with Mozzarella, basil and oregano. Bake uncovered at 375 degrees for 1 hr. Can be frozen.

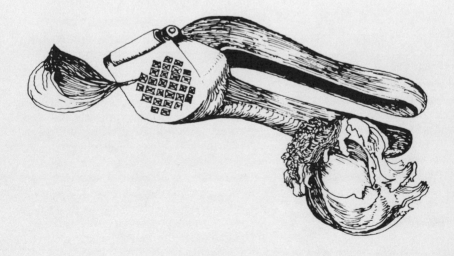

POULTRY & GAME
for 16

BAKED CHICKEN

Preparation: 15 min.
Baking: 2 hr.

16 whole chicken breasts, boned, skinned and split
4 pkg. onion soup mix
4 cans cream of mushroom soup
4 pts. sour cream

Combine onion soup mix, mushroom soup and sour cream. Add chicken and turn into baking dish. Bake uncovered at 325 degrees for 2 hr. Garnish as desired.

CHAMPAGNE CHICKEN

Preparation: 2 hr.

20 whole chicken breasts, boned, skinned, and split
3/4 c. butter
salt and pepper to taste
2 c. finely chopped onion
1/2 tsp. nutmeg
2 c. flour
1/2 c. cognac
2 bay leaves
12 c. chicken broth
1 qt. dry champagne
1 tsp. dried thyme
6 cans (4-oz. size) sliced mushrooms
5 c. heavy cream
paprika

In ovenproof kettle, toss chicken in 4 tbsp. butter over medium heat. Stir until well-coated. Add salt, pepper, onions and nutmeg. Continue cooking 5 min. Bake uncovered at 350 degrees for 30 min. Sprinkle with flour and stir to coat pieces. Bake 20 min longer. stirring occasionally. Add cognac, bay leaves, broth, champagne, thyme, mushrooms and 1 cup cream. Cover and simmer on top of stove 45 min. Remove chicken and keep warm. Boil sauce and reduce by one-third. Add remaining cream and simmer, covered, 1 hr. stirring frequently. Remove from heat and swirl in 8 tbsp. butter. Pour over chicken and sprinkle with paprika.

CHICKEN WITH GRAPES

Preparation: 40 min.
Baking: 45 min.

14 whole chicken breasts, boned and split
1/2 c. butter
3 cans (1-lb. size) potatoes
1-1/2 lb. mushroom caps
1/2 c. chopped onion
3 lb. white seedless grapes
1/2 c. flour
4 c. white wine
6 egg yolks, well beaten

Brown chicken breasts in butter. Remove to 5-6 qt. buttered casserole. Brown potato balls and add to casserole. Simmer mushrooms and onions until tender and add to casserole. Brown grapes quickly and add to casserole. Add flour to frying pan and blend with pan juices. Add white wine and stir over medium heat until thickened. Stir in egg yolks, correct seasoning and pour over chicken. Bake uncovered at 325 degrees for 45 min.

POULTRY & GAME
for 16

CHICKEN HAWAIIAN

Soaking: 8 hr.
Preparation: 20 min.
Browning: 15 min.

10 chicken cutlets, diced
4 eggs, lightly beaten
1 c. flour
1 c. soy sauce

SAUCE:

2 cans (28-oz. size)
　pineapple tidbits
juice of 1 lemon
2 c. brown sugar
3 c. water
2 tbsp. cornstarch
parsley sprigs

Soak chicken 8 hr. in soy sauce. Dip in egg and dredge with flour. Brown on both sides in oil in large frying pan. Drain on paper towel.

Use pineapple juice from cans, saving tidbits. Add cornstarch smoothly dissolved in lemon juice. Add brown sugar and water and cook over low flame until thick. Add pineapple and pour over chicken. Heat to serving temperature. Garnish with parsley sprigs.

ORIENTAL CHICKEN

Preparation: 20 min.
Cooking: 1 hr.

6 chickens, quartered
1/2 c. oil
3 cans (11-oz. size) mandarin
　orange sections
2 cans (5-3/4-oz. size) black
　olives, drained and pitted
1 lrg. can frozen orange juice

Fry chicken quarters in oil until lightly browned. Pour off oil. Add oranges including liquid, olives and orange concentrate. Place in large covered casserole and bake at 375 degrees for 1 hr.

PEACHY CHICKEN

Preparation: 45 min.
Baking: 30 min.

16 whole chicken breasts,
　boned, skinned and split
1 c. flour
1/4 tsp. garlic powder
1/4 tsp. onion salt
1/4 tsp. seasoned salt
1/8 tsp. pepper
6 tbsp. bacon fat
2 lb. fresh mushrooms,
　sliced
4 tsp. soy sauce
salt and pepper to taste
32 Freestone peach halves
2 pt. sour cream

Shake chicken breasts in bag with flour, garlic powder, onion salt, seasoned salt, and pepper. Brown in large skillet in hot fat. Lower heat and cook covered until done. Remove. Simmer mushrooms with soy sauce in same skillet about 10 min. stirring frequently. Sprinkle 4 tbsp. seasoned flour over mushrooms and stir until sauce is thickened. Arrange chicken in large baking dish with 1 peach half inverted on each piece. Cover with sour cream and top with mushroom gravy. Cover and bake at 300 degrees for 30 min. or until tender.

POULTRY & GAME
for 16

CHICKEN RONZINI

Preparation: 10 min.
Baking: 1 hr. 15 min.

10 lrg. chicken breasts, boned and split
4 jars (10-1/2-oz. size) marinara sauce
2 c. dry vermouth
1 lb. Mozzarella cheese, cubed

Place chicken breasts, sauce and vermouth in casserole. Stir to blend. Bake uncovered at 300 degrees for 1 hr. Remove chicken and cut into small pieces. Return to casserole and cover with cheese. Bake at 300 degrees for another 10 min. or until cheese is melted.

CHICKEN LIVERS MARSALA

Preparation: 10 min.
Cooking: 10 min.

4 lb. chicken livers
1 c. butter
1 tbsp. salt
1 tsp. pepper
1 tsp. sage
1 c. Marsala wine

Cut livers in half. Simmer in 1/2—3/4 cup butter together with seasonings for 5-10 min. Remove livers to warm platter. Add wine to pan gravy and cook for 3 min. Add remaining butter, mix well and pour over livers.

TURKEY FOR A CROWD

Preparation: 10 min.
Baking: 3-3/4 hr.

7-8 lb. boneless turkey roll
1/2 c. butter
2 tbsp. lemon juice
1/2 tsp. salt
1/4 tsp. pepper
1/4 tsp. dried tarragon
1/8 tsp. poultry seasoning
4 cans (10-1/2-oz. size) chicken giblet gravy
1/2—3/4 c. water or white wine

Melt butter and stir in lemon juice, salt, pepper, tarragon and poultry seasoning. Use for basting. Roast turkey at 325 degrees for 3-1/2 hr. basting frequently. Do not cover unless it gets too brown. When done, remove from roasting pan. Add water or wine to juices in pan and loosen the drippings. Add canned gravy. Heat and serve alongside thinly sliced turkey.

POULTRY & GAME
for 16

TURKEY TETRAZZINI

Preparation: 15 min.
Baking: 1 hr.

8 c. cooked, shredded turkey meat
1-1/2 lb. very thin noodles
8 c. med. white sauce (see index)
1/2 c. sherry
3 cans (8-oz. size) sliced mushrooms, drained
1/2 c. grated Parmesan cheese
salt and pepper to taste
chopped parsley

Cook noodles according to pkg. directions. Drain and combine with remaining ingredients except cheese and parsley in large casserole. Sprinkle with cheese. Bake uncovered at 375 degrees for 45-60 min. Remove from oven and garnish with parsley.

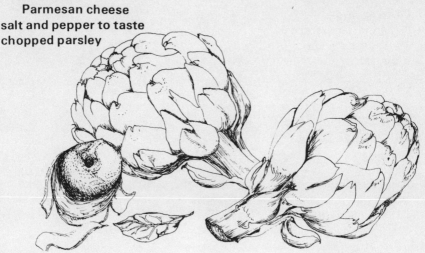

PATSY'S POTPOURRI

Preparation: 1 hr.
Baking: 40 min.

8 whole chicken breasts, cooked and diced
4 lb. shrimp, cooked and cleaned
3 cans (14-oz. size) non-marinated artichoke hearts, drained
3 lb. fresh mushrooms, sliced
3 tbsp. butter
2 tbsp. Worcestershire
6 c. white sauce (see index)
salt and pepper to taste
1 c. sherry
1/2 c. grated Parmesan cheese
paprika
chopped parsley

Arrange artichokes in bottom of large shallow buttered casserole. Add shrimp and chicken. In large skillet saute mushrooms in butter and add to casserole. Add Worcestershire to white sauce. Stir and pour over casserole. Add salt and pepper. Add sherry and stir gently. Sprinkle top with cheese and dust with paprika. Bake uncovered at 375 degrees for about 40 min. or until bubbly. Top should be brown. Garnish with parsley.

NOTE: Serves 20.

SEAFOOD
for 16

AVOCADO STUFFED WITH CRABMEAT

Preparation: 20 min.
Chilling: 30 min.

8 ripe avocados
2 lb. fresh crabmeat, flaked and chilled

Halve avocados and remove pits. Fill cavities with crabmeat.

SAUCE:

1 c. sour cream
1/2 c. lemon juice
1/2 c. tomato paste
2 tbsp. grated onion
1-1/2 tbsp. sugar
1-1/2 tsp. dry mustard
2 tsp. Worcestershire
3/4 tsp. salt

Mix sauce ingredients and spoon over crabmeat.

CRABMEAT MOUSSE

Preparation: 30 min.
Chilling: 2 hr.

2 env. unflavored gelatin
6 tbsp. cold water
1/2 c. mayonnaise
1/4 c. lime juice
1/4 c. lemon juice
2 tbsp. chopped parsley
2 tbsp. chopped chives
2 tbsp. prepared mustard
salt and pepper to taste
4 c. crabmeat, flaked
1-1/2 c. heavy cream, whipped
thin slices of lime
2 avocados
lime juice
chopped chives

Soften gelatin in water in large mixing bowl. Dissolve over hot water. Mix with mayonnaise, lime and lemon juices, parsley, chives, mustard, salt and pepper. Fold in crabmeat and whipped cream. Pour mixture into 8 cup ring mold and chill until set about 2 hr. Unmold onto a chilled platter and garnish with lime slices. Dice avocados and dip in lime juice. Mound in center and garnish with chives.

SEAFOOD
for 16

VERSATILE CRAB

Preparation: 30 min.
Baking: 30 min.

3/4 c. butter
3/4 c. flour
3 c. chicken stock or broth
1 c. heavy cream
2 tsp. salt
1/2 tsp. white pepper
1/2 c. sherry
4 lb. crabmeat, cooked
1 c. chopped green onions
3 tbsp. dry mustard
1/2 c. grated Parmesan cheese

Melt butter, add flour, stock, cream, sherry, salt and pepper and stir over low heat until thickened. Add crabmeat, onions and dry mustard. Blend well. Correct seasonings. Top with Parmesan cheese. Bake at 375 degrees for 30 min.

NOTE: May be used as filling for crepes.

SALMON LUNCHEON CASSEROLE

Preparation: 20 min.
Baking: 30 min.

4 cans (16-oz. size) salmon
3 pkg. frozen asparagus tips cooked and drained
4 eggs, hard-boiled and coarsely chopped
3/4 c. butter
3/4 c. flour
6 c. light cream or milk
pepper to taste
salt and pepper to taste
1 c. buttered bread crumbs

In saucepan melt butter, add flour and cook for 1-2 min. Add milk and wine. Whisk until smooth and thickened. Add salt and pepper. In large buttered casserole put drained and flaked salmon, asparagus, eggs and sauce. Stir gently to blend. Cover with bread crumbs. Bake at 350 degrees for 30 min. or until heated through, then brown under broiler for 2 or 3 min.

SAN ANTONIO SHRIMP

Preparation: 40 min.
Cooking: 20 min.

3/4 c. butter
3/4 c. flour
6 c. light cream or milk
pepper to taste
1 tbsp. salt
paprika
4 tbsp. chopped green pepper
10 lb. shrimp, cooked and cleaned
3 lb. fresh mushrooms, sliced
2 jars pimentos
1 med. onion, chopped
several sprigs parsley

In large saucepan, melt butter. Add flour and stir in cream. Continue stirring over medium heat until slightly thickened. Add seasonings, green pepper, shrimp, mushrooms, pimentos and onion and mix together. Cook uncovered over low heat for 20 min. Stir in snipped parsley.

SEAFOOD
for 16

SHRIMP AND CRABMEAT CASSEROLE

Preparation: 15 min.
Baking: 45 min.

4 lb. cooked shrimp
4 cans (6-oz. size) king crabmeat
2 lrg. onions, chopped
4 c. chopped celery
4 c. mayonnaise
1 c. bread crumbs
1/2 c. butter, melted

Combine first 5 ingredients and place in buttered 5 qt. casserole. Sprinkle with bread crumbs and drizzle with melted butter. Bake uncovered at 350 degrees for 45 min. or until mayonnaise is dissolved.

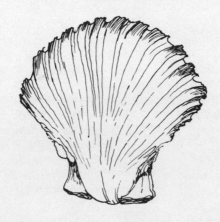

EASY SEAFOOD CASSEROLE

Preparation: 30 min.
Baking: 1 hr.

1/2 lb. butter
1/2 lb. mushrooms, sliced
1 c. milk
1-1/2 c. light cream
1 can cream of celery soup
1 can cream of mushroom soup
1/2 lb. pimento cheese
1-1/2 lb. lobster meat
1 lb. scallops, cooked
2 cans (7-oz. size) shrimp
2 cans (7-oz. size) crabmeat
salt and pepper to taste

In large skillet, over low heat, saute mushrooms in butter. Add milk, cream, soups and cheese, stirring until smooth. Add seafoods and sherry. Season to taste with salt and pepper. Pour into large casserole. Bake at 350 degrees for about 1 hr. or until thoroughly warmed.

SEAFOOD
for 16

COLD PAELLA

Preparation: 25 min.
Chilling: 8 hr.
Assembling: 20 min.

1/2 c. cooking oil
1 c. finely chopped onion
4 chicken bouillon cubes
2-2/3 c. boiling water
1/4 tsp. Tabasco
1/2 tsp. turmeric or curry
3-4 strands saffron
2-2/3 c. instant rice
2 qt. mixed cooked seafood (mussels, crabmeat, shrimp, lobster, tuna, etc.)
2 green peppers, diced
2 cans (6-oz. size) whole mushrooms, drained

Heat oil in large skillet. Add onions and cook until golden. Dissolve bouillon cubes in boiling water. Add broth, Tabasco, curry, and saffron to skillet. Bring to full boil and stir in uncooked rice. Cover, remove from heat and let stand 5 min. Fluff with fork to mix in seasonings. Chill 8 hr. At least 1 hr. before serving, combine seafood, green pepper, mushrooms and chilled rice with 1 cup dressing. Arrange in salad bowl and chill again. Just before serving, toss thoroughly with dressing. Have extra dressing on hand.

DRESSING:

1 tsp. salt
1 tsp. sugar
1 tsp. dry mustard
1 tsp. paprika
1-1/3 c. salad oil
1/2 tsp. Tabasco
2/3 c. wine vinegar

Mix dry ingredients well. Add oil and Tabasco and stir until blended. Add vinegar. Beat or stir well.

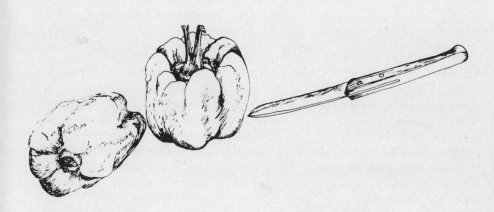

CHEESE & EGGS
for 16

FABULOUS CHEESE CASSEROLE

Preparation: 30 min.
Chilling: 8 hr.
Baking: 1 hr.

18 slices day-old bread
3 tbsp. minced white onion
3 tbsp. minced scallions
2 lb. Cheddar cheese, grated
8 eggs, slightly beaten
5 c. milk
2 tsp. dry mustard
2 tsp. Worcestershire
salt and pepper to taste

Cut 6 slices of bread in 3 strips each and fit tightly on bottom of lightly greased 4 qt. casserole. Sprinkle with salt and pepper and 1/3 of each kind on onion. Add 1/3 grated cheese evenly over top and press down. Repeat twice. Add eggs, milk, mustard and Worcestershire sauce and pour over casserole. Refrigerate 8 hr. Remove and let it reach room temperature. Bake uncovered at 325 degrees for about 1 hr.

CREPES

Preparation: 15 min.
Chilling: 1 hr.
Cooking: 3 min. (per crepe)

6 c. flour
12 eggs
7-1/2 c. milk
3/4 c. butter, melted
1-1/2 tsp. salt
freshly grated
    Parmesan cheese

Put all ingredients into 4 qt. bowl and whisk until smooth. Refrigerate for 1 hr. and whisk again. Grease 6"-7" skillet. Heat until drop of water skips around. Remove from heat and pour in 3 large tbsp. batter. Tilt pan to coat bottom evenly with a thin film. Return to heat 1-2 min. When bottom is light brown, turn carefully with large spatula. Cook other side less than 1 min. (It will be shiny yellow with brown spots.) To save for future use, put wax paper between crepes and cover closely.

BROCCOLI FILLING FOR CREPES

Preparation: 30 min.
Baking: 15 min.

3/4 c. butter
3/4 c. flour
4-1/2 c. milk
2 tsp. salt
1/2 tsp. pepper
1 c. shredded Swiss cheese
5 pkg. frozen chopped
    broccoli, cooked
32 crepes (above)
1/4 c. grated Parmesan cheese

Melt butter, add flour and 4 cups milk and stir over low heat until thickened. Reserve 1 cup. Add seasonings and cheese. Stir in drained broccoli. Spoon about 2 tbsp. mixture onto center of each crepe. Roll up crepes and place seam side down in buttered shallow baking dish-(es). Thin reserved sauce with remaining milk. Pour over crepes and top with cheese. Bake at 375 degrees for 15 min.

CHEESE & EGGS
for 16

CHICKEN A LA KING FOR CREPES

Preparation: 30 min.
Baking: 15 min.

32 crepes (see page 164)
3/4 c. butter
3/4 c. flour
3-1/2 c. chicken stock or broth
1 c. heavy cream
2 tsp. salt
1/2 tsp. white pepper
1/2 c. sherry
8 c. diced cooked chicken
2 cans (8-oz. size) chopped mushrooms
1 c. chopped pimento
1/4 c. chopped parsley
1/2 c. grated Parmesan cheese

Melt butter, add flour, 3 cups stock, cream, salt and pepper and stir over low heat until thickened. Reserve 1 cup of sauce. Add chicken, mushrooms and pimento. Blend well. Correct seasonings. Spoon about 2 tbsp. of mixture onto center of each crepe. Roll up crepe and place seam side down in buttered shallow baking dish(es). Thin reserved sauce with remaining 1/2 cup stock and add parsley. Stir and pour over crepes and top with Parmesan cheese. Bake at 375 degrees for 10-15 min.

CREAMY HAM AND MUSHROOM FILLING FOR CREPES

Preparation: 30 min.
Heating: 15 min.

32 crepes (see page 164)
8 c. cooked cubed ham
4 tbsp. oil
1-1/2 lb. fresh mushrooms, sliced
5 stalks celery, diagonally sliced
1/4 c. butter
1 c. flour
1 tbsp. salt, or to taste
pepper to taste
2 qt. milk
4 tbsp. chopped scallions

In a large saucepan, cook mushrooms and celery in oil until celery is tender-crisp. Add butter and melt. Stir in flour, salt and pepper until well-blended. Gradually add milk, stirring constantly, and cook, continuing to stir, until thick. Reserve about 2 cups sauce. Add ham to larger part of sauce. Cook until heated through. Fill each crepe with ham mixture. Place seam side down on serving platter. Pour reserved hot sauce over and sprinkle with scallions.

POTATOES, RICE & PASTA
for 16

CREAMED POTATOES

Preparation: 10 min.
Cooking: 3-1/2 hr.

18 med. potatoes, diced
2-1/2 pt. heavy cream
3 tbsp. chopped parsley
1 tsp. lemon pepper
1 tsp. paprika
1 tsp. salt
2 tbsp. Worcestershire

Place potatoes in top of large double boiler. Cover with cream and add parsley, lemon pepper, paprika and salt. Cook covered over boiling water for 3 hr. Add Worcestershire and cook additional 30 min. To reheat place in buttered casserole and bake covered at 350 degrees for 45 min.

GARLIC MASHED POTATOES

Preparation: 5 min.
Cooking: 30 min.

2-1/2 lb. potatoes
2 heads garlic
3/4 c. butter
1 c. milk
2 tsp. salt
4 tbsp. minced parsley
pepper to taste

Pare potatoes and boil until tender. Peel garlic and divide into cloves. Boil in water for 2 min. Saute garlic in 4 tbsp. butter for 20 min. Mash all ingredients together.

POTATO CHEESE BAKE

Preparation: 25 min.
Baking: 30 min.

16 med. potatoes
2 pt. sour cream
2 lb. cottage cheese
2 med. onions, minced
salt and pepper to taste

Peel and cube potatoes. Boil until tender and drain. Place in large greased casserole with remaining ingredients. Bake at 350 degrees for 30 min. or until bubbling.

SWEET POTATO AND MARRON BALLS

Preparation: 15 min.
Chilling: 30 min.
Baking: 45 min.

2 jars marrons glacees
3 cans (16-oz. size) sweet potatoes
1/2 c. butter
1 tsp. salt
1/2-1 c. crumbled cornflakes

Drain marrons and reserve syrup. Mash sweet potatoes and mix with marrons, butter and salt. Mold into balls and refrigerate. When firm, roll in crumbled cornflakes. Place in large buttered casserole and bake uncovered at 350 degrees for 45 min. Heat drained syrup and pour over balls just before serving.

POTATOES, RICE & PASTA
for 16

ALL-IN-ONE RISOTTO

Preparation: 25 min.
Cooking: 25 min.

1 tbsp. butter
1 tbsp. vegetable oil
3 slices bacon, diced
2 med. onions, chopped
3 med. potatoes, diced
4 carrots, cut-up
2 celery stalks, cut-up
3 zucchini, cut-up
1/2 sml. cabbage, chopped
2 tsp. salt
3/4-1 tsp. pepper
3 c. beef broth
2 c. uncooked rice
2 cans (10-oz. size) red kidney beans, drained
Parmesan cheese, grated

Melt butter and oil in large kettle. Add bacon and onion. Fry gently, until golden brown. Add potatoes, carrots, celery, zucchini, cabbage, salt and pepper. Simmer 5 min. stirring occasionally. Add broth and simmer 10 min. Vegetables should remain firm. Cook and drain rice. Add rice and beans to vegetables and heat through. Sprinkle with lots of cheese.

NOTE: Can be done ahead and reheated uncovered at 325 degrees for 20 min.

OVEN RICE

Preparation: 5 min.
Baking: 1 hr. 15 min.

4 c. rice
4 cans beef consomme
4 soup-cans water
2 beef bouillon cubes
1 pkg. onion soup mix
1 c. sweet butter

Blend all ingredients in 4 qt. casserole. Cover and bake at 350 degrees for 1 hr. 15 min.

NOTE: When serving chicken, substitute chicken broth for consomme.

SPANISH RICE

Preparation: 35 min.
Cooking: 15 min.

2 c. uncooked white rice
5 tbsp. butter
4 c. sliced onions
1 tbsp. salt
4 cans (1-lb. size) tomatoes
2/3 c. diced green pepper
4 tsp. sugar

Cook rice according to pkg. directions. In skillet saute onions in butter. Add salt, tomatoes, green pepper and sugar. Simmer uncovered for 15 min. Add rice and mix.

POTATOES, RICE & PASTA
for 16

NOODLE PUDDING

Preparation: 30 min.
Chilling: 8 hr.
Baking: 3/4 hr.

1 lb. broad noodles
6 eggs
1 pt. sour cream
12 oz. cream cheese
1/2 c. sugar (opt.)
1/2 c. butter
1/2 c. margarine
2 c. crushed cornflakes (not crumbs)
2 tsp. orange rind

Boil noodles according to pkg. directions. Drain and rinse in cold water. In mixer, beat eggs, sugar, sour cream and cream cheese until texture is smooth. Melt margarine and half of butter and pour over noodles (which you have rinsed again with hot water). Fold cheese mixture into noodles. Pour mixture into large greased casserole. Sprinkle cornflakes over top until competely covered. Melt remaining butter and drizzle over top. Add 2 tsp. orange rind. Cover tightly with foil and refrigerate 8 hr. Bake uncovered at 325 degrees for 1-3/4 hr.

NORFOLK NOODLES

Preparation: 10 min.
Baking: 40 min.

2 boxes (12-oz. size) wide noodles
1-1/2 c. chopped fresh parsley
2 pt. large curd cottage cheese
1-1/2 tsp. Worcestershire
dash Tabasco
1 bunch green onions, chopped
salt to taste
1 c. grated sharp cheese
1/2 tsp. paprika

Boil noodles according to pkg. directions and drain. Into hot noodles mix all remaining ingredients except grated cheese and paprika. Place in shallow baking dish. Top with grated cheese and paprika. Bake uncovered at 350 degrees for 40 min. or until hot through and cheese is melted.

POTATOES, RICE & PASTA
for 16

SPINACH OR BROCCOLI NOODLE CASSEROLE

Preparation: 15 min.
Baking: 20 min.

3 pkg. frozen chopped spinach
or 3 pkg. frozen chopped broccoli
3/4 lb. wide noodles
3/4 lb. narrow noodles
1-1/2 pt. sour cream
3/4 c. butter
salt to taste
lemon pepper to taste
freshly grated Parmesan cheese

Cook vegetables and noodles separately according to pkg. directions for minimum time. Drain. Mix together and add all other ingredients. Bake at 350 degrees for 20 min.

VEGETABLES
for 16

STRING BEANS DELUXE

Preparation: 20 min.
Cooking: 20 min.

4 pkg. frozen string beans
2 cans (6-oz. size)
 water chestnuts
1/2 c. butter
salt and pepper to taste

Cook string beans according to pkg. directions until barely done. Drain water chestnuts and slice thin. In double boiler, combine chestnuts with butter, salt, pepper and beans. Heat over boiling water for about 20 min.

PICKLED BEETS

Preparation: 10 min.
Chilling: 2 hr.

2 cans (16-oz. size) sliced
 beets, drained
1 c. beet juice from cans
1/2 c. sugar
1 c. cider vinegar
4 med. onions, sliced
salt to taste
1 sml. head lettuce

In large saucepan combine beets, beet juice, sugar and vinegar. Bring to a boil and remove from heat. Add onions and salt. Chill at least 2 hr. Serve on lettuce leaves.

BROCCOLI TOMATO STACK-UPS

Preparation: 30 min.
Cooking: 10-12 min.

8 lrg. tomatoes
salt
2 pkg. frozen chopped
 broccoli, cooked and
 drained
8 oz. Swiss cheese,
 shredded
1 c. chopped onion

Cut tomatoes into 3/4" slices. Sprinkle each lightly with salt. Set aside 1/4 cup cheese. Combine remaining cheese, broccoli and onion. Place tomato slices on baking sheet. Spoon broccoli mixture onto tomatoes. Sprinkle with reserved cheese. Broil 7-8" from heat for 10-12 min. or until cheese bubbles and tomato slices are hot.

BRUSSELS SPROUTS AND CHESTNUTS

Preparation: 20 min.
Cooking: 10 min.

2 qt. Brussels sprouts
 or 5 pkg. frozen
1/2 c. butter
4 tsp. sugar
2 c. boiled chestnuts, cubed
1 c. chicken stock or broth
salt and pepper to taste

Boil Brussels sprouts, then saute in small amount of butter until well-coated. Remove sprouts, add remaining butter and sugar and stir over medium heat until brown. Add chestnuts and cook until brown. Add Brussels sprouts and broth and combine well. Just before serving, return to near boil.

VEGETABLES
for 16

CORN PUDDING

Preparation: 20 min.
Baking: 30 min.

16 ears fresh corn, uncooked
5 egg yolks
salt to taste
2 tbsp. butter
2 c. heavy cream

Cut kernels from corn, but not too close to cob. Mix well with egg yolks, salt, butter and cream. Bake uncovered at 350 degrees for 30 min.

SPICY TOMATO EGGPLANT

Preparation: 1 hr.
Cooking: 30 min.

4 med. eggplants, pared and cubed
2 c. diced onion
2 c. diced celery
1 c. diced green pepper
4 c. tomato sauce
1-1/2 c. wine vinegar
2 tbsp. caraway seed
3 tsp. salt
1 tbsp. Worcestershire
pepper

Plunge eggplant into rapidly boiling, lightly salted water and cook 5 min. Remove from heat, drain well and combine with other vegetables. Add vinegar and seasonings to tomato sauce. Pour over vegetables. Bake at 300 degrees for 30 min.

OKRA AND CORN

Preparation: 30 min.
Cooking: 45 min.

1 lb. slab bacon
2 cans (16-oz. size) stewed tomatoes
1-1/2 c. water
2 pkg. frozen okra, chopped
2 pkg. frozen corn
1/2 tsp. thyme
1/4 tsp. onion powder
1/4 tsp. garlic powder
salt and pepper to taste

Cut bacon into small cubes. Fry until golden brown in large skillet. Pour off grease. Add water and stewed tomatoes. Mix well and let simmer for a few min. Add okra and corn and mix well. Add remaining ingredients to skillet. Blend, cover and simmer 30-45 min. Add more water during cooking if necessary.

SAUERKRAUT

Preparation: 30 min.
Cooking: 2 hr.

6 lb. sauerkraut
3/4 c. butter
2 lrg. onions, chopped
3 c. brown sugar
3 c. ketchup
3 c. canned tomatoes, strained

Wash sauerkraut 3 or 4 times in cold water. Drain. Brown onion in butter in large saucepan. Add sauerkraut, sugar, ketchup and tomatoes. Cover and simmer for 2 hr.

VEGETABLES
for 16

SNOW PEAS AND WATER CHESTNUTS

Preparation: 10 min.
Cooking: 15 min.

2 cans (6-oz. size) water chestnuts, sliced
5 pkg. frozen snow peas
4 tbsp. butter
1/2 c. water
2 chicken bouillon cubes
1/2 tsp. ground ginger
2 tsp. soy sauce

Combine all ingredients in large skillet. Saute, stirring constantly for 10-15 min. until peas are cooked but still crisp. Serve with pan sauce.

SPINACH CASSEROLE

Preparation: 20 min.
Baking: 45 min.

8 pkg. frozen chopped spinach
4 c. sour cream
2 pkg. onion soup mix
1 c. buttered bread crumbs
salt and pepper to taste

Cook spinach according to pkg. directions, drain and put in 5-6 qt. ungreased casserole. Add sour cream, onion soup mix, salt and pepper. Stir to mix. Top with bread crumbs. Bake covered at 350 degrees for 45 min.

BAKED ACORN SQUASH

Preparation: 10 min.
Baking: 60 min.

8 acorn squash
3 c. brown sugar
1 c. butter
2 c. sherry

Cut squash in half. Scrape cavity clean. Melt butter and mix with brown sugar and sherry. Pile in each cavity. Bake at 375 degrees for 45 min. to 1 hr.

BAKED SQUASH

Preparation: 5 min.
Baking: 30 min.

2 lb. Hubbard squash, peeled and thinly sliced
1 tsp. salt
1/2 c. sugar (brown, or white)
1 c. heavy cream
2 tsp. cinnamon

Place squash in well-greased baking dish. Sprinkle with salt and sugar. Add cream. Sprinkle with cinnamon and bake at 300 degrees for about 30 min. or until tender.

VEGETABLES
for 16

CREOLE TOMATOES

Preparation: 20 min.
Baking: 30 min.

16 firm tomatoes
salt and pepper to taste
1 c. brown sugar (the soft kind)
1/2 lb. butter
5 tbsp. + 2 tsp. minced onion
5 tbsp. + 2 tsp. minced green pepper

Cut tomatoes in half, crosswise. Top each half with salt, pepper, 1 tbsp. brown sugar, 1 tbsp. butter, 2 tsp. mixed green pepper and onion. Bake at 350 degrees for 30 min.

SPICY TOMATOES

Preparation: 40 min.
Baking: 1 hr.

6 cans (28-oz. size) tomatoes
24 whole cloves
24 whole peppercorns
3 bay leaves
salt to taste
1-1/2 yellow onions, chopped
2-1/2 c. brown sugar
9-12 slices white bread, bite-size pieces
6 tbsp. butter

Put cloves, pepper and bay leaves in cheesecloth bag. Cook undrained tomatoes, cheesecloth bag and salt very slowly in ovenproof casserole on top of stove for 30 min. Stir occasionally. Add onion, sugar, bread and butter. Place in greased baking dish. Remove cheesecloth bag and its contents. Bake at 400 degrees for 1 hr.

FANNED ZUCCHINI

Preparation: 20 min.
Baking: 30 min.

16 lrg. or 32 sml. zucchini
1 c. grated Parmesan cheese
4 cans tomatoes or 16 fresh tomatoes
4 med. onions, sliced
2 c. chicken broth
1/2 c. oil
1/2 c. chopped parsley
salt and pepper to taste

If zucchini is tender and young, use it fresh. Otherwise, parboil. Slice each zucchini down to stem 4 times. Make fan of each. Divide between 2 large frying pans. Add 1/4 cup oil to each covered pan, cooking over low heat until zucchini is softish, about 10 min. Transfer to large casserole. Fan zucchini out and cover with sliced onion, broth, tomatoes, cheese, salt and pepper. Bake covered at 350 degrees for 20 min. Garnish with parsley.

SALADS
for 16

NOTE: *A selection of Salad Dressings for tossed green or mixed salads appears in the Accompaniments Chapter.*

ZIPPY GREEN BEAN SALAD

Preparation: 40 min.
Chilling: 2 hr.

6 pkg. frozen French style green beans
1 c. chopped onion
1 c. salad oil
1/2 c. vinegar
1 tsp. salt
1/8 tsp. pepper
12 eggs, hard-boiled
2 tsp. prepared mustard
2 tbsp. lemon juice
1/2 c. mayonnaise
   or 1/2 c. salad dressing
1 tsp. salt
lettuce leaves
12 slices bacon, cooked and crumbled
12 stuffed olives, chopped
1 jar (2-1/2 oz.) tiny shrimp
   or 1 jar (4 oz.) pimento

Cook beans according to pkg. directions. Drain and place in large bowl. Stir in onions, salad oil, vinegar, salt and pepper. Chill 2 hr. Chop eggs, add mustard, lemon juice, mayonnaise (or salad dressing) and salt. Blend and chill about 2 hr. Just before serving, drain beans. Place in bowl lined with lettuce leaves. Spread egg mixture on top. Garnish with bacon, olives and drained shrimp (or pimento).

SALADS
for 16

SALAD BEULAH

Preparation: 30 min.

1-1/2 lb. fresh spinach
4 scallions
2 tbsp. parsley
celery greens from 2 stalks
1/4 lb. fresh mushrooms
1 head iceberg lettuce
oil and vinegar dressing

Wash and de-stem spinach. Chop scallions, parsley and celery tops. Slice mushrooms. Tear lettuce. Place all ingredients in plastic bag and seal. Refrigerate. Toss with oil and vinegar dressing just before serving.

BUNNY SALAD

Preparation: 30 min.

16 canned pear halves
32 leaves Boston lettuce
32 blanched almonds
48 pink jelly beans
  or gumdrops
16 lrg. marshmallows
French dressing

Shred lettuce. Invert pear halves on beds of lettuce. Insert 2 blanched almonds for ears. Use jelly beans for eyes and nose and marshmallow for tail. Serve with dressing in a separate bowl.

FRESH MUSHROOM SALAD

Preparation: 30 min.

2 lb. fresh mushrooms, sliced
1 c. lemon juice
1/2 c. chopped fresh parsley
4 scallions, finely chopped
4 bunches watercress
1-1/2 c. olive oil
3 tbsp. dry vermouth
2 tbsp. dry red wine
salt and pepper to taste
1 tbsp. chopped thyme
1 tbsp. chopped marjoram
1 tbsp. chopped rosemary
1/2 tsp. dry mustard

Place mushrooms, lemon juice, parsley, scallions and chopped watercress in salad bowl. Place remaining ingredients in jar and shake to mix. Add one-half the dressing and toss. Add more dressing as needed.

SALADS
for 16

MRS. SCHULTZ'S TOMATO AND CREAM CHEESE SALAD

Preparation: 10 min.
Chilling: 2 hr.

2 cans cream of
   tomato soup
32 oz. cream cheese
3 env. unflavored gelatin
2 c. mayonnaise
3 c. chopped celery
3 tbsp. chopped onion

Heat undiluted soup. Add cream cheese and stir. Dissolve gelatin in a little cold water and add to mixture stirring until dissolved. Add mayonnaise, celery and onion. Stir to mix well. Pour into 2 qt. mold and chill until set.

HEARTS OF PALM SALAD

Preparation: 20 min.
Chilling: 2 hr.

1 head iceberg lettuce
2 heads Boston lettuce
1 lb. fresh spinach
2 avocados, peeled
   and diced
3 cans (14-oz. size)
   hearts of palm,
   drained and thinly sliced
1/4 c. vinegar
3/4 c. salad oil
1 tsp. salt
1/4 tsp. pepper

Wash and dry lettuce and spinach. Wrap in towels and refrigerate. Toss lettuce, spinach, avocado and hearts of palm in large bowl. In a jar, place remaining ingredients and shake to mix. Pour over salad and toss.

A SIMPLE SALAD

Preparation: 30 min.
Chilling: 2 hr.

1 head escarole
2 heads Boston lettuce
1/2 head chicory
1 lb. fresh spinach
1/2 head broccoli
1/2 head cauliflower
1 lb. fresh mushrooms, sliced
2 cans (14-oz. size)
   hearts of palm
salt and pepper to taste
1 bottle herb and
   garlic dressing

Wash and dry all lettuces and vegetables. Refrigerate until well-chilled. Break leaves into bite-size pieces and break broccoli and cauliflower into flowerets. Mix all ingredients in large bowl. Shake dressing and pour over salad. Toss well to coat salad ingredients. Add salt and pepper and toss again.

SALADS
for 16

VEGETABLE SALAD

Preparation: 30 min.
Chilling: 12 hr.

2 lb. fresh spinach, chopped
10 eggs, hard-boiled and sliced
1 lb. bacon, cooked and crumbled
1 med. head lettuce, shredded
1 c. sliced shallots
1 pkg. frozen peas
2-1/2 c. mayonnaise
2-1/2 c. sour cream
Worcestershire to taste
Tabasco to taste
lemon juice to taste
salt and pepper to taste
1-1/2 c. grated Swiss cheese

In large salad bowl put layer of spinach, layer of egg slices sprinkled with bacon, layer of shredded lettuce, layer of shallots and layer of frozen peas (poured right from the box). Blend mayonnaise and sour cream flavored with Worcestershire, Tabasco, lemon juice, salt and pepper. Pour over peas. Add layer of shredded cheese. Cover and chill about 12 hr. Do not toss.

DESSERTS
for 16

> NOTE: A large selection of Cakes, Pies, Cookies and Squares appears in the Accompaniments Chapter.

CHERRIES JUBILEE
Preparation: 10 min.

3 cans (1-lb. size) pitted cherries
6 oz. brandy
1/2 gal. vanilla ice cream

Place cherries in chafing dish and cover with brandy. Ignite brandy and spoon flaming cherries over vanilla ice cream.

DELUXE CHOCOLATE MOUSSE
Preparation: 25 min.
Chilling: 1 hr.

2 env. unflavored gelatin
1/2 c. cold water
2/3 c. creme de cacao
1 pkg. (12 oz.) semi-sweet chocolate bits
1-1/2 c. brown sugar
1/2 tsp. salt
8 eggs, separated
2 c. heavy cream

Soften gelatin in water in large saucepan. Add creme de cacao, heat and mix over low flame. Mix in chocolate bits and 3/4 cup brown sugar. Stir until melted. Beat in egg yolks one at a time keeping flame low. Cool. Whip egg whites until firm but not stiff. Fold remaining brown sugar and carefully fold into chocolate mixture. Whip cream and fold in. Pour into large serving bowl or individual bowls. Chill.

ORANGES AND GRAND MARNIER
Preparation: 20 min.
Baking: 40 min.

16 seedless oranges
16 oz. Grand Marnier
2 c. sugar
4 c. heavy cream, whipped
8 tbsp. orange juice

Peel oranges, leaving no pith. Slice across. Arrange slices in large, shallow ovenproof dish. Mix orange juice and Grand Marnier and pour over oranges. Melt sugar in frying pan over high heat but do not burn. Pour over orange slices. Bake at 250 degrees for 40 min. or until warmed through but not hot. Top with whipped cream.

DESSERTS
for 16

PEARS IN WINE

Preparation: 20 min.
Cooking: 40 min.

12 firm pears, peeled and quartered
1 bottle red wine
1 c. sugar
1 lemon, thinly sliced
1 stick cinnamon
1 c. heavy cream, whipped
1 tsp. ground cinnamon

Put pears in large saucepan with wine, sugar, lemon slices and cinnamon stick. Simmer for 40 min. Put hot pears in individual dishes. Pour sauce over pears and top with dollop of whipped cream and sprinkling of cinnamon.

RASPBERRY CHARLOTTE

Preparation: 30 min.
Chilling: 3 hr.

2 pkg. (3-oz. size) raspberry gelatin
1 c. raspberry jam
1 c. heavy cream, whipped
1 pkg. frozen raspberries or 1 pt. fresh raspberries

Prepare gelatin according to pkg. directions and chill until slightly thickened. Beat until fluffy and thick. Fold in whipped cream and raspberry jam. Beat until blended and chill in large mold, pre-rinsed in cold water, until firm. Unmold and decorate with whipped cream and raspberries.

ICE CREAM PUDDING

Preparation: 20 min.
Freezing: 3 hr.

1-1/2 pt. heavy cream, whipped
1/4 tsp. confectioners' sugar
16 lrg. meringue kisses (see index)
2 lrg. cans fruit salad
1 c. chopped nuts

Whip sugar into cream. Reserve 1 cup. Crush meringues into small pieces and add to larger amount of cream. Spoon into large ring mold. Freeze for at least 3 hr. Unmold on serving platter. Fill center with drained fruit. Garnish with reserved whipped cream and nuts.

INSTANT DINNER PARTY DESSERT

Preparation: 30 min.
Chilling: 2 hr.

2 boxes lady fingers
2 pkg. (6-oz. size) fruit-flavored gelatin
1 lrg. container Cool Whip

Line large bowl or mold with lady fingers. Make gelatin according to pkg. directions using ice cubes instead of cold water. As mixture cools whip with eggbeater over ice until thick and fluffy. Mix with 3/4 of the Cool Whip and pour into lined bowl or mold. Refrigerate. Turn out onto platter and trim with remaining Cool Whip.

DESSERTS
for 16

CREPES SUZETTE

Preparation: 1-1/2 hr.
Cooking: 10 min.

All ingredients for Crepes (see index)
3 tbsp. sugar
1 tbsp. vanilla

SAUCE:
1-1/2 c. butter
1 c. sugar
1-1/2 c. orange juice
1-1/2 c. orange liqueur
1-1/2 c. brandy

Make crepe batter using additional ingredients and follow method suggested. When crepes are removed from pan, fold carefully in quarters so that each looks like a pie slice.

In large chafing dish combine butter, liqueur, orange juice and sugar. Heat until bubbling. Arrange folded crepes in pan and simmer until sauce is slightly thickened, basting frequently. Warm brandy and pour over crepes. Ignite and serve immediately, spooning flaming sauce over crepes.

STRAWBERRY CREPES

Preparation: 1-1/2 hr.
Baking: 10 min.

All ingredients for Crepes (see index) plus:
3 tbsp. sugar
1 tbsp. vanilla
4 pt. fresh strawberries
1 c. granulated sugar
1/2 c. confectioners' sugar
1-1/2 c. heavy cream, whipped

Make crepe batter using additional ingredients and follow method suggested.

Wash strawberries and remove stems. Reserve 16 strawberries. Slice remaining ones and put about 2 tbsp. in center of each crepe. Sprinkle with sugar, roll crepes and place in ovenproof platter. Heat at 350 degrees for about 10 min. Sprinkle with powdered sugar. Cover with whipped cream and garnish with reserved whole strawberries.

FORGOTTEN PUDDING

Preparation: 20 min.
Baking: 4 hr.
Chilling: 12 hr.

10 egg whites, stiffly beaten
3 c. sugar
1 tsp. cream of tartar
2 tsp. vanilla
1/2 tsp. salt
2 c. heavy cream
2 qt. fresh strawberries, peaches or blueberries

Preheat oven to 450 degrees. Beat egg whites until stiff. Gradually beat sugar, into egg whites. Add cream of tartar, salt and vanilla. Spread evenly in greased 9" x 13" pan. Set in oven and TURN OVEN OFF. Leave pudding in oven for 4 hr. Whip cream and spread on top. Refrigerate all day. Cut into squares and serve topped with fresh fruit.

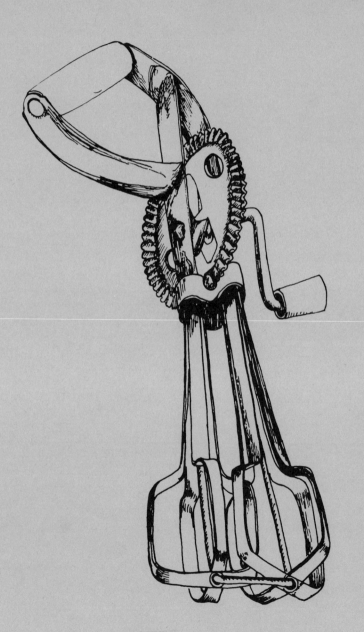

ACCOMPANIMENTS

BREADS

✓ BANANA BREAD

Preparation: 10 min.
Baking: 50 min.

2-1/2 c. firmly packed brown sugar
3/4 c. butter
5 med. ripe bananas, mashed
5 eggs
4-3/4 c. flour
2-1/2 tsp. salt
3 tsp. baking powder
1 c. chopped walnuts or pecans
3/4 c. sour cream
1/2 tsp. baking soda

Cream sugar and butter together. Add eggs and bananas. Mix well. Blend in flour, salt, baking powder and nuts. Stir in sour cream to which baking soda has been added. Pour into buttered loaf pans and bake at 325 degrees for 40-50 min. Serve warm or cold. Can be frozen.

YIELD: (3) regular loaves, or 5 tea loaves

(Aluminum foil pans)

BATTER BREAD

Preparation: 10 min.
Baking: 45 min.

1-1/2 c. white cornmeal
1-1/4 c. boiling water
2 tbsp. butter, melted
2 eggs, well-beaten
2 c. milk
1 tsp. salt
2 tsp. baking powder

In a large bowl pour boiling water over cornmeal and stir. Add butter, eggs, milk, salt and baking powder. Put in a 9" x 13" buttered and floured baking pan. Bake uncovered at 350 degrees for 45 min. or until golden brown. Do not overcook as it tends to dry out.

NOTE: Virginia water-ground cornmeal should be used if possible.

BLUEBERRY COFFEE CAKE

Preparation: 15 min.
Baking: 45 min.

✓ 1/2 c. butter
1 c. sugar
2 eggs
1-1/2 c. flour
1/2 c. milk
1 tsp. vanilla
1 c. blueberries
1 tsp. baking powder

Cream butter and sugar together. Add remaining ingredients, one at a time, in order given, beating by hand after each addition. Pour into greased and floured 8" square pan. Bake at 350 degrees for 45 min.

BREADS

COFFEE CAKE

Preparation: 10 min.
Baking: 20 min.

1 egg, beaten
1/2 c. sugar
3/4 c. milk
2 c. flour
4 tsp. baking powder
1/2 tsp. salt
3 tsp. shortening, melted

Blend egg, sugar and milk. Mix and sift dry ingredients and add to egg mixture. Add shortening and beat thoroughly. Pour into greased 9" square pan. Add topping mixture and bake at 400 degrees for 20 min.

TOPPING:

3 tbsp. flour
2 tbsp. sugar
1 tbsp. shortening *(melt or cut in)*
3-4 tsp. cinnamon

Blend all ingredients together and sprinkle on top of cake mixture before baking.

CORN BREAD

Preparation: 10 min.
Baking: 30 min.

3/4 c. sifted flour
2 tbsp. sugar
2 tsp. baking powder
1 tsp. salt
1-1/2 c. yellow cornmeal
2 eggs, beaten
1-1/4 c. milk
1/4 c. shortening, melted

Sift flour, sugar, baking powder and salt together. Stir in cornmeal. Combine eggs and milk and add to dry ingredients. Blend. Stir in shortening. Pour into greased and floured 9" square pan. Bake at 425 degrees for 25-30 min. Cut when slightly cooled.

CRANBERRY ORANGE BREAD

Preparation: 15 min.
Baking: 1 hr.

2 c. sifted, all-purpose flour
1/2 tsp. salt
1/2 tsp. baking soda
1-1/2 tsp. baking powder
1 c. sugar
grated peel of 1 orange
1/2 c. orange juice
2 tbsp. shortening
1/4 c. boiling water
1 egg, beaten
1 c. chopped cranberries
1 c. raisins
   or chopped walnuts

Sift together flour, salt, baking soda, baking powder and sugar. Combine orange peel, juice, shortening and water. Blend into dry ingredients. Add egg and beat well. Fold in cranberries and raisins. Pour into greased 9" x 5" loaf pan. Bake at 350 degrees for 1 hr. Let cool 10 min. before removing from pan onto wire rack. Cool completely and let stand overnight before slicing.

YIELD: 1 loaf

BREADS

CRULLERS

Preparation: 15 min.
Cooking: 20 min.

1/4 c. butter
1 c. sugar
2 eggs, separated
1 c. milk
1 tsp. vanilla
4 c. flour
1/4 tsp. salt
4 tsp. baking powder
1 tsp. ginger
1 tsp. nutmeg
fat
powdered sugar

Cream butter and sugar together. Add beaten egg yolks, milk, vanilla, flour sifted with salt, baking powder and spices. Beat well. Add egg whites, beaten to a froth. Mix well. On a floured board, roll to 1/4" thickness and cut into doughnut shapes. Deep fry until golden brown. Drain on absorbent paper and sprinkle with sugar.

YIELD: Approx. 45 medium crullers

CRUNCHY GRANOLA

Preparation: 5 min.
Baking: 30 min.

3 c. rolled oats
1 c. rolled wheat or
   Roman meal
1 c. shredded coconut
1/2 c. wheat germ
1/4 c. brown sugar
1/2 c. oil
1 tbsp. vanilla
1/2 c. honey or corn syrup

Mix first 5 ingredients together in large mixing bowl. Mix oil, honey and vanilla together. Add to grain mixture very slowly while tossing well. Spread on large cookie sheet and toast at 300 degrees turning every 10 min. until browned, about 30 min.

YIELD: 1 lb.

HERB SEASONED DINNER ROLLS

Preparation: 20 min.
Baking: 15 min.

2 c. flour
2 tsp. sugar
2-1/2 tsp. baking powder
1/2 tsp. salt
A blend of 2 or more of:
   marjoram ⎫
   basil   ⎬ 1 – 1-1/2 tsp.
   thyme   ⎪
   parsley ⎭
   garlic salt ⎫
   fennel   ⎬ 1/2 tsp.
   savory   ⎭
5 tbsp. butter or shortening
1 c. milk
poppy or sesame seeds

Stir dry ingredients into bowl. Add herb blend of choice. Blend in shortening or butter, or a blend of each. Add milk and stir lightly only to moisten. Drop by spoonfuls on greased baking sheet. Sprinkle with poppy or sesame seeds. Bake at 425-450 degrees for 15 min. or until top is golden brown.

YIELD: 12-15 rolls

NOTE: Butter holds roll together better, but shortening gives very light, fluffy roll.

BREADS

HERB TOAST

Preparation: 10 min.
Baking: 1 hr.

8 slices very thin bread
8 tbsp. butter, softened
1/4 tsp. celery salt
1/4 tsp. poppy seed
1/4 tsp. caraway seed
1/4 tsp. fines herbes

Cream butter and mix in herbs. Remove crusts from bread and spread on mixture. Cut each slice into three strips. Bake at 250 degrees for 1 hr. Serve warm.

HERBED GARLIC BREAD

Preparation: 10 min.
Baking: 20 min.

1 lrg. loaf Italian bread
1/2 c. butter, softened
1 clove garlic, crushed
2 tbsp. chopped fresh parsley
1 tsp. lemon juice
1/4 tsp. basil
1/4 tsp. oregano
black pepper to taste

Slice bread leaving slices attached at bottom. Combine remaining ingredients and mix well. Spread on cut surface of bread. Wrap in foil and bake covered at 375 degrees for 10 min. Open foil and bake for 10 min. more to brown.

GRANDMOTHER'S HOLIDAY NUT BREAD

Preparation: 10 min.
Baking: 50 min.

1 egg, beaten
3/4 c. brown sugar, tightly packed
2 c. flour, sifted
1 tsp. baking soda
3/4 c. warm water
1 tsp. vanilla
3/4 c. chopped walnuts
1/4 c. raisins

Beat egg and sugar together until very light and creamy. Add flour, baking soda, water and vanilla and mix well. Add nuts and raisins. Bake in well-greased small loaf pan at 350 degrees for 50 min. Best wrapped in foil and aged a week.

BREADS

HOLIDAY SQUASH BREAD

Preparation: 15 min.
Baking: 1 hr. 15 min.

1 c. sugar
1/2 c. butter
1 egg
1 pkg. (12 oz.) frozen squash, cooked and drained
1-3/4 c. flour
1 tsp. baking powder
1 tsp. salt
1 tsp. cinnamon
1/2 tsp. ground cloves
1 c. raisins
1 c. chopped walnuts

Cream sugar and butter. Add egg and beat until fluffy. Blend in squash and gradually add dry ingredients. Fold in raisins and walnuts. Bake in 9" x 5" pan at 325 degrees for 1 hr. 15 min.

NUT BROWN BREAD

Preparation: 15 min.
Baking: 1 hr.

2 c. graham flour
2 c. white flour
1/2 tsp. salt
1 c. chopped nuts
2 c. milk
3/4 c. molasses
1 level tsp. baking soda

Blend flours and salt and mix in nuts. Add milk gradually, beating constantly. Dissolve baking soda in molasses and beat into mixture. Place in 2 floured 9" x 5" x 3" loaf pans. Bake at 300 degrees for 1 hr. or more.

SCONES

Preparation: 15 min.
Baking: 10 min.

1 c. flour
1/2 tsp. salt
1 tsp. baking soda
2 tsp. cream of tartar
4 tbsp. butter
1/4 c. sugar
1/2 c. milk (approx.)
1 egg, beaten

Sift together flour, salt, baking soda and cream of tartar. Cut in butter and add sugar. Add milk gradually, just enough to make soft dough. Roll out on lightly floured board until 3/4"-1" thick. Cut with round cookie cutter. Place on greased and floured cookie sheet. Brush with egg. Bake at 450 degrees for 5-10 min.

YIELD: 30 medium scones

FRUIT SCONES:

Above ingredients, plus:
2 oz. currants
2 oz. sultana figs

Follow same method, adding fruit after butter, then continue as above.

NOTE: Serve warm with butter, or cool with strawberry jam and whipped cream.

BREADS

SPOON BREAD

Preparation: 15 min.
Baking: 45 min.

1 scant c. cornmeal
3 c. milk
1 tsp. salt
3 eggs, well-beaten
3 tsp. baking powder
1 full tbsp. butter, melted

In a medium saucepan stir cornmeal into 2 cups milk and bring to boil, making a mush. Add remaining milk, salt, eggs, baking powder and butter. Stir well. Place in greased baking dish and bake uncovered at 350 degrees for 45 min. or until done.

WHEAT BREAD

Preparation: 2 hr.
Baking: 35 min.

2 tbsp. sugar
1 tbsp. salt
2 c. milk, lukewarm
500 mg. vitamin C
2 pkg. dry yeast mix
5 c. whole wheat flour
1/2 c. butter, melted

In large mixing bowl, put sugar, salt, milk, and vitamin C. Stir to moisten and dissolve. Add yeast and 3 cups flour. Stir slowly and thoroughly. Add 4 tbsp. butter which has cooled slightly but is still liquid. Stir. Add 1-1/2–2 cups more flour and stir. Let stand covered for 10 min. Knead 7 min. pushing outward. Let stand covered 1-1/2 hr. in warm place. Knead again. Divide into 2 equal portions and put in buttered loaf pans. Let rise 45 min. if desired. Pour remaining melted butter on top of loaves and bake at 350 degrees for 35 min.

WHITE BREAD

Preparation: 30 min.
Rising: 2 hr.
Baking: 30 min.

1-1/4 tbsp. fat
2 tsp. salt
500 mg. vitamin C
2-1/2 tbsp. sugar
2 c. milk, scalded
2 pkg. dry yeast
6-7 c. flour
1/4 lb. butter, melted

Put fat, salt, vitamin C and sugar in bowl. Add milk and mix briefly with electric beater. When lukewarm, add yeast and mix again with beater. Add 4 cups flour and mix. Add more flour until dough does not adhere to bowl. Knead on floured surface for at least 4 min. Separate dough into 2 pieces, one larger than the other. Place in floured loaf pans, cover and let stand to rise for at least 2 hr. Pour melted butter over (to form crust) and bake at 375 degrees for about 30 min. until golden brown. Remove from pans to wire rack and let cool.

BREADS

HOMEMADE BREAD

Preparation: 45 min.
Rising: 1-1/2 hr.
Baking: 15 min.

8 c. unbleached flour
1 tbsp. salt
3-1/2 c. warm water
2 tbsp. honey
1 pkg. dry yeast

Dissolve yeast in 1/2 cup warm water and add to rest of ingredients, reserving 2 cups flour. Beat. Stir in remaining flour and mix briefly with hands. Cover and let rise in warm place. When double in size, separate into 3 loaves and put into greased loaf pans. Let rise 1/2—3/4 hr. Bake at 400 degrees for 10 min. Lower oven to 375 degrees and continue baking for another 35 min. Can be frozen.

THE PANCAKE

Preparation: 5 min.
Baking: 20 min.

4 tbsp. butter
1/2 c. flour
1/2 c. milk
2 eggs
pinch nutmeg
   or cinnamon
maple syrup
   or jam

Melt butter in a large ovenproof frying pan. Blend other ingredients except syrup or jam in a bowl using an egg beater. Pour into frying pan with butter. Bake at 425 degrees for 15-20 min. until pancake rises and is golden brown. Serve with maple syrup or jam.

YORKSHIRE PUDDING

Preparation: 15 min.
Baking: 25 min.

3 eggs, slightly beaten
1 c. milk
1 c. all-purpose flour
3/4 tsp. salt
1/2-1/3 c. drippings
   from pan in which
   roast beef was cooked

In a medium bowl mix eggs with milk. Sift and measure flour then resift into milk/egg mixture, adding salt. Beat until smooth. Add drippings and pour into greased 13" x 9" pan. Bake uncovered at 450 degrees for 20-25 min. Cut into squares and serve immediately with roast beef.

CAKES

APPLE CAKE

Preparation: 40 min.
Cooking: 10 min.
Chilling: 2 hr.

7 oz. dried bread crumbs
6 oz. granulated sugar
6 oz. butter
2 lb. stewed apples
2 oz. port (opt.)
1/2 pt. heavy cream, whipped
strawberry
  or raspberry jam

Mix bread crumbs and sugar. Saute until golden in butter. Place alternate layers of bread crumbs and stewed apples mixed with port if desired in a glass bowl, beginning and ending with bread crumbs. To serve warm, decorate with jam and put whipped cream in a separate dish. To serve cold decorate with whipped cream and jam.

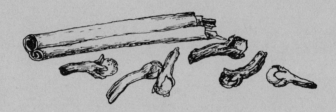

APPLESAUCE CAKE

Preparation: 10 min.
Baking: 45 min.

1-1/3 c. + 2 tbsp.. flour
1 tsp. baking soda
1/2 tsp. salt
1/2 tsp. cinnamon
1/4 tsp. ground cloves
1/4 tsp. allspice
1/4 c. soft shortening
1 c. sugar
1 egg
1 c. applesauce
1/4 c. pecans or walnuts
1/2 c. raisins

ICING:

1/4 c. butter
1/2 tsp. vanilla
1 c. sifted confectioners'
  sugar
1 tsp. grated orange rind
2 tbsp. orange juice

Sift together 1-1/3 c. flour, baking soda, cinnamon, cloves, allspice and salt. Beat shortening, sugar and egg in mixing bowl until light and fluffy. Add flour mixture alternately with applesauce, beginning and ending with flour. Scrape bowl frequently during mixing. Mix nuts, raisins and remaining flour together. Fold into batter. Pour into greased 9" square pan. Bake at 350 degrees for 40-45 min. Cool in pan 10 min. Frost if desired with orange butter cream icing.

Blend butter, vanilla and sugar thoroughly. Beat in orange rind and orange juice. Beat until spreading consistency. (It may require a little more juice.) Spread on top of cake.

CAKES

BLACK FOREST CHERRY CAKE

Marinating: 4 hr.
Preparation: 2 hr.
Baking: 20 min.

2 cans (1-lb. size) sour pitted cherries
1 c. kirsch
2 sq. unsweetened chocolate
1 pkg. (1-lb. 3-oz.) yellow cake mix
1/2 c. butter
4 c. powdered sugar
red food coloring
1 env. unflavored gelatin
4 c. heavy cream
maraschino cherries with stems
grated semi-sweet chocolate

Drain sour cherries, cut in half and marinate in 1/4 cup or more kirsch. Cover tightly and let stand for at least 4 hr. Grease and flour four 9" cake pans. Melt unsweetened chocolate and prepare cake mix according to pkg. directions. Pour one-half of the mix into 2 of the pans. Add melted chocolate to remaining batter and pour in equal parts into other 2 pans. Bake at 350 degrees 15-20 min. until springy. Let stand 10 min. and turn out on rack. When cool, slice each cake into 2 layers. Drain kirsch from cherries and reserve. Cream butter and blend in 3-1/2 cup powdered sugar, alternating with reserved kirsch. Color mixture to a bright pink and set aside. Soften gelatin in 1/4 cup kirsch, and dissolve over hot water. Cool. Whip cream thick. Gradually beat in cooled gelatin and remaining kirsch and powdered sugar. Beat until peaks form.

ASSEMBLING:

1. One chocolate layer
   Cover with 1/3 cherry/cream mixture
   Cover with 1/3 sour cherries

2. One yellow layer
   Cover with 1/3 whipped cream mixture

3. Keep repeating, but omit the 4th yellow layer and end, instead, with chocolate one. Cover top and sides with whipped cream mixture.

Garnish with maraschino cherries, stems up, and grated chocolate. For freezing, remove maraschino cherries and freeze solid before wrapping tightly.

CAKES

✓ BROWNIE CAKE

9 x 13"
55 min.

Preparation: 20 min.
Baking: 35 min.

2 c. cake flour
2 tsp. baking powder
1/2 tsp. salt
1/2 c. butter
2 c. sugar
2 eggs
4 sq. unsweetened chocolate, melted
1-1/2 c. milk
1 tsp. vanilla
1 c. chopped walnuts

Grease and flour 3-9" cake pans. Sift together flour, salt and baking powder. In large bowl, cream butter and sugar until light and fluffy. Beat in eggs, one at a time. Stir in chocolate. Add flour mixture and milk alternately, beating after each addition. Stir in vanilla and nuts. Pour into pans. Bake at 350 degrees for 30-35 min. and cool in over 10 min. Remove from oven and continue cooling on wire racks. Frost as desired.

CARROT CAKE

Preparation: 35 min.
Baking: 50 min.

2 c. sugar
1-1/2 c. cooking oil
1/2 tsp. salt
4 eggs
2 c. flour
2 tsp. baking soda
2 tsp. cinnamon
3 c. shredded carrots
1/2 c. chopped walnuts
1/2 c. raisins (opt.)
cream cheese frosting
   or lemon icing
   or powdered sugar

Mix sugar, oil and salt together. Add eggs, mixing in one at a time. Add remaining dry ingredients plus carrots, nuts and raisins. Pour into greased and floured tube pan and bake at 350 degrees for 45 min.

OPTIONAL:

When cool, frost with cream cheese or lemon icing or just cover with powdered sugar.

CHEESE CAKE

Preparation: 30 min.
Baking: 1 hr. 45 min.

1-1/2 c. fine graham cracker crumbs
2 tbsp. butter, melted
2 tbsp. sugar
8 oz. cream cheese, softened
1 c. sugar
3 eggs, room temp.
1 tsp. vanilla
1 pt. sour cream, room temp.

Grease 9" spring-form pan and sprinkle sides with 2 tbsp. graham cracker crumbs. Mix remaining crumbs with butter and sugar and pack firmly into bottom of pan. Beat cheese until fluffy and gradually beat in sugar. Add eggs one at a time, beating after each egg. Fold in vanilla and sour cream. Pour into pan. Bake at 375 degrees for 45 min. Turn off oven and LEAVE cake in for 1 hr. more.

CAKES

CHEESE CAKE

Preparation: 30 min.
Baking: 45 min.
Chilling: 24 hr.

CRUST:
1 c. graham cracker crumbs
1/4 c. butter, melted
2 tbsp. sugar

Stir all ingredients together and press into a 9" pie pan.

FILLING:
16 oz. cream cheese, softened
1/2 tsp. vanilla
3/4 c. sugar
3 eggs

Beat cheese with wooden spoon until creamy. Add vanilla, sugar and eggs one at a time continuing to beat. Pour into crust and bake at 375 degrees for 20 min. Remove from oven and set aside. Turn oven down to 350 degrees.

TOPPING:
1 pt. sour cream
1/4 c. sugar
1/2 tsp. vanilla

When pie has cooled for 15 min. stir all three topping ingredients together and spread on pie. Bake at 350 degrees for 10 min. Cool and chill 24 hr.

CHOCOLATE MOCHA LAYER CAKE

Preparation: 30 min.
Baking: 20 min.

1-1/2 sq. bitter chocolate or 6 tbsp. unsweetened cocoa powder
4 tbsp. butter
1 c. flour
2 tsp. baking powder
1 c. sugar
2 eggs
1/2 c. milk
1 tsp. vanilla

In top of double boiler melt chocolate and butter. Sift together flour, baking powder and sugar. Break eggs into mixture, stir and add milk. Stir and add butter and chocolate. Stir in vanilla. Pour into 2 buttered 8" cake pans. Bake at 350 degrees for 15-20 min. or until knife comes out clean. Remove from pan and place cakes on rack. Frost when cool.

MOCHA FROSTING:
2 c. confectioners' sugar
1 sq. bitter chocolate
4 tbsp. butter, melted
1 tsp. vanilla
1/2 c. strong black coffee

Melt butter and chocolate, remove from fire and add sugar and vanilla. Moisten with warm coffee to spreading consistency. Frost cake dipping knife into coffee while spreading.

CAKES

CHRISTMAS CAKE

Preparation: 30 min.
Soaking: Overnight
Baking: 1 hr.
Storing: 7 days

- 1 box (15 oz.) seedless raisins
- 1 box (16 oz.) currants
- 1 can (8 oz.) chopped walnuts
- 1 c. brandy
- 1 c. butter
- 1 c. sugar
- 2 c. cake flour
- 6 eggs, separated

Soak first 4 ingredients overnight in a large covered bowl. Cream butter and sugar together and add egg yolks. Sprinkle flour (about 1/4 cup) on marinated fruit to coat. Fold fruit into butter/sugar mixture. Fold rest of flour into mixture. Beat egg whites until stiff but not dry and fold into mixture. Bake in greased and floured tube pan at 350 degrees for 1 hr. Cool and wrap in wax paper. Store in tin for 7-10 days before cutting.

FAIRY CAKE

Preparation: 45 min.
Baking: 20 min.
Chilling: 2 hr.

FIRST PART (Cake):

- 1/4 lb. butter
- 1/2 c. sugar
- 4 egg yolks, beaten
- 4 tbsp. milk or pineapple juice
- 2/3 c. all-purpose flour
- 1 tsp. baking powder
- 1/4 tsp. salt

Cream together butter and sugar. Add egg yolks and sifted dry ingredients, alternately with milk or juice. Spread batter on 2 well-buttered 9" cake pans. (This makes a very thin layer.)

SECOND PART (Meringue):

- 4 egg whites
- 3/4 c. sugar
- 1 tsp. vanilla

Beat egg whites until they stand in peaks. Fold in sugar and vanilla. Spread meringue mixture over raw batter. Bake at 350 degrees for 20 min. Cool.

THIRD PART (Filling):

- 1 c. heavy cream
- 1 c. crushed pineapple, drained
- 1-1/2 tbsp. powdered sugar

Whip cream until stiff. Add sugar to thoroughly drained pineapple. Fold pineapple and sugar mixture into whipped cream. Remove cakes from pans, invert so meringue side of cakes form top and bottom, Spread filling over cake part of one cake and place second cake on top. Serve fresh or place in refrigerator for serving as ice-box cake.

CAKES

FUDGE CAKE

Preparation: 15 min.
Baking: 45 min.

1 c. flour
2 tsp. baking powder
1/4 tsp. salt
1/4 c. sugar
1-1/2 tbsp. cocoa powder
1/2 c. milk
1 tsp. vanilla
2 tbsp. butter, melted
1 c. chopped nuts

In a large bowl sift flour 3 times before measuring. Add baking powder, salt and cocoa and mix thoroughly. Combine milk, vanilla and butter and stir into mixture. Beat until smooth. Blend in nuts. Spread in greased and floured 8" square pan.

SAUCE:

1 c. brown sugar, tightly packed
1 tbsp. cocoa
1-3/4 c. boiling water

In a medium bowl, mix brown sugar and cocoa. Add water and mix. Pour over cake mixture in pan. Bake at 350 degrees for 45 min.

GARNISH:

1 c. heavy cream, whipped

Serve with whipped cream.

GRANDMA HUME'S STRAWBERRY SHORTCAKE

Preparation: 30 min.
Baking: 20 min.
Assembling: 10 min.

2 c. flour
4 tsp. baking powder
1 tsp. salt
1/3 c. shortening
3/4 c. milk
2 qt. strawberries
  or 2 pkg. frozen strawberries
1/3 c. water (if fresh strawberries are used)
1/4 c. sugar
1 c. heavy cream, whipped

Sift flour 3 times before measuring. Add salt and baking powder and mix thoroughly. Cut in shortening with a knife and finish by rubbing between palms of hands. Add milk gradually. Divide dough into 2 parts. Put on floured board and roll lightly to fit 2 buttered and floured 9" layer cake pans. Bake at 450 degrees for 20 min. or until brown. Sweeten strawberries with sugar. Keep a few for garnish. Crush remaining berries lightly (add water if fresh are used). Heat to lukewarm over low flame. Pour half on top of bottom layer, cover with other layer, and put remaining berries on top. Cover with whipped cream and garnish with reserved strawberries.

CAKES

ITALIAN CREAM CAKE

Preparation: 15 min.
Baking: 25 min.
Frosting: 10 min.

1/4 lb. margarine
1/2 c. shortening
2 c. sugar
5 eggs, separated
2 c. flour
1 tsp. soda
1 c. buttermilk
1 tsp. vanilla
1 sml. can shredded coconut
1 c. chopped pecans

FROSTING:

8 oz. cream cheese, softened
1/4 c. margarine, softened
1 lb. powdered sugar
1 tsp. vanilla
chopped nuts

Cream margarine, shortening and sugar together and beat until smooth. Add egg yolks and beat well. In a separate bowl combine flour and soda and add to creamed mixture alternately with buttermilk. Stir in vanilla, coconut, and nuts. Beat egg whites until stiff and fold in. Bake in three greased and floured layer pans at 350 degrees for 25 min. Cool.

Beat cream cheese and margarine together until smooth. Add powdered sugar and vanilla and beat until smooth. Cool layers and spread frosting on each layer. Put layers on top of each other and spread frosting on top and sides. Sprinkle top and sides with chopped nuts.

MOLASSES CAKE

Preparation: 35 min.
Baking: 40 min.

2 c. flour
1/2 tsp. salt
1 tsp. ginger
1/2 tsp. ground cloves
1 tsp. cinnamon
1/2 c. butter, melted
1 c. molasses
1 egg, well-beaten
1/2 c. coffee
1 tsp. baking soda
1 tbsp. vinegar

In medium bowl sift flour 3 times and add salt, ginger, cloves and cinnamon. In large bowl mix butter, molasses, egg and lukewarm coffee in which baking soda has been dissolved. Beat thoroughly and add dry mixture to wet mixture, a little at a time, beating constantly to prevent lumping. At the last minute add vinegar. Bake in a greased and floured loaf pan at 350 degrees for 40 min.

CAKES

NIXIES CUP CAKE

Preparation: 15 min.
Baking: 20 min.

1 c. butter
1 c. sugar
1 egg
1/2 c. milk
1-1/4 c. flour
1/4 c. flour sifted with
   1 tsp. baking powder
1/8 tsp. salt
1 tsp. vanilla
powdered sugar

Cream butter and sugar, add unbeaten egg and beat with wooden spoon. Add milk and 1-1/4 cup flour. Beat until light and smooth. Add flour and baking powder mixture, salt and vanilla. Mix well, but do not beat. Bake at 400 degrees in tiny cupcake tins for 20 min. Serve warm, sprinkled with powdered sugar.

NUSSTORTE

Preparation: 25 min.
Baking: 1 hr.
Chilling: Overnight.
Final Chilling: 2 hr.

6 lrg. eggs, separated
   and room temp.
8 oz. ground hazelnuts
3/4 c. sugar
pinch salt

Beat yolks until lemon-colored. Add salt and sugar and beat until smooth. Add nuts and mix well. Fold in stiffly beaten egg whites. Pour into buttered, floured 10" springform. Bake at 325 degrees for about 1 hr. Cool. Chill overnight.

FILLING:

1/2 pt. heavy cream
2 tbsp. sugar
1 tsp. vanilla

Whip cream and stir in sugar and vanilla. Mix well. Cut cake into two layers. Spread filling on top of bottom layer. Replace top layer.

GLAZE:

1 jar (18 oz.) apricot jam
6-8 maraschino cherries
   and/or whole hazelnuts

Heat jam. Pour through sieve over top and sides of cake. When cool, decorate with cherries and/or nuts. Chill.

CAKES

PARTY CHIFFON CAKE

Preparation: 30 min.
Baking: 1 hr. 10 min.

2 c. sifted all-
   purpose flour
1-1/2 c. sugar
3 tsp. baking powder
1 tsp. salt
1/2 c. oil
7 eggs, separated
3/4 c. cold water
2 tsp. vanilla
1/2 tsp. cream of tartar

Sift first 4 ingredients together in large mixing bowl. Mix well and add oil, yolks, water and vanilla. Beat with electric beater at medium speed 1 min. until smooth. Add cream of tartar to egg whites in another large mixing bowl and beat until whites form very stiff peaks. Pour egg yolk mixture gradually over beaten egg whites, gently folding with rubber scraper until just blended. Do not stir. Pour immediately into ungreased 10" x 4" tube pan. Bake at 325 degrees for 55 min. then increase to 350 degrees for 10-15 min. or until top springs back when lightly touched. Hang pan upside down on bottleneck until cool.

PRUNE CAKE

Preparation: 1 hr.
Baking: 1 hr.

1 c. oil
2 c. sugar
2 tsp. cloves
2 tsp. cinnamon
2 tsp. allspice
2 tsp. nutmeg
3/4 tsp. salt
2 tsp. vanilla
3 eggs
1 tsp. baking soda
1 c. buttermilk
2 c. sifted flour
1 c. pitted prunes, cut-up
1 c. chopped pecans

Combine oil, sugar, spices, salt and vanilla. Add eggs one at a time. Add baking soda and buttermilk alternately with flour. Add prunes. Stir well and add nuts. Bake in 2 buttered and floured small loaf pans at 350 degrees for 40-45 min. or bake in a tube pan at 325 degrees for 1 hr. or until done. Glaze while still warm.

GLAZE:

1 c. sugar
1/2 c. buttermilk
1/4 tsp. soda
1/4 c. butter

Mix ingredients, boil 5 min. and pour over cake.

NOTE: Cut glaze recipe in half when making tube pan cake.

CAKES

RED VELVET CAKE

Preparation: 25 min.
Baking: 30 min.

1/2 c. butter
2 eggs
2 tsp. cocoa powder
1 tsp. vinegar
1/2 tsp. salt
1 tsp. vanilla
1 tsp. raspberry flavoring
1-1/2 c. sugar
2 oz. red food coloring
2 tsp. baking soda
2-1/2 c. sifted flour
1 c. buttermilk

Cream butter, sugar and eggs together thoroughly. Make paste of cocoa and food coloring and add to creamed mixture. Add salt, vanilla and raspberry flavoring to buttermilk and alternately add with flour to creamed mixture. Mix baking soda with vinegar and fold into creamed mixture. Pour into two greased and floured 9" layer pans. Bake at 350 degrees for 30 min. Cool.

ICING:

1 c. milk
1 c. butter
6 tsp. flour
1 c. sugar
1 tsp. vanilla
1 c. shredded coconut

Mix milk and flour, making a paste, and cook until thick. Cool. Cream butter and sugar together and add vanilla. Combine with cooled mixture and beat until fluffy. Spread on bottom layer, then assemble cake and ice top and sides. Decorate with shredded coconut.

RUM CAKE

Preparation: 15 min.
Freezing: 24 hr.

6 eggs, separated
3 env. unflavored gelatin
3 c. milk
1-1/4 c. sugar
1 tbsp. vanilla
6 oz. rum
1/2 lb. stale macaroons
1 pt. heavy cream, whipped
1/2 c. chopped walnuts

Mix egg yolks with a fork. Dissolve gelatin in 1 cup cold milk. Add remaining milk to egg yolks, pour into saucepan and bring to boil. Add gelatin. Turn off heat as soon as it begins to boil. Cool and fold in stiffly beaten egg whites. Add vanilla and rum and blend carefully. Line a 10" springform pan with crumbled macaroons, pour mixture on top and freeze 24 hr. Unmold onto serving platter and top with whipped cream and chopped walnuts.

CAKES

SACHER TORTE

Preparation: 20 min.
Baking: 50 min.
Chilling: Overnight

1/2 c. butter
1/2 c. + 2 tbsp. sugar
6 eggs, separated
5 sq. semi-sweet chocolate,
3/4 c. flour
1/2 c. ground almonds
1 jar (18 oz.) apricot jam

CHOCOLATE FROSTING:

3 sq. unsweetened chocolate
1 c. heavy cream
1 tbsp. corn syrup
1 c. granulated sugar
1 egg, lightly beaten
1 tsp. vanilla
1 c. heavy cream (opt.)

Cream together butter and 1/2 cup sugar. Beat in egg yolks (one at a time) and melted chocolate. Mix in flour and ground almonds. Beat egg whites with remaining sugar until stiff and fold into mixture. Bake in cake pan at 350 degrees for 50 min. Chill overnight. Slice into 2 layers and spread middle and sides with apricot jam.

Combine chocolate, cream, corn syrup and sugar in a saucepan. Heat, stirring until smooth. Cook until mixture forms a soft ball when dropped into cold water. Stir occasionally. Beat in egg and vanilla. Pour over cake and chill to set. If desired whip cream stiff and spoon onto cake.

SAUERKRAUT CAKE

Preparation: 20 min.
Baking: 40 min.

1/2 c. butter
1-1/2 c. sugar
3 eggs
1 tsp. vanilla
2 c. all-purpose flour
1 tsp. baking powder
1 tsp. baking soda
1/4 tsp. salt
1/2 c. cocoa powder
1 c. water
1 c. sauerkraut, drained, rinsed and snipped

SOUR CREAM/CHOCOLATE FROSTING:

1 pkg. (6 oz.) semi-sweet chocolate bits
4 tbsp. butter
1/2 c. sour cream
1 tsp. vanilla
1/4 tsp. salt
2-1/2 — 2-3/4 c. confectioners' sugar, sifted

Cream butter and sugar until light. Beat in eggs, one at a time and add vanilla. In a separate bowl sift together flour, baking powder, soda, salt and cocoa. Add to creamed mixture alternately with water, beating after each addition. Stir in sauerkraut. Turn into greased and floured 13" x 9" baking pan. Bake at 350 degrees for 35-40 min. Cool in pan. Frost.

Melt chocolate and butter together over low heat. Remove from heat and blend in sour cream, vanilla and salt. Gradually beat in sifted sugar until mixture reaches spreading consistency. Beat well and spread on cake.

CAKES

PINEAPPLE UPSIDE-DOWN CAKE

Preparation: 15 min.
Baking: 40 min.

6 tbsp. butter
1-1/2 c. brown sugar
1 can (20 oz.) crushed pineapple, drained
2 c. cake flour
2-1/2 tsp. baking powder
6 tbsp. shortening
1-1/4 c. sugar
2 eggs
3/4 c. pineapple juice or milk

Put first three ingredients in #8 ovenproof skillet in the order given. Heat until melted. Mix other ingredients in large bowl and place on top of first mixture. Bake at 375 degrees for 30-40 min. Invert to serve.

WACKY CAKE

Preparation: 10 min.
Baking: 30 min.

1-1/2 c. flour
1 tsp. baking soda
3 tbsp. cocoa powder
1 c. sugar
1/2 tsp. salt
5 tbsp. shortening
1 tsp. vanilla
1 tbsp. vinegar
1 c. cold water

FROSTING:
2 c. confectioners' sugar
1 tsp. vanilla
2 tbsp. margarine, softened
water

In a large bowl sift together first 5 ingredients. Mix in remaining ingredients. Bake in a 9" x 9" pan at 350 degrees for 30 min.

Mix ingredients together with enough water to make mixture of spreading consistency.

QUICK NO-COOK FLUFFY CAKE FROSTING

Preparation: 10 min.

1 lrg. sour apple, peeled
pinch salt
1 c. sugar
1 egg white
1/4 tsp. lemon juice (opt.)

Grate apple with fine side of grater. (It will turn brown.) Mix all ingredients in bowl at high speed until peaks form. (Mixture will look like marshmallows.) If not tart enough, add lemon juice a little at a time.

YIELD: Enough to cover two 8" layers or one 9" x 13" cake.

COOKIES

BUTTER COOKIES

Preparation: 30 min.
Chilling: 1 hr.
Baking: 18 min.

1 lb. butter
1 c. + 2 tbsp. sugar
2 eggs, separated
juice of 1/2 lemon and
   1 tsp. almond extract and
   1 c. chopped almonds
   or
2 tbsp. brandy and
   1 tbsp. vanilla extract
   and 1 c. chopped walnuts
1 tsp. baking powder
5 c. flour

Cream butter and 1 cup sugar together. Add slightly beaten egg yolks, lemon juice or brandy, and almond or vanilla extract. Mix well. Sift baking powder and flour into mixture, beating constantly. If more flour is needed, add 1 tbsp. at a time. Form into a ball and roll out on floured surface. Cut into shapes with cookie cutters. Beat egg whites and brush a little on each cookie. Mix chopped nuts with 2 tbsp. sugar and sprinkle some on each one. Bake at 350 degrees for 15-18 min. until light brown. (Dough should be chilled before rolling.)

COCONUT COOKIES

Preparation: 10 min.
Baking: 10 min.

1/2 c. brown sugar
1/2 c. white sugar
1/2 tsp. salt
1/2 tsp. baking powder
1 egg
1/2 c. shortening
1/2 c. flour
1 c. quick cooking oatmeal
1 c. coconut
1 tsp. vanilla

Sift brown sugar, white sugar, salt and baking powder together. Break egg into mixture and beat. Add shortening and beat thoroughly. Sift flour 3 times before measuring, and add with oatmeal and coconut to mixture. Add vanilla. Drop dough onto greased cookie sheet from a teaspoon. Bake at 350 degrees for 10 min. or until brown.

CREAM CHEESE COOKIES

Preparation: 10 min.
Baking: 15 min.

1 c. shortening
3 oz. cream cheese
1 c. sugar
1 egg yolk
1/2 tsp. vanilla
2-1/2 c. flour

Cream together first 5 ingredients. Add flour and mix until smooth. Put through cookie press or take about 1 tsp. of dough, roll into a ball and flatten with fork. Dip cookies in flour and place on lightly greased baking sheet. Bake at 350 degrees for 15 min. or until light golden brown.

COOKIES

FRENCH LACE COOKIES

Preparation: 25 min.
Baking: 10 min.

1/4 c. corn syrup
1/2 c. butter
1/3 c. brown sugar
1/2 c. flour
1/2 c. finely chopped pecans

In a saucepan bring first 3 ingredients just to boiling point. Remove from heat immediately. Blend together flour and pecans and add syrup to mixture, beating until smooth. Drop from a teaspoon onto greased cookie sheet, 3" apart. Bake at 325 degrees for 8-10 min. Cool for 1 min. Remove carefully with spatula.

GOURMANDS

Preparation: 15 min.
Chilling: 2 hr.

3 c. cake crumbs
1/2 c. strawberry jam
1/2 c. dark rum
1/2 c. chopped orange peel
chocolate glaze
  or chopped nuts

In a medium bowl combine first 4 ingredients. Roll into sausage shape 1-1/2" thick. Chill at least 2 hr. Cut into 1" slices. Flatten a bit. Either glaze with chocolate or roll in chopped nuts.

YIELD: 24 cookies

OATMEAL COOKIES

Preparation: 15 min.
Baking: 15 min.

1 c. margarine
3/4 c. brown sugar
3/4 c. white sugar
1-1/2 c. flour
1 tsp. baking soda
1/2 tsp. salt
2 eggs
1 tsp. vanilla
2 c. steel-cut Irish oatmeal
1-1/2 c. raisins
1-1/2 c. chocolate bits

In a large bowl, combine margarine and sugars. Mix in remaining ingredients. Form into balls and place on ungreased cookie sheet. Bake at 325 degrees for 15 min. or until golden brown.

COOKIES

MERINGUE KISSES

Preparation: 30 min.
Baking: 1 hr.

4 egg whites
2 c. sugar
1 tbsp. lemon juice
1/8 tsp. vanilla

Beat egg whites with electric mixer until stiff. Add sugar, a little at a time, while continuing to beat. Fold in lemon juice and vanilla. Drop from teaspoon into mounds on greased cookie sheet. Bake at 250 degrees for 1 hr. or more until crisp outside and slightly tan.
YIELD: Approx. 48 kisses

OVERNIGHT MERINGUE

Preparation: 15 min.
Baking: 8 hr.

2 egg whites
pinch salt
2/3 c. sugar
1/4 tsp. almond flavoring
1/4 tsp. orange flavoring (opt.)
1/2 tsp. vanilla
1 c. walnut halves

Preheat oven to 250 degrees. Beat egg whites until foamy. Very gradually add sugar and beat until quite stiff. Fold in flavorings. Stir in nuts. From teaspoon drop onto greased cookie sheet. They will not spread. Place in oven and turn off heat. Allow to stay in oven all night or all day, for at least 8 hr. DO NOT OPEN OVEN DOOR no matter how curious you may be.

EASY SCOTTISH SHORTBREAD

Preparation: 30 min.
Chilling: 2 hr.
Baking: 10 min.

1 part fine sugar
  or 1 part Parmesan cheese
2 parts butter
3 parts flour

In a bowl mix all ingredients together and shape into a loaf 1/2" thick. Let rest in refrigerator 2 hr. Cut into thin slices and bake at 400 degrees for 10 min.

SCOTTISH SHORTBREAD

Preparation: 20 min.
Baking: 40 min.

1 c. confectioners' sugar
1/2 lb. butter
2 c. plain flour
1 c. cornstarch

Cream sugar and butter together until fluffy. Mix in flour and cornstarch and knead on a board. Flatten to about 1/2". Put on cookie sheet and bake at 350 degrees for 10 min. Turn heat to 300 degrees and bake 30 min. more.

PIES

CHEESE PIE WITH STRAWBERRY GLAZE

Preparating: 30 min.
Baking: 20 min.
Chilling: 2 hr.
Glazing: 15 min.

3 tbsp. butter, melted
1 c. graham cracker crumbs
1 lb. cream cheese
3/4 c. sugar
2 eggs
1 tsp. vanilla
3/4 c. sour cream

Make pie crust by adding butter to crumbs, mixing and pressing into greased 9" pie plate. Place cream cheese, sugar, eggs and vanilla in bowl and beat at high speed with electric beater for 10 min. Pour mixture into pie crust and spread thin layer of sour cream on top. Bake at 350 degrees for 20 min. Refrigerate at least 2 hr. preferably overnight.

GLAZE:
1 pkg. frozen strawberries
1 tbsp. cornstarch

Thaw strawberries and drain, reserving juice. In a saucepan mix half the berries with about 1 cup juice and cornstarch. Cook over medium heat stirring until thick. Let cool. Spread over top of pie and garnish with reserved strawberries.

CHESS PIE

Preparation: 10 min.
Baking: 45-55 min.

1-1/2 c. sugar
6 tbsp. butter
3 eggs
1 tsp. vinegar
1 tsp. corn meal
1 tsp. vanilla
dash salt
unbaked 9" pie shell
whipped cream

Cream sugar and butter together. Add remaining ingredients and mix well. Pour into pie shell. Bake at 350 degrees until filling is firm about 45-55 min. Decorate with whipped cream.

CHOCOLATE FUDGE PIE

Preparation: 15 min.
Baking: 45 min.

1 unbaked 9" pie crust
1/2 c. butter
1 c. sugar
1 tsp. vanilla
2 eggs, separated
2 sq. bitter chocolate
1/3 c. sifted flour
1/8 tsp. salt
1 c. heavy cream, whipped
chocolate sprinkles

Cream butter and gradually add sugar. Continue creaming until light. Add vanilla. Beat in egg yolks, one at a time. Melt chocolate and mix with flour. Beat egg whites with salt until stiff. Fold into mixture. Put filling into pie shell and bake at 350 degrees for 45 min. Cool. Top with whipped cream and decorate with chocolate sprinkles.

PIES

CRANBERRY WALNUT PIE

Preparation: 20 min.
Baking: 45 min.

1-1/2 c. cranberries
1/4-1/2 c. sugar
1/4-1/2 c. chopped walnuts
1/4 c. butter, melted
1/2 c. sugar
1/2 c. flour
1 egg
ice cream

Mix first 3 ingredients and pour into 9" pie plate. Mix last 4 ingredients thoroughly to form dough. Spread dough on top of cranberry mixture. Bake at 350 degrees for 45 min. Serve warm with ice cream.

GRAHAM CRACKER PIE

Preparation: 20 min.
Baking: 25 min.

2 eggs, separated
3/4 c. sugar
1/2 tsp. baking powder
1 c. graham cracker crumbs
1 c. chopped nuts
1 tsp. vanilla
1/4-1/3 c. butter, melted
whipped cream

In a large bowl beat egg whites until stiff. Add sugar and baking powder and mix well. In a separate bowl combine graham cracker crumbs, chopped nuts, vanilla, slightly beaten egg yolks and butter. Fold into egg whites. Press into greased 9" pie plate and bake at 350 degrees for 20-30 min. Serve warm with whipped cream.

GRASSHOPPER PIE

Preparation: 20 min.
Chilling: 2 hr.

14-16 chocolate wafers
3/4 c. sugar
1/4 c. butter, melted
1 env. unflavored gelatin
1/8 tsp. salt
1/2 c. water
3 eggs, separated
1/4 c. creme de cacao
1/4 c. green creme de menthe
1 c. heavy cream, whipped
1/4 c. crushed mint-flavored chocolate bits

With a rolling pin, crush chocolate wafers to make fine crumbs. Mix with 1/4 c. sugar and butter. Press firmly against bottom and sides of buttered 9" pie plate. Bake at 450 degrees for 5 min. Cool. Combine gelatin, 1/4 cup sugar and salt in top of double boiler. Add water and egg yolks, one at a time, stirring to blend well. Place over boiling water, stir until gelatin is dissolved and mixture is slightly thickened, about 5 min. Remove from water. Stir in creme de cacao and creme de menthe. Chill, stirring occasionally until mixture is consistency of unbeaten egg whites. Beat egg whites until stiff but not dry. Gradually add 1/4 cup sugar, beating until very stiff. Fold in gelatin mixture. Fold in whipped cream. Turn into pie shell and chill 2 hr. or overnight. Sprinkle with crushed chocolate.

PIES

HEATH BAR PIE

Preparation: 10 min.
Chilling: 2 hr.

1 pkg. lady fingers, cut crosswise
1 lrg. container Cool Whip
1 pkg. (6-10¢ size) Heath Bars

Place half the lady fingers into bottom and sides of a pie pan, standing curved ends up. Chop finely, or put in blender, the Heath Bars. Reserve some crumbs. Mix with Cool Whip. Put half the mixture over the lady fingers. Add another layer of lady fingers and remaining mixture. Sprinkle with crumbs and refrigerate at least 2 hr.

LEMON PIE

Preparation: 30 min.
Baking: 8 min.
Cooking: 10 min.

1 pkg. shortbread cookies
4 tsp. grated almonds
1/4 lb. butter, melted
grated rind and juice of 4 lrg. lemons
7 eggs, separated
1 c. sugar
1 env. unflavored gelatin
1/4 c. water

Mix first 3 ingredients together and press into a 9" pie plate. Bake at 375 degrees for 8 min. Cool. Beat yolks and 1/4 c. sugar. Dissolve gelatin in water and add juice and rind. Mix together in top of double boiler about 10 min. until slightly thickened. Remove from flame and stir until cool. Beat egg whites with remaining sugar and fold into lemon mixture. Pour into crust. Chill 2 hr.

LEMON MERINGUE PIE

Preparation: 30 min.
Baking: 10 min.
Browning: 5 min.

1 unbaked 9" pie shell
4 eggs, separated
3 whole eggs
rind of 1 lemon, grated
juice of 2 lemons
1 c. + 3 tbsp. sugar

Prick bottom of pie crust and bake at 400 degrees about 10 min. Cool. In top of double boiler, beat together egg yolks, whole eggs, lemon rind, lemon juice and 1 cup sugar. Continue beating until thick, about 10-15 min. Pour into pie shell. Whip egg whites with 3 tbsp. sugar until very stiff. Spread over custard. Brown lightly at 400 degrees (about 5 min.).

PIES

MYSTERY TORTE

Preparation: 15 min.
Baking: 30 min.

16 Ritz crackers
2/3 c. chopped nuts
3 egg whites
1/2 tsp. baking powder
1 c. sugar
1 tsp. vanilla
1 c. heavy cream, whipped
shredded chocolate

Chop crackers and nuts together in blender until very fine. Beat egg whites until stiff. Sift together baking powder and sugar and add gradually to egg whites. Fold in nuts and cracker mixture all at once and add vanilla. Pour into lightly greased 8" pie plate and bake at 350 degrees for 30 min. Cool. Top with whipped cream and garnish with shredded chocolate. Can be frozen.

CREAMY PEACH PIE

Preparation: 15 min.
Baking: 45 min.
Chilling: 2 hr.

3/4 c. sugar
1/4 c. flour
1/4 tsp. salt
1/4 tsp. nutmeg
4 c. sliced and peeled peaches
  or 1 can (1-lb. 13-oz.) peaches drained and rinsed
1 9" unbaked pie shell
1/2 c. heavy cream

In medium bowl mix sugar, flour, salt and nutmeg. Add to peaches and toss lightly. Turn into pie shell. Pour cream over top. Bake at 400 degrees for 35-40 min. or until firm. Chill at least 2 hr.

PEANUT BRITTLE PIE

Preparation: 30 min.
Freezing: 3 hr.

1 graham cracker pie crust (9")
2 c. heavy cream
1 tbsp. instant coffee
1 tsp. vanilla
1-1/2 c. crushed peanut brittle

Prepare crust according to pkg. directions and cool. Whip heavy cream with vanilla and coffee. Fold in 1 cup peanut brittle crumbs. Spoon mixture into pie shell. Top with remaining crumbs. Freeze at least 3 hr. Remove about 30 min. before serving.

NOTE: Put peanut brittle through meat grinder to crush.

PIES

PECAN PIE

Preparation: 10 min.
Baking: 30 min.

1 unbaked 9" pie shell
3 eggs
1 c. brown sugar, firmly packed
1/2 c. dark corn syrup
1/4 tsp. salt
6 tbsp. rum
1/4 c. butter, melted
1 c. pecans, coarsely chopped
1/2 c. heavy cream, whipped
1 tbsp. sugar
or ice cream

Beat eggs in medium-size bowl until light colored and fluffy. Add brown sugar, corn syrup, salt and 4 tbsp. rum and thoroughly mix. Stir in butter and pecans. Pour into pie shell and bake at 375 degrees for 40 min. or until knife inserted in the filling comes out clean. Serve with whipped cream to which the remaining rum and sugar have been added, or ice cream.

PUMPKIN PIE

Preparation: 10 min.
Chilling: 8 hr.
Baking: 40 min.

1 unbaked 9" pie crust
1/2 tsp. mace
1/2 tsp. grated nutmeg
1 tsp. cinnamon
2 tsp. ginger
3/4 c. sugar
1/8 c. dark molasses
1 c. evaporated milk
2 eggs beaten
1 (16 oz.) can pumpkin

Mix together all filling ingredients except eggs. Cover and refrigerate 8 hr. Add eggs and blend well. Pour into pie crust and bake at 450 degrees for 10 min. Lower oven to 350 degrees and continue baking until knife inserted comes out clean about 20-30 min.

RUM PIE

Preparation: 30 min.
Chilling: 4 hr.

9" graham cracker pie crust
6 egg yolks
1 c. sugar
1 env. unflavored gelatin
1/2 c. rum
1 pt. cream, whipped
shaved bittersweet chocolate or minced pistachio nuts

Prepare crust according to pkg. directions. In large bowl beat egg yolks until light and add sugar. Mix well. Dissolve gelatin in 1/2 cup cold water in small saucepan. Heat until boiling and pour over sugar/water mixture, stirring briskly. Fold whipped cream into mixture and flavor with rum. Cool slightly and pour into pie shell. Chill for 4 hr. or more. Sprinkle the top with chocolate shavings or pistachio nuts.

SQUARES

BUTTERSCOTCH BROWNIES

Preparation: 15 min.
Baking: 50 min.

1/4 lb. butter
2 c. dark brown sugar
2 eggs, slightly beaten
1-1/2 c. flour
2 tsp. vanilla
1/2 tsp. salt

In a saucepan, melt butter and add brown sugar. Remove from heat and add eggs, flour, vanilla and salt. Mix until blended. Put in a 9" x 9" greased pan and bake at 275 degrees for 50 min. or until soft. Cool before cutting.

CINNAMON BARS

Preparation: 15 min.
Baking: 1 hr.

1 c. sugar
1 c. butter
1 egg, separated
2 c. sifted flour
1 tsp. cinnamon
1 c. chopped pecans or walnuts

Cream butter and sugar together. Add egg yolk, flour and cinnamon. Mix well. Press batter into greased 15" x 10" jelly roll pan. Brush top of batter with whipped egg white. Press nuts into dough. Bake at 275 degrees for 1 hr. Cut into squares when slightly cooled.

COCONUT DELIGHT SQUARES

Preparation: 15 min.
Baking: 30 min.

2 tbsp. butter, softened
1 sml. pkg. chocolate chips
1 sml. pkg. butterscotch chips
1 c. graham cracker crumbs
1 can condensed milk
1 sml. pkg. coconut
1 c. chopped nuts (opt.)

Spread butter evenly on bottom of 9" x 9" pan. Sprinkle in graham cracker crumbs. Pour butterscotch and chocolate chips on top and cover with coconut. Pour milk slowly, covering all ingredients. Sprinkle with nuts. Bake for about 30 min. at 325 degrees. Cool at least 15 min. before cutting in small squares.

SQUARES

CONGO SQUARES

Preparation: 30 min.
Baking: 50 min.

1 lb. light brown sugar
3/4 c. shortening, melted
3 eggs, beaten
2-1/2 c. sifted slour
1/4 tsp. salt
2-1/2 tsp. baking powder
1 tsp. vanilla
1 pkg. (12 oz.) sweet chocolate chips
3/4 c. chopped walnuts

Mix sugar and shortening and add eggs. Add dry ingredients and vanilla. Fold in chocolate chips and nuts. Spread in 9" x 13" pan. Bake at 350 degrees until brown about 50 min. Cut into squares while warm.

LEMON DREAMS

Preparation: 15 min.
Baking: 45 min.

1/2 c. butter
1/2 c. confectioners' sugar
1 c. + 1 tbsp. flour
2 eggs
1 c. granulated sugar
2 tbsp. flour
1/2 tsp. baking soda
dash salt
3 tbsp. grated lemon rind
4 tbsp. lemon juice
powdered sugar

Cream together butter and confectioners' sugar. Cut in all but 2 tbsp. flour making soft dough. Press into buttered and floured 9" square pan. Bake at 350 degrees for about 20 min. or until mixture is consistency of shortbread. Meanwhile, beat eggs and remaining 2 tbsp. flour, sugar, baking soda, salt, lemon rind and juice. Spread on baked mixture. Bake again at 350 degrees for 20-25 min. Sprinkle with powdered sugar. Cut while warm.

MARGARET TURNER'S SQUARES

Preparation: 15 min.
Mixing: 15 min.
Baking: 25 min.

3/4 c. butter (not margarine)
3 tbsp. sugar
1/2 c. flour
3 eggs, separated
2-1/2 c. brown sugar
1 c. chopped pecans
3/4 c. coconut

Cream butter and sugar. Add flour and blend thoroughly. Put mixture in greased baking dish 7" x 11" or 11" round and bake at 350 degrees for 15 min. While baking, combine beaten egg yolks, brown sugar, nuts and coconut. Fold in stiffly beaten egg whites. Pour over hot baked mixture and bake 25 min. more. Cut at once.

SQUARES

MARGO'S FUDGE

Preparation: 20 min.
Cooling: 15 min.

2 oz. unsweetened chocolate
2 c. sugar
1/2 c. milk
2 heaping tbsp. butter
1 heaping tsp. vanilla

Place chocolate, sugar and milk in saucepan. Bring to boil over medium heat, stirring occasionally to keep from burning. Boil for exactly 7 min. Remove from heat. When slightly cooled add butter and vanilla. Beat a few minutes until mixture thickens. Pour into buttered 8" square pan. Cool before cutting.

NUTTIES

Preparation: 15 min.
Baking: 30 min.

1/2 c. butter
1 tbsp. light corn syrup
1 c. brown sugar
2 c. rolled oats
1/2 tsp. salt
1/2 tsp. vanilla
1/2 c. chopped walnuts

In medium saucepan melt butter, syrup and sugar. Mix in remaining ingredients. Spread in greased 9" square baking pan and press down with spoon. Bake at 350 degrees for 30 min. Cut into fingers while still warm and leave in pan to cool.

SQUARES FOR THE GODS

Preparation: 15 min.
Baking: 35 min.

1 c. chopped dates
1 c. chopped walnuts
3 heaping tbsp. flour
1 tsp. baking powder
1 c. sugar
3 eggs, beaten

In a large bowl combine all ingredients. Pour into greased 9" sq. pan. Bake at 350 degrees for 35 min. Cut into squares.

TANNIES

Preparation: 15 min.
Baking: 35 min.

4 sq. semi-sweet chocolate
1 c. butter
1-1/2 c. sugar
1 c. sifted flour
4 eggs
2 tsp. vanilla

Melt chocolate and butter together in top of double boiler, stirring occasionally. Add sugar and stir. Add flour and eggs, one at a time, stirring constantly. When thoroughly mixed, add vanilla. Put mixture into greased 8" square pan. Bake at 350 degrees for 30-35 min.

SALAD DRESSINGS

ALMOND SALAD DRESSING

Preparation: 10 min.
Chilling: 30 min.

1 pkg. (3 oz.) slivered almonds
1 tbsp. butter
1 tbsp. mayonnaise
1/3 c. blue cheese dressing
milk

Saute almonds in butter and allow to cool. Mix blue cheese dressing and mayonnaise until blended. Add milk until dressing is consistency of heavy cream. Combine dressing and almonds. Chill 30 min.

YIELD: Approx. 1 cup

BLUE CHEESE SALAD DRESSING

Preparation: 5 min.
Chilling: 1 hr.

6 oz. blue cheese
2 c. mayonnaise
1-1/2 tsp. Worcestershire
1/2 tsp. garlic powder
3 tbsp. chopped chives
1-1/2 tsp. pepper
1 c. sour cream
1/2 c. buttermilk

Crumble cheese with other ingredients and mix well. Chill at least 1 hr.

YIELD: 4 cups

COOKED SALAD DRESSING

Preparation: 5 min.
Cooking: 3 min.
Cooling: 30 min.

3 tbsp. cider vinegar
3 egg yolks, well-beaten
2 tbsp. butter
pinch salt
pinch pepper
pinch dry mustard
sour cream

Combine all ingredients, except sour cream, in top of small double boiler. Cook until thickened. Cool in refrigerator for at least 30 min. When ready to serve, thin to desired consistency with sour cream. Serve with cold asparagus, artichokes, meat, etc.

SALAD DRESSINGS

CROWELL'S SALAD DRESSING

Preparation: 10 min.

2 tbsp. wine vinegar
1/2-1 tsp. salt
1/4 tsp. pepper
1/2 tsp. dry mustard
1/4 tsp. MSG (opt.)
1/2 tsp. paprika
1/2 tsp. garlic salt
  or rub salad bowl with
    cut side of garlic clove
1 tsp. fresh basil, chopped
1 tsp. fresh oregano, chopped
1 tsp. fresh chives, chopped
1 tsp. fresh garden cress, chopped
  or 1 tsp. fresh watercress,
    chopped
6 tbsp. olive oil

Put chopped herbs with other ingredients except oil in a pint glass jar. Seal and shake to mix. Add oil and shake again.

YIELD: About 3/4 cup

HORSERADISH DRESSING

Preparation: 5 min.
Chilling: 30 min.

1/2 pt. sour cream
1/2 pt. mayonnaise
1 tbsp. sherry
1 tbsp. lemon juice
horseradish to taste
salt to taste

Mix all ingredients until smooth. Chill at least 30 min. Correct seasoning just before serving. Serve on molded salads.

MASON JAR DRESSING

Preparation: 10 min.

1/4 c. sugar
2 tsp. dry mustard
2 tsp. salt
1/4 tsp. paprika
1/8 tsp. black pepper
1-1/2 tbsp. Worcestershire
1 tsp. onion juice
1 can cream of tomato soup
1-1/2 c. oil
1/2 c. wine vinegar (scant)
basil or other herbs to taste

Combine dry ingredients in 1 qt. mason jar. Add soup, oil and vinegar slowly. Shake vigorously to mix.

YIELD: About 1 quart

SALAD DRESSINGS

MAYONNAISE

Preparation: 20 min.
Cooling: 30 min.

3/4 c. water
3/4 c. vinegar
2 eggs, beaten
5 tsp. flour
4 tbsp. sugar
1 tsp. salt
1 tsp. dry mustard
2 c. sour cream

In a medium saucepan, bring water and vinegar to a boil. In a medium bowl add flour, sugar, salt and dry mustard to eggs. Stir in half the boiling mixture. Stir and mix into remaining boiling mixture. Bring to boil again stirring constantly for no more than 1 min. Cool 30 min. Stir sour cream into cooled mixture. Cover and store in refrigerator.

YIELD: Approx. 1 quart

ROQUEFORT CREAM DRESSING

Preparation: 5 min.

3/4 c. olive oil
2 tbsp. wine vinegar
3 tbsp. cream
1/2 clove garlic
1/4" slice of onion
3 oz. Roquefort cheese
1 tsp. salt
1/2 tsp. pepper
dash cayenne

Put all ingredients into a blender in the order given. Blend for 30 sec. For lumpy dressing blend only half the cheese. Mash the rest and add later. Keep refrigerated. Dressing solidifies as it chills but readily softens at room temperature.

YIELD: 1-3/4 cups

SALAD DRESSING

Preparation: 15 min.
Chilling: 30 min.

3/4 c. salad oil
1/4 c. wine vinegar
1 tbsp. lemon juice
1 tbsp. ketchup
1 tbsp. grated onion
1 clove garlic, minced
1/2 tsp. dry mustard
1 tsp. salt
1-1/4 tsp. sugar
2 tsp. Tabasco
1 c. mayonnaise

Blend all ingredients except mayonnaise for 3 min. in electric blender. Add mayonnaise and blend another 3 min. Chill at least 30 min.

NOTE: Serve with cold vegetables.

SALAD DRESSINGS

SOUR CREAM DRESSING

Preparation: 5 min.

1/2 tsp. salt
1 tsp. sugar
dash cayenne pepper
a few good grinds of black pepper
1/2 tbsp. lemon juice
1 tbsp. cider vinegar
1/2 c. sour cream

Mix salt, sugar, cayenne and pepper. Add lemon juice and vinegar and beat until smooth. Add sour cream and beat again until dressing is well-mixed.

YIELD: 1/2 cup

SPICY LOW CALORIE FRENCH DRESSING

Preparation: 15 min.
Chilling: 1 hr.

1/2 c. water
1/2 c. red wine vinegar
2 tsp. cornstarch
1 tsp. lemon juice
1/4 tsp. paprika
1/2 tsp. dry mustard
1-1/2 tsp. salt
pepper to taste
chopped herbs to taste

Bring water and vinegar to boiling point and remove from heat. Add cornstarch, dissolved in lemon juice. Heat over low flame, stirring to a boil. Remove from heat. Beat in other ingredients. Cool and chill.

YIELD: 1 cup

SWEET SALAD DRESSING

Preparation: 10 min.

1-1/2 c. sugar
2 tsp. salt
2 tsp. dry mustard
2/3 c. vinegar
3 tbsp. onion juice
2 c. salad oil (not olive)
3 tbsp. poppy seeds

With electric blender at medium speed mix sugar, mustard, salt and vinegar. Add onion juice and mix thoroughly. Add oil slowly blending constantly until thickened. Add poppy seeds and blend a few more min. Keep refrigerated.

YIELD: Approx. 3 cups

NOTE: Use on fresh grapefruit sections, avocados, bananas, Boston lettuce, pears or other fruit.

SAUCES

BEARNAISE SAUCE

Preparation: 15 min.

2 egg yolks
2 tbsp. lemon juice
1 tbsp. water
6 tbsp. butter
1 tsp. chopped parsley
1 tsp. chopped tarragon
1/2 tsp. salt
paprika

Mix egg yolks, lemon juice and water in a cold pan. Add butter, parsley and tarragon and stir constantly over low heat until thickened. Season with salt and paprika. Do not let mixture get too hot. Serve warm.

YIELD: 3/4 cup

CREAM CHEESE HOLLANDAISE

Preparation: 15 min.

6 oz. cream cheese
2 egg yolks
2 tbsp. lemon juice
1/2 tsp. mustard
salt and pepper to taste

Melt cheese in top of double boiler. Add remaining ingredients and beat until well-blended. Serve hot or at room temperature.

YIELD: 3/4 cup

HOLLANDAISE SAUCE

Preparation: 30 min.
Cooking: 10 min.

1/4 lb. butter
3 egg yolks
2 tbsp. lemon juice
salt to taste

Cut butter into small pieces and put in top of double boiler. Let stand at room temperature for 30 min. Add egg yolks and lemon juice. Put over simmering water which does not touch bottom of double boiler. Stir constantly until thickened. Season to taste.

YIELD: 3/4 cup

INSTANT BLENDER HOLLANDAISE

Preparation: 10 min.

7 egg yolks
4 tbsp. lemon juice
1/2 tsp. salt
dash cayenne
1 c. butter, melted

In blender, combine egg yolks, lemon juice, salt and cayenne. Cover. Turn motor on and off once quickly. At high speed gradually and steadily add hot butter. Serve immediately, or keep warm by putting blender container in 2" hot water.

YIELD: 2 cups

SAUCES

MOCK MORNAY SAUCE

Preparation: 5 min.
Cooking: 10 min.

1/2 med. onion, grated
1 tbsp. butter
1 can cream of mushroom soup
1/2 soup-can milk
1/2 soup-can light cream
1 tsp. dry mustard
3/4 tsp. Worcestershire
1 tbsp. sherry
salt and pepper to taste

In saucepan saute onion in butter. Add remaining ingredients and stir over low heat until thickened. Add more milk or cream if desired.

YIELD: 2-1/2 cups

MORNAY SAUCE

Preparation: 5 min.
Cooking: 10 min.

1/2 med. onion, grated
2 tsp. butter
2 tsp. flour
1/2 c. milk
1 c. cream
1 tsp. dry mustard
1/2 tsp. Worcestershire
1 tbsp. sherry
salt and pepper to taste

In a saucepan saute onion in butter. Add remaining ingredients and cook over low heat, stirring constantly, until thickened. Add more milk or cream if desired.

YIELD: 1-1/2 cups

PEAR CHUTNEY

Preparation: 40 min.
Cooking: 2 hr.
Mellowing: 2 mos.

4-1/2 lb. ripe pears
1/2 c. minced green peppers
1-1/2 c. seeded raisins
2-1/2 c. brown sugar
1 c. crystallized ginger, in sml. pieces
3 c. cider vinegar
1/2 tsp. salt
1/2 tsp. ground cloves
1 c. water
1/2 tsp. cinnamon
1/4 tsp. nutmeg
1/4 tsp. allspice
6 bay leaves
1/2 c. liquid pectin

Pare, core and slice pears. Mix with green peppers, raisins, sugar, ginger, vinegar, salt and water. In a cheesecloth bag, tie securely cinnamon, nutmeg, allspice and bay leaves. Add to pears and simmer until pears are tender and mixture is thick, about 2 hr. Remove bag, add liquid pectin and boil 1 min. Pour at once into jars for storing. Store for at least 2 months since sauce requires mellowing.

YIELD: 2-3/4 quarts

SAUCES

WHITE SAUCE-MEDIUM

Preparation: 15 min.

1/4 c. butter
1/4 c. flour
2 c. milk
salt and pepper to taste

In saucepan, slowly melt butter. Remove from heat. Add flour and stir until smooth. Add milk a little at a time stirring constantly. Return to medium heat and bring to boil, stirring constantly. Reduce heat and simmer 1 min.

YIELD: 2 cups

WHITE SAUCE (BECHAMEL)

Preparation: 10 min.

TO MAKE 2 CUPS mix the following over low heat until thickened:

THIN: 2 tbsp. melted butter and 2 tbsp. flour with 2 cups milk (consistency of thin soup)

MEDIUM: 3 tbsp. melted butter and 3 tbsp. flour with 2 cups milk (consistency of thick cream soup)

THICK: 8 tbsp. melted butter and 8 tbsp. flour with 2 cups milk (consistency of hot cooked cereal)

FOR VARIATIONS BELOW stir in the added ingredients:

CHANTILLY: 2 c. med. white sauce plus 1/2 c. heavy cream, whipped

CREAM SAUCE: 2 c. med. white sauce plus 1/2 c. heavy cream

MORNAY: 2 c. med. white sauce plus: 2 egg yolks, 2 tbsp. heavy cream, 2 tbsp. grated Parmesan cheese

VELOUTE SAUCE (BLOND): same as white sauce except stock or broth is used in place of milk.

SMITAINE SAUCE: 1-1/2 c. med. veloute sauce plus: 1 tbsp. butter, 1/4 c. chopped onion, 1/3 c. dry white wine, 1/2 c. sour cream.

ADD SALT AND PEPPER TO TASTE FOR EACH SAUCE.

EXOTICA

EXOTICA

EARTH TART

Select 64 sq. centimeters of fine loam. Sift, removing detritus. Place in large pan. Add 1 cup lukewarm water. Season with pinch of salt and dash of oregano. Preheat oven to 348 degrees and bake for 35 min.

To make crust:

Rinse in cold water, then pat dry with paper towel:
    4 c. finely chopped Kentucky lawn
Add: 2 tbsp. arrowroot
       1/2 c. Neat's Foot Oil

Divide equally into 6 parts and roll on floured board until 1/4" thick. Line 6 tart tins with rolled pastry and prick sides and bottom. Place in oven and cook for 25 min. at 372 degrees. Cool for 10 min. Add filling, sprinkle with paprika and bake at 425 degrees for 35 min. Let cool.

GLAZE A LA ATLANTIC BEACH HOTEL (opt.)

1 c. confectioners' pebbles
1/4 c. water
dash of cinnamon
Stir until smooth. Glaze cooled tarts.
Return to oven 2-5 min. at 274 degrees.

NOTE: Some settling of contents normally occurs during handling and shipping.

EXOTICA

TO PRESERVE LOVE

Of Love, first take two glowing fruits.
    Remove the rind of Doubt:
And all the seeds of Discontent
    and Jealousy take out.

Next, add the spice of Thoughtfulness,
    The salt of Constancy,
The essence of Devotion, and
    The oil of Harmony.

Pour in a quart of Merriment,
    And spirits of Good Cheer,
Then add two teaspoonsful of Wit,
    And mix til they adhere.

Carefully strain all troubles out
    With Courage, Tact and Art;
And serve it up, forevermore,
    Warm-simmering in the Heart.

            Anonymous, ca. 1859

HOW TO PRESERVE A HUSBAND

    Be careful in your selection. They are better if not too fresh. Some choose them young, others want them old, but this is a matter of personal taste. DO NOT BOIL. Many insist on keeping them in hot water, but this always makes them sour and hard. Be careful not to chill with indifference. Instead, keep them warm with sunshine and smiles. Even the poor varieties may be made sweet, tender and good if spiced with essence of love and a dash of play.
    If treated this way, they will last for years.

EXOTICA

SCRIPTURE CAKE

1 c. Judges 5:25
3-1/2 c. I Kings 4:22
3 c. Jeremiah 6:20
2 c. I Samuel 30:12
1 c. Genesis 24:17
1 c. Genesis 43:11
6 c. Isaiah 10:14
1 tbsp. Exodus 16:21
pinch of Leviticus 16:13
to taste I Kings 10:10
2 tbsp. I Corinthians 5:6

Follow Solomon's directions in Proverbs 23:14 and bake 350 degrees for 1 hr.

HOMEMADE SOAP

HOMEMADE SOAP — with a healthy respect for the treatment of lye — please.

Boil any mixture of fats in twice the amount of water for 20 min. to eliminate salt. Measure 6 lb. skimmed off the top when chilled. (Particles will have settled in the bottom.) Use ONLY enamelware from here on.

Slowly empty a can of lye into 5 c. cold water in an enamel saucepan out-of-doors. Stir with wooden spoon with long handle, which is to be kept for this purpose, only.

Warm 6 lb. fat in enamel pail until liquid, not fat. Add lye and water mixture when tepid, not hot. Stir with the same wooden spoon until mixture starts to thicken. Pour into enamel roasting pan and let set until it leaves the edges of the pan (about 2 days).

Cut in any desired size with sharp knife.

NOTE: A flat carton or solid wooden box may be substituted for enamel roasting pan, but mixture must be cooler and more solid if this method is used.

MEASUREMENTS SHOULD BE EXACT.

EXOTICA

AGNUM TARPEIANUM

From Marcus Apicius, a food-lover of ancient Rome.

Antequam coquatur, ornatus consuitur. Piper, rutam, satureiam, cepam, thymum modicum. Et liquamine collues agnum, macerabis in furno in patella, quae oleum habet. Cum percoxerit, perfundes in patellam impensam, teres satureiam, cepam, rutam, dactylos, liquamon, vinum caroenum, oleum. Cum bene duxerit impensam, in disco pones, piper asperges et inferes.

DULCE DE LECHE

South American Sweet

3 litros de leche
3/4 kilos de azucar

Modo de hacer dulce de leche:

En 3 litros de leche 3/4 kilos de azucar. Hacer hervir en fuerte hasta que tome la consistencia necesaria para que al dejar caer una gota en un plato, que de pegada. Generalmente a los 40 minutos esta a pumto. Revolver con cudiaro de madera hasta que se enfrie. Asi se hace el duce en la provincia de Salt (Uruguay).

PERDRIX AU CHOU

D'abord, allez chasser votre perdrix!

Mettez le chou, coupe en quartiers, dans de l'eau bouillante non salee. Laissez bouillir environ 20 minutes (2 livres de chou par perdrix).
Pendant que le chou blanchit, mettez dans une casserole un morceau de beurre (2 oz. par perdrix). Faites blondir le beurre et mettez-y du porc sale coupe en petits morceaux. Quand le porc sera bien dore (2 oz. par perdrix) ajoutez les perdrix. Faites rotir lentement, ajoutez le chou bien egoutte et de petits ognons (6 par perdrix), salez avec precaution a cause du porc. Couvrez la casserole et laissez cuire a feu doux pendant 1-1/2 heures ou plus.

EXOTICA

SOMERSET ROOK PIE WITH FIGGY PASTRY

6 rooks, skinned
weak stock
pieces of fat bacon
   cut in chunks
salt and pepper to taste

FOR THE PASTE:

1 lb. flour
1/2 lb. fat
4 oz. currants
4 oz. raisins
salt and pepper to taste

Preparation: 2 hr.
Soaking: Overnight:
Cooking: 3 hr.

Bake rooks using only legs and breasts as all other parts are bitter. Soak overnight in salted water. In the morning, drain brine and put meat in a good-size pie dish, adding bacon. Cover with stock and soak well, adding salt and pepper.

Rub fat well into flour, adding salt, pepper, currants and raisins. Mix well and add sufficient water to make a stiff paste. Roll out to 3/4" thick and place over pie, letting it come well over the sides. Place a piece of wax paper over pie and a pudding cloth on top. Tie well down and see that water has no chance of getting in. Place in kettle with water to cover. Do not put pie in until water is boiling. Cook 3 hr. Serve with gooseberry jelly.

BLACK PUDDING

1 qt. fresh pig's blood
1 qt. skimmed milk
1 c. rice
1/2 loaf bread, cut
   into cubes
1 c. barley
1/2 lb. fresh beef suet
2-3 handfuls oatmeal
salt and pepper to taste
dried mint to taste

Place the bread in a large pie plate. Pour milk over and place in 200 degree oven to warm gently. Do not allow to get too hot. Have the blood ready in a large bowl and pour into the warm bread and milk. Prepare rice and barley by basting with water and cooking well in a 300 degree oven. Add this to the blood mixture as well, then add grated beef suet and stir in oatmeal. Season. Put into well-greased baking pans up to three-fourths full. Bake at 350 degrees until cooked through.

RECIPE CONTRIBUTORS

*Asterisks indicate those who tested recipes for this book.

Mrs. Thomas Ackerman	Laurel Hollow, N.Y.
Miss Mimi Adams	Cambridge, Mass.
Mrs. William H. Adams	Lawrence, N.Y.
Mr. Anthony J. Alexandre	New Canaan, Conn.
Mrs. Anthony J. Alexandre	New Canaan, Conn.
Mrs. Lawrence Alexandre	Radnor, Pa.
Mrs. Benjamin R. Allison	Hewlett, N.Y.
Mr. Zinn Arthur	Cedarhurst, N.Y.
Mrs. Joseph Atkinson	Atlantic Beach, N.Y.
Mr. Crowell Baker	Lawrence, N.Y.
* Mrs. Crowell Baker	Lawrence, N.Y.
Mr. Frank C. Baker	New York, N.Y.
Miss Alice Baldridge	Lawrence, N.Y.
Mrs. Robert Baldridge	Lawrence, N.Y.
Mr. Montague Ball	Hewlett, N.Y.
Miss Louise Bancroft	Ocean City, N.J.
Mr. Anthony V. Barber	Tuxedo Park, N.Y.
Mrs. Robert Baur	Woodmere, N.Y.
Mr. Frank Behne	Lynbrook, N.Y.
Mrs. Frank Behne	Lynbrook, N.Y.
Mrs. Charles Benedict	New York, N.Y.
* Mrs. Donald Benkhart	Lawrence, N.Y.
Mrs. E. Patrick Bernuth	Lawrence, N.Y.
Mr. John C. Bierwirth	Lawrence, N.Y.
Mrs. John C. Bierwirth	Lawrence, N.Y.
Mrs. John E. Bierwirth	Lawrence, N.Y.
Miss Susan Bierwirth	Lawrence, N.Y.
Mrs. James D. Bloodworth	Texarkana, Tex.
Mrs. Steven P. Borner	Bedford, N.Y.
Mrs. C. Warren Bowring	Lawrence, N.Y.
* Mrs. William B. Bowring	Lawrence, N.Y.
Mrs. L. Lincoln Brown	Winslow, Me.
Mrs. Peter C. Browne	Lawrence, N.Y.
Mrs. William H. N. Brune	Raybrook, N.Y.
Mrs. David R. Bundy	Washington, D.C.
Mrs. Adrian P. Burke, Jr.	Lawrence, N.Y.
Miss Jane Ellen Burt	Hewlett, N.Y.
Mrs. Frederic G. Cammann	New York, N.Y.
Mr. Marsden B. Candler	Lawrence, N.Y.
Mrs. Marsden B. Candler	Lawrence, N.Y.
Mrs. Howard Cantus	San Juan, Puerto Rico
* Mrs. David H. Carnahan Sr.	Lawrence, N.Y.
Mrs. Edward N. Carpenter	Lawrence, N.Y.
* Mrs. Ryland E. D. Chase	Lawrence, N.Y.
* Mrs. John H. Claiborne, Jr.	Lawrence, N.Y.
Mrs. John H. Claiborne III	Arlington Heights, Ill.
Miss Patricia Claiborne	Lawrence, N.Y.
Mr. Ralph M. Clark	Danbury, Conn.

RECIPE CONTRIBUTORS

Mrs. Ralph M. Clark	Danbury, Conn.
Mrs. Timothy Clark	Milford, Conn.
* Mrs. Henry E. Coe III	Lawrence, N.Y.
Mrs. C. Payson Coleman	Lawrence, N.Y.
Mrs. George Conroy	Oceanside, N.Y.
* Mrs. John Conway	Lawrence, N.Y.
Mrs. Robert F. Corroon	Lawrence, N.Y.
Mrs. A. P. Cousins, Jr.	Old Square, Va.
Mrs. Rosemary Crane	Saugus, Cal.
Mrs. Warren Crunden	Lawrence, N.Y.
Mrs. Henry A. Dall	Saranac Lake, N.Y.
Mrs. Stewart M. Dall	Lawrence, N.Y.
* Mrs. Daniel Davis	Hewlett, N.Y.
Mrs. Lewis L. Delafield	Hewlett, N.Y.
Mrs. Julie Denison	Atlantic Beach, N.Y.
* Mrs. William D. Denson	Lawrence, N.Y.
Mrs. Duncan Devereux	Virginia Beach, Va.
* Mrs. Peter DiCapua	Lawrence, N.Y.
* Mrs. Lawrence Dilg	Garden City, N.Y.
* Mrs. Camilla Dinan	Lawrence, N.Y.
* Mrs. Courtlandt P. Dixon, Jr.	Lawrence, N.Y.
Mrs. Jonathan W. Dodge, Jr.	Los Angeles, Cal.
Mrs. Parke Doland	New London, Conn.
Mrs. John Doody	Lawrence, N.Y.
Mr. John Doody, Jr.	Lawrence, N.Y.
Mrs. Walter B. Eaton	New York, N.Y.
Mr. Robert V. Edgar	Concord, N.H.
Mrs. William Edgar, Jr.	Geneva, Switzerland
Mrs. Robert Edmunds	New York, N.Y.
* Mrs. Ralph J. Edsell, Jr.	Lawrence, N.Y.
Mrs. Ethel O. Elwell	Lawrence, N.Y.
* Mrs. John M. Emery	Lawrence, N.Y.
Mrs. Robert Fear	Southampton, N.Y.
Mrs. Peter J. Ferrara	Cornwall, N.Y.
Mrs. Clark M. Fosdick	Woodmere, N.Y.
Miss Hilary Fowler	Lawrence, N.Y.
Mrs. Albert Francke, Jr.	New York, N.Y.
Mr. Albert Francke III	New York, N.Y.
Mrs. Robert Freeman	Atlantic Beach, N.Y.
Mrs. Alfred Galka	Hewlett, N.Y.
Miss Laurey Galka	Hewlett, N.Y.
Mrs. Shockley Gamage	Woodmere, N.Y.
Miss Susan Gamage	New York, N.Y.
Mr. Howard X. Geoghegan, Jr.	Coconut Grove, Fla.
Mrs. Howard X. Geoghegan, Jr.	Coconut Grove, Fla.
Mrs. Peter Gilmour	Victoria, Australia
Miss Linda Gleig	Hewlett, N.Y.
Mrs. Robert Goner	Atlantic Beach, N.Y.

RECIPE CONTRIBUTORS

Mrs. Robert Goodale, Jr.	Minneapolis, Minn.
Mrs. F. Abbot Goodhue	Hewlett, N.Y.
Mrs. Michael D. Grant, Jr.	Lawrence, N.Y.
Mrs. David Green	Montclair, N.J.
Mrs. Ehler O. Gregory	Woodmere, N.Y.
Mr. Henry S. Grew	Dublin, N.H.
Mrs. Chalmers Handy	Lawrence, N.Y.
Mrs. William F. Haneman	Woodmere, N.Y.
Mrs. William F. Haneman, Jr.	Bronxville, N.Y.
Mrs. Alden Hatch	Sarasota, Fla.
Mrs. Geoffrey Hazard	New Haven, Conn.
Mrs. Daniel Healy	Woodmere, N.Y.
Mrs. Lawrence S. Heath, Jr.	Lawrence, N.Y.
Mrs. Harold E. Herrick, Jr.	Lawrence, N.Y.
Mrs. N. Lawrence Herrick, Jr.	Weston, Conn.
Miss Carolyn Hewlett	New York, N.Y.
Mr. Frederick V. W. Hewlett, Jr.	Woodmere, N.Y.
Mrs. Frederick V. W. Hewlett, Jr.	Woodmere, N.Y.
Mrs. Roger S. Hewlett	Woodmere, N.Y.
Mrs. G. Dana Hicks	Lawrence, N.Y.
Mrs. Harold Hild	Delray Beach, Fla.
Miss Verlinde Hill	Glen Coe, Md.
Mrs. George Hobson, Jr.	Granby, Conn.
Mrs. Townsend Hoen	Cockeysville, Md.
Mrs. E. Williams Holmes	Lawrence, N.Y.
The Rev. E. Donald Hood	Hewlett, N.Y.
Mrs. Lester Horne	Far Rockaway, N.Y.
Mrs. Martin McG. Horner	Lawrence, N.Y.
Mrs. Norman P. Hunte	Rochdale Village, N.Y.
Mrs. Sue Tidy Hurst	London, England
Mrs. Frank Hutchison	Polson, Mont.
* Mrs. Seton Ijams	Lawrence, N.Y.
Mrs. Maynard C. Ivison	New York, N.Y.
Mrs. George B. Jackson	Lawrence, N.Y.
Mrs. Jervis S. Janney	Dayton, Ohio
Mrs. Patricia Johnson	Far Rockaway, N.Y.
Mr. Ward L. Johnson	Cocoa Beach, Fla.
Mr. Robert N. Kay	Fitchburg, Mass.
* Mrs. Robert N. Kay	Fitchburg, Mass.
Mrs. H. Donnelly Keresey	New York, N.Y.
* Mrs. James B. Ketcham	Lawrence, N.Y.
Mrs. William T. Ketcham	Lawrence, N.Y.
Mrs. Harold N. Kingsland	Woodmere, N.Y.
Mrs. Howard S. Kniffin	Lawrence, N.Y.
Mrs. William Koch	Inwood, N.Y.
Mrs. Richard S. Koehne	Sutton, Vt.
* Miss Linda Krummel	Valley Stream, N.Y.
Mrs. Alfred N. Lawrence	Lawrence, N.Y.

RECIPE CONTRIBUTORS

Mrs. James H. LeFeaver, Jr.	Chevy Chase, Md.
Mrs. Jessie M. Linicus	Wethersfield, Conn.
Miss Julia Littlefield	New York, N.Y.
Mr. Charles Lovering	Woodmere, N.Y.
Mrs. Alden R. Ludlow	Lawrence, N.Y.
Mrs. G. Philip Lynch	Lawrence, N.Y.
Mrs. Simon Lynn	Lawrence, N.Y.
Mr. David McCallum	New York, N.Y.
Mrs. Donald R. McGuirk	Bronxville, N.Y.
Mrs. Robert M. McLane	Locust Valley, N.Y.
* Mrs. Michael T. McNichols	Lawrence, N.Y.
Mrs. Edward C. MacEachron	Morrisville, Vt.
Miss Leith MacLean	Washington, D.C.
* Mrs. Malcolm O. MacLean	Lawrence, N.Y.
* Mrs. Clarence L. MacNelly	Lawrence, N.Y.
Mrs. Charles R. Martin	Winnetka, Ill.
Mrs. John Mel	Santa Cruz, Cal.
Miss Lucinda Mellen	Lawrence, N.Y.
Mrs. Stanley W. Merrell	Darien, Conn.
Mrs. Lewis Merrill	Westport, Conn.
Mrs. Schuyler Merritt II	Lawrence, N.Y.
Mrs. Daniel Millett	Lawrence, N.Y.
Mrs. Paul E. Monath	Skillman, N.J.
Mrs. Daniel L. Monroe	Lawrence, N.Y.
Mrs. Hugh Montgomery	Lookout Mountain, Tenn.
Mrs. John A. Morris	New York, N.Y.
Mr. L. Van B. Morris	Lawrence, N.Y.
* Mrs. Mandeville Mullally	Lawrence, N.Y.
* Mrs. Arthur M. Murray, Jr.	Woodmere, N.Y.
Mrs. Matthew T. Murray	New York, N.Y.
* Mrs. Morgan T. Murray	Lawrence, N.Y.
New York without Tears	New York, N.Y.
Mrs. Frank Nielsen	Pompano Beach, Fla.
* Ninth Grade Gourmets	Hewlett, N.Y.
Mrs. Richard Oller	Belvedere, Cal.
Miss Elizabeth Oller	Belvedere, Cal.
Mrs. Shelby Page	Lawrence, N.Y.
Mrs. Trevor Pardee	Huntington, N.Y.
Mrs. Andrew Perni	Woodmere, N.Y.
Mrs. Robert Pike	Lawrence, N.Y.
* Mrs. Peter Posmantur	Lawrence, N.Y.
Mrs. Joseph Pratt II	Farmington, Conn.
Mrs. Richard J. Prentiss	Hewlett, N.Y.
Mrs. William F. Prescott	East Islip, N.Y.
Miss Ann Quinton	Hewlett, N.Y.
Mrs. Willis L. M. Reese	Hewlett, N.Y.
* Mrs. Edgar B. Robbins	Atlantic Beach, N.Y.
Mrs. Powell Robinson	Morristown, N.J.

RECIPE CONTRIBUTORS

* Mrs. William Roth	Atlantic Beach, N.Y.
* Mrs. John A. Rutter	Lawrence, N.Y.
Mrs. John T. Savage	Lawrence, N.Y.
* Mrs. Arthur Scharf	Hewlett, N.Y.
Mrs. Toby Schoyer	St. Croix, V.I.
Mrs. William G. T. Shedd, Jr.	Fairfield, Conn.
Mrs. Richard Silver	Far Rockaway, N.Y.
Mrs. Paul Singstad	New York, N.Y.
Mrs. Robert N. Sloan	Lawrence, N.Y.
Miss Anna M. Smith	Croyers, N.Y.
Mrs. George B. Smith	Freeport, N.Y.
Mrs. Morton Spinner	North Woodmere, N.Y.
Mrs. John L. Squire	Lawrence, N.Y.
Mrs. Foye F. Staniford, Jr.	New York, N.Y.
Mrs. David M. Stewart	Wilton, Conn.
Mrs. Clay Stites	South Dartmouth, Mass.
Mrs. Charles R. Supin	Lawrence, N.Y.
Mr. Benjamin Swan	Farmington, Conn.
Mrs. Prentice Talmage	Lawrence, N.Y.
Mr. Ronald Teller	Hewlett, N.Y.
Mrs. T. Redmond Thayer	Asheville, N.C.
Mrs. Roger M. Thomas	Weston, Mass.
* Mrs. McKean Thompson	Lawrence, N.Y.
Mrs. Thomas Thomson	Edinburgh, Scotland
Mrs. James Thornton	New York, N.Y.
Mr. George H. Tilghman	Lawrence, N.Y.
Mrs. Joan A. Tompkins	Lawrence, N.Y.
Mrs. Erich Traugott	Forest Hills, N.Y.
Mrs. Bruce Tucker	Lawrence, N.Y.
Mrs. John H. Tyner	Lawrence, N.Y.
* Mrs. W. James Wade	Lawrence, N.Y.
Mrs. Edward Waesche	Melville, N.Y.
Mrs. George Ward	Lawrence, N.Y.
Mrs. Allen Wardwell	New York, N.Y.
Mrs. Thomas J. Waters	Hingham, Mass.
Miss Toni Waters	Gainesville, Fla.
Mr. Edward T. Weiner	Long Beach, N.Y.
* Mrs. Martin Weiner	Long Beach, N.Y.
Mrs. Herman Weiss	Lawrence, N.Y.
Mrs. William B. White	Woodmere, N.Y.
Mrs. Alexander Whitman	Lawrence, N.Y.
Mr. Frank C. Whittelsey II	Fayeston, Vt.
Mrs. Michael Wiley	Arverne, N.Y.
Mrs. I. T. Williams	Lawrence, N.Y.
Mrs. Lawrence Woolson	Springfield, Vt.
Mrs. Martin Yarvis	Long Beach, N.Y.

INDEX

Numbers in parentheses indicate number of servings.

A

Acorn Squash, Baked (16) 172
Acorn Squash, Baked
    with Pineapple (12) 128
Almond:
    Ball, Cheese (12) 94
    Mold, Strawberry (12) 136
    Salad Dressing 212
    Soup (8) 48
Antipasto Salad (8) 84
Apple:
    Betty (4) 40
    Cake 189
    Crumble (12) 132
    Pancake (4) 40
    Dessert, Scandinavian (8) 92
    Yam Stuffed (12) 123
Applesauce Cake 189
Apricot Cheese Delight (8) 86
Artichokes and Peas (4) 30
Artichoke Soup (12) 98
Asparagus:
    au Fromage (12) 124
    en Casserole (4) 30
    Roll-up (16) 138
    Salad, and Carrot (12) 130
    Tomatoes, stuffed with (12) 131
Aspic, Tomato (8) 85
Avocado:
    Guacamole (12) 94
    Mold (8) 84
    Mold (12) 130
    Mousse (4) 36
    Soup (4) 8
    Soup (8) 48
    Stuffed with Chicken (12) 112
    Stuffed with Crabmeat (16) 160

B

Banana Bread 182
Banana Dessert (12) 132
Banana Fritters (8) 78
Barbecue Chicken (4) 18
Barbecue Lamb, Butterfly (12) 106
Bars, Cinnamon 209
Batter Bread 182
Beans:
    Baked, Pressure Cooker (12) ...124
    Black, Soup, Zaragozana (16) ...143
    Green, in Mustard Sauce (12) ...124
    Green, Lively (4) 30
    Green, Salad (8) 85
    Italian (8) 78
    Lima, Curried (12) 125
    Lima Roquefort Salad (4) 37
    Salad, Zippy (16) 174
    Soup, and Zucchini (12) 101
    String, Deluxe (16) 170
    String, Puree (8) 78
    Texas (12) 125
Bearnaise Sauce 216
Bechamel Sauce 218
Beef:
    Bourguignon (12) 103
    Cabbage, stuffed with (8) 52
    Cabbage, stuffed with (12) 103
    Casserole (20) 154
    Casserole, Divine (12) 105
    Casserole, Oriental
        Hamburger (16) 147
    Chili Bowl (12) 104
    Chowder, Hamburg (12) 100
    Dried Deluxe (16) 149
    Goulasche-Suppe (8) 54
    Goulash, Good (16) 149
    Goulash, Imperial (16) 149
    Hash, Texas (16) 150
    Lasagne (30) 205
    Manicotti, Baked (12) 102
    Meat Loaf, Different (12) 104
    Meat Loaf, Turkish (4) 13
    Meat Loaf, with Blue Cheese (16) 146
    Meatballs, Baked (16) 146
    Meatballs, California (16) 146
    Meatballs, Saucepot (4) 13
    Meatballs, Swedish (12) 105
    Meatballs, Sweet and Sour (8) ...55
    Meatballs, Sweet and Sour (12) ...97
    Meatballs, Sweet and Sour (16) ..141
    Milanese and Noodles (4) 12
    Parmigiana, Eggplant (8) 52
    Piccadillo (8) 55
    Puffs, Meat and Vegetable (8) ...45
    Roast, Cocktail Party (16) 148
    Roast, Inebriated (4) 13
    Roast, Pot, Dinah's (8) 54
    Roll, Stuffed (4) 14
    Roll-ups (8) 52
    Sandwich, Quick Dip (4) 14
    Sauce, Hearty Italian Meat (16) ..148
    Sauce, Uncle Peter's Meat (12) ..105
    Soup, Vegetable and Barley (16) .142
    Steak, Flank, with
        Howard's Sauce (16) 150

Beef . . . Continued
- Steak, Salisbury (4) 14
- Steak, Tartare (16) 141
- Stew (8) 53
- Stew, Burgundy (16) 150
- Stew, Gaston (8) 53
- Stew, Monte's (16) 151
- Stew, Oven (12) 104
- Stroganoff (12) 102
- Stroganoff, Hamburger (16) 147
- Trittini (20) 154
- Zucchini, Stuffed with (4) 12

Beets:
- a la Schultz (8) 78
- Buttered, Spiced (12) 125
- in Sour Cream (4) 30
- Pickled (16) 170

Black Bean Soup, Zaragozana (16) . . 143
Black Forest Cherry Cake 190
Blue Cheese Salad Dressing 212
Blueberry Coffeecake 182
Boeuf Bourguignon (12) 103
Bourekakia (12) 94

Breads: 182-188
- Banana 182
- Batter 182
- Blueberry Coffeecake 182
- Coffeecake 183
- Corn 183
- Cranberry Orange 183
- Crullers 184
- Crunchy Granola 184
- Grandmother's Holiday Nut 185
- Herb Seasoned Dinner Rolls 184
- Herb Toast 185
- Herbed Garlic 185
- Holiday Squash 186
- Homemade 188
- Nut Brown 186
- Scones 186
- Spoon 187
- The Pancake 188
- Wheat 187
- White 187
- Yorkshire Pudding 188

Bread Pudding (12) 132

Broccoli:
- Noodle Casserole (16) 169
- Filling for Crepes (16) 164
- Ring (12) 130
- Soup, Cream of (4) 8
- Stack-ups, Tomato (16) 170

Broth, Chicken (8) 49
Brownie Cake 191
Brownies, Butterscotch 209
Brussels Sprouts and Cauliflower (8) . 79
Brussels Sprouts, Party (12) 126
Brussels Sprouts, Souffle (4) 31
Brussels Sprouts
 with Chestnuts (16) 170
Butter Cookies 201
Butterscotch Brownies 209
Butterscotch Crunch (8) 86

C

Cabbage:
- Coleslaw (8) 85
- Stuffed with Beef (8) 52
- Stuffed with Beef (12) 103

Cakes: 189-200
- Apple 189
- Applesauce 189
- Brownie 191
- Carrot 191
- Cheesecake 191, 192
- Cherry, Black Forest 190
- Chiffon, Party 197
- Chocolate, Mocha Layer 192
- Christmas 193
- Fairy 193
- Fudge 194
- Italian Cream 195
- Molasses 195
- Nixies Cupcake 196
- Nusstorte 196
- Prune 197
- Red Velvet 198
- Rum 198
- Sauerkraut 199
- Shortcake, Strawberry 194
- Torte, Sacher 199
- Upside-down Pineapple 200
- Wacky 200

Calf's Liver Milanese (4) 16
Calf's Liver, Speedy Pate (4) 7

Carrots:
- Cake 191
- Deviled (12) 126
- Glazed (12) 128
- Marinated (8) 79
- Salad, and Asparagus (12) 130
- Souffle (4) 31
- Soup (8) 48

Casseroles, Beef:
- and Noodles Milanese (4) 12
- Chili Bowl (12) 104
- Company Beef (20) 154
- Divine (12) 105
- Dried Deluxe (16) 149
- Good Goulash (16) 149
- Goulasche Suppe (8) 54
- Hamburger Stroganoff (16) 147
- Imperial Goulash (16) 149
- Oriental Hamburger (16) 147
- Piccadillo (8) 55
- Stroganoff (12) 102
- Texas Hash (16) 150
- Trittini (30) 154

231

Casseroles, Chicken:
  a l'Orange (4) 18
  and Artichoke au Gratin (8) 61
  and Lamb Algerique (8) 62
  Asopao (12) 110
  Baked (16) 156
  Baked and Sherried (12) 110
  Breasts and Chipped Beef (4) 18
  Breasts Piquant (4) 19
  Broccoli (12) 110
  Casserole (8) 61
  Casserole (12) 111
  Casserole, Lady Metcalf (12) 112
  Champagne (16) 156
  Hawaiian (16) 157
  in Rose Wine (8) 62
  Maricado (12) 111
  Marsala (4) 20
  Oriental (16) 157
  Patsy's Potpourri (16) 159
  Ronzini (16) 158
  Rosemary (8) 61
  Viva la (12) 113
Casseroles, Crabmeat:
  Baked Seafood (4) 25
  Deviled Seafood (8) 71
  Easy Seafood (16) 162
  Versatile Crab (16) 161
  with Shrimp (16) 162
Casseroles, Ham:
  and Eggplant (8) 56
  and Noodles (16) 151
  and Spinach (8) 55
  Creamy and Mushrooms (16) 165
  Swiss (12) 106
  with Endive (16) 151
Casseroles, Lamb:
  and Artichoke (16) 152
  and Eggplant (4) 15
  Cairo (12) 107
  Curry (8) 56
  Moussaka (8) 56
  Scallop (12) 107
Casseroles, Liver:
  Chicken, in Red Wine (4) 20
  Chicken, in Red Wine (8) 63
  Chicken Marsala (16) 158
Casseroles, Lobster:
  Deviled Seafood (8) 71
  Easy Seafood (16) 162
Casseroles, Salmon:
  Luncheon (16) 161
  Rice (12) 116
Casseroles, Scallops:
  Easy Seafood (16) 162
Casseroles, Shrimp:
  and Crabmeat (16) 162
  Baked Seafood (4) 25

  Casserole (8) 69
  Delight (12) 117
  Deviled Seafood (8) 71
  Jambalaya (8) 69
  Patsy's Potpourri (20) 159
Casseroles, Tuna:
  Easy Seafood (16) 162
Casseroles, Turkey:
  for a Crowd (16) 158
  Rice Gourmet (4) 21
  Tetrazzini (16) 159
Casseroles, Veal:
  and Mushrooms (16) 152
  and Water Chestnuts (12) 109
  Italian, and Peppers (12) 108
  Kidneys (4) 17
  Palarma (12) 109
Cauliflower and Brussels Sprouts (8) .79
Cauliflower, Baked (4) 31
Cauliflower, Chopin (8) 79
Caviar and Cream Cheese (4) 6
Celery Amandine (8) 80
Celery Baked, and Peas (12) 127
Celery, Chinese (12) 126
Celery Root Remoulade (4) 36
Chantilly Sauce 218
Cheese:
  Ball (8) 44
  Ball, Almond (12) 94
  Bits (8) 44
  Bourekakia (12) 94
  Casserole, Fabulous (16) 164
  Cream, and Caviar (4) 6
  Cream, and Crabmeat (8) 45
  Cream, Cookies 201
  Fondue, Swiss (4) 26
  Galettes Lausannoise (12) 118
  Liptauer a la Bartlett (16) 138
  Omelet, Noodle (8) 72
  Pie 204
  Quiche Lorraine (8) 73
  Roll (16) 138
  Salad Dressing, Blue 212
  Salad Dressing, Roquefort 214
  Sandwich, Monte Cristo (4) 27
  Souffle, Ham (4) 26
  Souffle, Overnight (12) 119
  Souffle, Swiss (12) 119
  Soup (16) 143
  Spread, Chutney (4) 6
  Welsh Rarebit (8) 73
Cheesecake 191, 192
Cheesecake, Onion (8) 72
Cherries:
  Cake, Black Forest 190
  Jubilee (16) 178
Chess Pie 204

Chestnut Soup (16) 144
Chicken:
   a la King (16) 165
   a l'Orange (4) 18
   and Artichoke au Gratin (8) 61
   and Lamb Algerique (8) 62
   Asopao (12) 110
   Baked (16) 156
   Baked and Sherried (12) 110
   Balls, Curried (8) 45
   Barbecued (4) 18
   Bermuda (4) 18
   Breasts and Chipped Beef (4) 18
   Breasts in Sauce (8) 60
   Breasts Piquant (4) 19
   Broccoli Casserole (12) 110
   Broth (8) 49
   Casserole (8) 61
   Casserole, Lady Metcalf (12) 112
   Champagne (16) 156
   Cotelettes a la Tourel (8) 63
   Hash a la Ritz (4) 19
   Hawaiian (16) 157
   in Rose Wine (8) 62
   Livers (12) 111
   Liver Casserole (8) 63
   Livers in Red Wine Sauce (4) 20
   Livers, Marsala (16) 158
   Livers, Pate Maison (8) 47
   Maricado (12) 111
   Marsala (4) 20
   Oriental (16) 157
   Paella, Spanish (8) 71
   Patsy's Potpourri (16) 159
   Peachy (16) 157
   Ronzini (16) 158
   Rosemary (8) 61
   Soup, Curried (12) 98
   Stuffed Bantams (8) 60
   Stuffed, in Avocados (12) 112
   Tour d'Argent (4) 20
   Viva la (12) 113
   with Grapes (16) 156
Chiffon Cake, Party 197
Chili Bowl (12) 104
Chocolate:
   Cake, Fudge 194
   Cake, Mocha Layer 192
   Delight (8) 87
   Fondue (8) 87
   Fudge, Margo's 211
   Mousse, Deluxe (16) 178
   Mousse, Quick (4) 42
   Pie, Fudge 204
   Ste. Emilion au (4) 42
   Waffles (4) 41
Choucroute Alsacienne (8) 81
Chowders:
   Clam (4) 8
   Crab Supreme (12) 99
   Hamburg (12) 100

Maine Fish (8) 50
Chutney Cheese Spread (4) 6
Chutney, Pear 217
Cinnamon Bars 209
Clams:
   Alexandre (16) 138
   Baked (12) 94
   Cataplana (8) 66
   Chowder (4) 8
   Dip, Hot (8) 44
   Linguine (8) 66
   Soup, Billi Bi (8) 49
   Steamed (16) 139
   Stuffed (4) 7
Coconut Cookies 201
Coconut Delight Squares 209
Coffee:
   Cake 183
   Cake Blueberry 182
   Cream (8) 87
   Icebox Delight (12) 133
   Souffle (8) 87
Coleslaw (8) 85
Congo Squares 210
Cookies: 201-203
   Butter 201
   Coconut 201
   Cream Cheese 201
   French Lace 202
   Gourmands 202
   Meringue Kisses 203
   Meringue, Overnight 203
   Oatmeal 202
   Shortbread, Scottish 203
Coquilles St. Jacques (8) 68
Corn:
   and Okra (16) 171
   Bread 183
   Pudding (8) 80
   Pudding (16) 171
   Seattle (12) 126
   Soup (12) 98
   Zesty (4) 32
Cornish Hens, Veronique (8) 64
Cottage Cheese Pancakes (4) 26
Crab:
   Alexander (12) 95
   and Cream Cheese (8) 45
   Ball (16) 139
   Canapes (12) 95
   Casserole, Baked Seafood (4) 25
   Casserole, Easy Seafood (16) ... 162
   Casserole, with Shrimp (16) 162
   Chowder Supreme (12) 99
   Cold Paella (16) 163
   Fish Hash (12) 114
   Hollandaise (4) 22
   Imperial (4) 22
   in Avocado (16) 160
   Johnny (12) 114

Crab ... Continued
- Meeting Street (8) 67
- Mousse (8) 67
- Mousse (16) 160
- Ravigote (8) 45
- Souffle (4) 22
- Soup (4) 8
- Soup (16) 144
- Versatile (16) 161

Cranberry Dessert (8) 88
Cranberry Orange Bread 183
Cranberry Walnut Pie 205
Cream Cheese:
- and Caviar (4) 6
- and Crabmeat (8) 45
- Cookies 201
- Hollandaise 216
- Salad, and Tomatoes (16) 176

Cream Sauce 218
Crepes (16) 164
Crepes, Strawberry (16) 180
Crepes Suzette (16) 180
Crullers 184
Cucumber Onion Mold (4) 37
Cucumber Soup (12) 99
Cupcakes, Nixies 196
Curried Dishes:
- Chicken Balls (8) 45
- Fillet of Sole East Indian (4) .. 24
- Fruit (8) 88
- Lamb (8) 56
- Lima Beans au Fromage (12) 125
- Soup, Chicken (12) 98
- Soup, Eggplant (8) 49
- Soup, Spinach (4) 10

Custard, Creamy (4) 41

D

Dandelion Greens (4) 37
Desserts:
- Almond Strawberry Mold (12) ... 136
- Apple Betty (4) 40
- Apple Crumble (12) 132
- Apple Pancake (4) 40
- Apple Scandinavian (8) 92
- Apricot Cheese Delight (8) 86
- Banana Dessert (12) 132
- Butterscotch Crunch (8) 86
- Cakes (listed under Cakes) .. 189-200
- Cherries Jubilee (16) 178
- Chocolate Delight (8) 87
- Chocolate Fondue (8) 87
- Chocolate Mousse, Deluxe (16) .. 178
- Chocolate Mousse, Quick (4) 42
- Chocolate Waffles (4) 41
- Coffee Cream (8) 87
- Coffee Icebox Delight (12) 133
- Coffee Souffle (8) 87
- Cookies (listed under Cookies) 201-203
- Cranberry Dessert (8) 88
- Crepes, Strawberry (16) 180
- Crepes, Suzette (16) 180
- Curried Fruit (8) 88
- Custard, Creamy (4) 41
- English Trifle (12) 133
- Fancy Jell-O (12) 134
- Forgotten Pudding (16) 180
- Fruit Meringue (12) 133
- Grapes Glacee (4) 41
- Ice Cream Mold (8) 88
- Ice Cream Pudding (16) 179
- Ice Cream, Strawberry (12) 136
- Instant Dinner Party Dessert (16) . 179
- La Pyramide (8) 91
- Lemon Bluff (4) 42
- Lemon Dessert (8) 89
- Lemon Mousse (8) 89
- Lemon Souffle (12) 134
- Lemon Souffle with Strawberries (8) 89
- Lemon Sponge (12) 134
- Mocha Dessert (12) 135
- Oranges and Grand Marnier (16) . 178
- Orange Marshmallow (8) 90
- Orange Mold (12) 135
- Peaches Flambe (8) 90
- Peaches in Brandy Sauce (12) .. 135
- Peach Melba, Easy (4) 41
- Pears in Wine (16) 179
- Pies (listed under Pies) 204-208
- Puddings, listed under Puddings.
- Raspberry Charlotte (16) 179
- Raspberry Mousse (8) 91
- Ste. Emilion au Chocolat (4) 42
- Squares 209-211
- Swedish Cream (8) 92
- Zweiback Torte (12) 136

Dips:
- Easy Shrimp (12) 97
- Guacamole (12) 94
- Hot Clam (8) 44

Duck, Wild (8) 65
Duckling, a l'Orange (4) 21

E

Egg Roll (12) 96
Eggplant:
- Baked (12) 127
- Casserole with Ham (8) 56
- Casserole with Lamb (4) 15
- Fried with Yoghurt (8) 80
- Moussaka (8) 56
- Parmigiana, Beef (8) 52
- Soup, Curried (8) 49
- Spicy Tomato (16) 171
- Stuffed with Itself (8) 81

Eggs:
- Benedictine (4) 27

Eggs . . . Continued
　　Escalloped with Ham (12) 118
　　Lisa (4) 27
　　Omelet, Cheese Noodle (8) 72
　　Stuffed with Salmon (4) 6
　　Tomatoes Benedict (8) 73
Endive, Braised (4) 32
Endive, with Ham (16) 151
English Trifle (12) 133
Escarole Soup (4) 9
Exotica: 220-224
　　Agnum Tarpeianum 223
　　Black Pudding 224
　　Dulce de Leche 223
　　Earth Tart 220
　　Homemade Soap 222
　　How to Preserve a Husband 221
　　Perdrix au Chou 223
　　Scripture Cake 222
　　Somerset Rook Pie 224
　　To Preserve Love 221

F

Fettucine Alfredo (8) 74
Fish Chowder, Maine (8) 50
Fish Dish, My Favorite (4) 24
Fish Eyes (4) 6
Fish Hash (12) 114
Fish Pudding, Norwegian (8) 70
Flank Steak
　　with Howard's Sauce (16) 150
Fondue, Chocolate (8) 87
Fondue, Swiss (4) 26
Fritters, Banana (8) 78
Frosting, Mocha 192
Frosting, Quick No-Cook 200
Frosting, Sour Cream 199
Fruit, Curried (8) 88
Fruit Meringue (12) 133
Fruits, listed by name.
Fudge Cake . . . . : 194
Fudge, Margo's 211
Fudge Pie 204

G

Galettes Lausannoise (12) 118
Game Hens Veronique (8) 64
Garlic Bread, Herbed 185
Garlic Grits (8) 77
Garlic Potatoes, Mashed (16) 166
Gazpacho (4) 9
Gazpacho (12) 99
Goulasche Suppe (8) 54
Goulash, Good (16) 149
Goulash, Imperial (16) 149
Gourmands 202
Granola, Crunchy 184
Grapes, Glacee (4) 41
Grasshopper Pie 205

Green Beans:
　　Deluxe (16) 170
　　in Mustard Sauce (12) 124
　　Lively (4) 30
　　Pureed (8) 78
　　Salad (8) 85
　　Salad, Zippy (16) 174
　　Soup, and Zucchini (12) 101
Grits, Garlic (8) 77
Guacamole (12) 94

H

Halibut, Marinated Green (4) 23
Ham:
　　Appetizer (16) 139
　　Baked, with Mustard Glaze (12) . 106
　　Casserole, and Eggplant (8) 56
　　Casserole, and Noodles (16) 151
　　Casserole, and Spinach (8) 55
　　Casserole, Swiss (12) 106
　　Creamy and Mushrooms (16) . . . 165
　　Eggs Lisa (4) 27
　　Escalloped and Eggs (12) 118
　　Puffs, Deviled (12) 95
　　Sandwich, Monte Cristo (4) 27
　　Souffle, Cheese (4) 26
　　Spread, Snow Cap (8) 47
　　Tomatoes Benedict (8) 73
　　with Endive (16) 151
Hamburger:
　　Cabbage Stuffed with (8) 52
　　Cabbage Stuffed with (12) 103
　　Casserole, Divine (12) 105
　　Casserole, Oriental (16) 147
　　Chili Bowl (12) 104
　　Chowder (12) 100
　　Hash, Texas (16) 150
　　Lasagne (30) 155
　　Manicotti, Baked (12) 102
　　Meat Loaf, Different (12) 104
　　Meat Loaf, Turkish (4) 13
　　Meat Loaf with Blue Cheese (16) 146
　　Meatballs, Baked (16) 146
　　Meatballs, California (16) 146
　　Meatballs, Saucepot (4) 13
　　Meatballs, Swedish (12) 105
　　Meatballs, Sweet and Sour (16) . 141
　　Meatballs, Sweet and Sour (12) . . 97
　　Meatballs, Sweet and Sour (8) . . . 55
　　Milanese and Noodles (4) 12
　　Parmigiana, Eggplant (8) 52
　　Piccadillo (8) 55
　　Puffs, Meat and Vegetable (8) 46
　　Sauce, Hearty Italian (16) 148
　　Sauce, Uncle Peter's (12) 105
　　Steak, Salisbury (4) 14
　　Steak Tartare (16) 141

Hamburger . . . Continued
   Stroganoff (16) 147
   Trittini (20) 154
   Zucchini, Stuffed with (4) 12
Hard Sauce (8) 40, 90
Hash, Chicken (4) 19
Hash, Fish (12) 114
Hash, Potato (4) 28
Hash, Texas (16) 150
Hearts of Palm Salad (16) 176
Heath Bar Pie 206
Hollandaise, Cream Cheese 216
Hollandaise, Instant Blender 216
Hollandaise Sauce 216
Hors D'Oeuvres:
   Asparagus Roll-ups (16) 138
   Bourekakia (12) 94
   Cheese-Almond Balls (12) 94
   Cheese Ball (8) 44
   Cheese Bits (8) 44
   Cheese, Chutney Spread (4) 6
   Cheese, Cream and Caviar (4) 6
   Cheese, Liptauer (16) 138
   Cheese Roll (16) 138
   Cherry Tomatoes, Stuffed (12) ... 97
   Chicken Balls, Curried (8) 45
   Clams Alexandre (16) 138
   Clams, Baked (12) 94
   Clam Dip, Hot (8) 44
   Clams, Steamed (16) 139
   Clams, Stuffed (4) 7
   Crabmeat Alexander (12) 95
   Crabmeat and Cream Cheese (8) .. 45
   Crabmeat Ball (16) 139
   Crabmeat Canapes (12) 95
   Crabmeat Ravigote (8) 45
   Egg Roll (12) 96
   Eggs, Stuffed with Salmon (4) 6
   Fish Eyes (4) 6
   Guacamole (12) 94
   Ham Appetizer (16) 139
   Mushroom Canapes (8) 46
   Mushroom Paste (12) 96
   Mushrooms, Stuffed (12) 97
   Mushrooms, Stuffed (16) 140
   Oysters Rockefeller (4) 7
   Pate, Frosted (12) 96
   Pate, Frosted (16) 140
   Pate Maison (8) 47
   Pate, Molded (16) 140
   Pate, Pheasant (16) 141
   Pate, Speedy (4) 7
   Pineapple Salami (8) 47
   Puffs, Deviled Ham (12) 95
   Puffs, Meat and Vegetable (8) .....
   Shrimp Dip (12) 97
   Snails in Mushrooms (8) 46
   Snow Cap Spread (8) 47
   Spanacopita (16) 141

   Steak Tartare (16) 141
   Sweet and Sour Meatballs (12) ... 97
   Sweet and Sour Meatballs (16) .. 141
Horseradish Dressing 213

I

Ice Cream Mold (8) 88
Ice Cream Pudding (16) 179
Ice Cream, Strawberry (12) 136
Italian Beans (8) 78
Italian Cream Cake 195

J

Jambalaya, Shrimp (8) 69
Jell-O, Fancy (12) 134

K

Kebabs, Lamb (4) 15
Kidneys:
   Rognons de Veau (4) 17
   Stew, Louisa (12) 107
Kirsch Syrup 91
Kisses, Meringue 203

L

Lamb:
   and Artichoke (16) 152
   and Chicken Algerique (8) 62
   Barbecue, Butterfly (12) 106
   Casserole, Cairo (12) 107
   Casserole and Eggplant (4) 15
   Curry (8) 56
   Kebabs (4) 15
   Kidney Stew, Louisa (12) 107
   Leg, Roast (4) 16
   Leg, with Mustard Coating (8) 57
   Moussaka (8) 56
   Scallop (12) 107
Lasagne (30) 155
Lemon:
   Bluff (4) 42
   Dessert (8) 89
   Dreams 210
   Mousse (8) 89
   Pie 206
   Pie, Meringue 206
   Souffle (12) 134
   Souffle with Strawberries (8) 89
   Sponge (12) 134
   Turkey (8) 65
Lenten Treat (12) 115
Lima Beans, Curried (12) 125
Lima Bean Roquefort Salad (4) 37
Linguine, Clams (8) 66
Liptauer Cheese (16) 138

Liver, Calf's, Milanese (4) 16
Livers, Chicken (12) 111
Livers, Chicken, Casserole (8) 63
Livers, Chicken, in Red Wine (4) 20
Livers, Chicken, Marsala (16) 158
Livers, Chicken, Pate Maison (8) ...47
Liver Pate, Frosted (12) 96
Liver Pate, Frosted (16) 140
Liver Pate, Molded (16) 140
Liver Pate, Speedy (4) 7
Lobster:
   Cold Paella (16) 163
   Deviled Seafood Casserole (8) 71
   Easy Seafood Casserole (16) 162
   Fish Hash (12)................114
   Pie (12) 115
   Tails a la Barber (4) 23

M

Macaroni Salad, Salmon (4) 38
Manicotti, Baked (12) 102
Marshmallow, Orange (8) 90
Mayonnaise 214
Meat Loaf, Different (12) 104
Meat Loaf, Turkish (4) 13
Meat Loaf with Blue Cheese (16) ...146
Meatballs:
   Baked (16) 146
   California (16) 146
   Saucepot (4) 13
   Swedish (12) 105
   Sweet and Sour (8) 55
   Sweet and Sour (12) 97
   Sweet and Sour (16) 141
Meeting Street Crab (8)............67
Meringues:
   Forgotten Pudding (16) 180
   Fruit (12) 133
   Kisses 203
   Lemon Pie 206
   Overnight 203
Minestrone (8) 50
Mocha Chocolate Layer Cake 192
Mocha Dessert (12) 135
Molasses Cake 195
Monte's Stew (16) 151
Monte Cristo Sandwich (4) 27
Mornay Sauce 217, 218
Mornay Sauce, Mock 217
Moussaka (8) 56
Mousses:
   Avocado (4) 36
   Chocolate Deluxe (16) 178
   Chocolate, Quick (4) 42
   Crabmeat (8) 67
   Crabmeat (16) 160
   Lemon (8) 89

Raspberry (8) 91
Sole (8) 70
Mushrooms:
   Canapes (8) 46
   Creamy Ham and (16) 165
   Paprika (8) 81
   Paste (12) 96
   Salad (16) 175
   Snails in (8) 46
   Souffle (4) 33
   Soup, Clear (8) 51
   Spinach Salad (4) 38
   Stuffed (4) 32
   Stuffed (12) 97
   Stuffed (16) 140
Mussels, Cold Paella (16) 163
Mystery Torte....................207

N

Nixie's Cupcake................. 196
Noodles:
   Casserole with Spinach (16) 169
   Cheese Omelet (8) 72
   Fettucine Alfredo (8) 74
   Milanese, and Beef (4) 12
   Norfolk (16) 168
   Pudding (8) 76
   Pudding (16) 168
   Spinach Toss (4) 28
Nusstorte 196
Nutties 211

O

Oatmeal Cookies 202
Okra and Corn (16) 171
Omelet, Cheese, Noodle (8) 72
Onion Cheesecake (8) 72
Onions, Creamed (4) 33
Onion Soup (4) 10
Onion Soup, Cream of (16) 145
Onion Soup, French (8) 51
Oranges and Grand Marnier (16) ...178
Orange Marshmallow (8) 90
Orange Mold (12) 135
Oriental Chicken (16).............159
Oysters Rockefeller (4) 7
Oyster Stew (16) 145

P

Paella, Cold (16) 163
Paella, Spanish (8) 71
Pancake, Apple (4) 40
Pancake, Cottage Cheese (4) 26
Pancake, The....................188
Pate, Frosted (12) 96
Pate, Frosted (16) 140

237

Pates: ... Continued
- Maison (8) 47
- Molded (16) 140
- Mushroom (12) 96
- Pheasant (16) 141
- Speedy (4) 7

Peaches:
- and Chicken (16) 157
- Flambe (8) 90
- in Brandy Sauce (12) 135
- Melba (4) 41
- Pie, Creamy 207
- Peachy Chicken (16) 157

Peanut Brittle Pie 207
Pear Chutney 217
Pears in Wine (16) 179
Peas and Artichokes (4) 30
Peas and Celery (12) 127
Pecan Pie 208
Pheasant Francke (12) 113
Pheasant in Sour Cream (8) 64
Pheasant Normandy (4) 21
Pheasant Pate (16) 141
Piccadillo (8) 55
Pies: 204-208
- Cheese 204
- Chess 204
- Chocolate Fudge 204
- Cranberry Walnut 205
- Creamy Peach 207
- Graham Cracker 205
- Grasshopper 205
- Heath Bar 206
- Lemon 206
- Lemon Meringue 206
- Mystery Torte 207
- Peanut Brittle 207
- Pecan 208
- Pumpkin 208
- Rum 208

Pilaf, Greek (4) 29
Pineapple Salami (8) 47
Pineapple Upside Down Cake 200
Pissenlit Salad (4) 37
Plum Pudding (8) 90
Pork:
- Chops in Plum Sauce (16) 152
- Chops in Vermouth (8) 57
- Chops, Oriental (8) 57
- Chops, Tahitian (12) 108
- Cutlets a la Charcutiere (4) 16
- Marinated (12) 108
- Soup, Special (12) 100

Potatoes:
- Bake, Cheese (16) 166
- Bake, Golden (12) 121
- Brown Braised (12) 120
- Casserole, Golden (8) 74
- Chantilly (12) 120
- Creamed (16) 166
- Hash (4) 28
- Mashed, Garlic (16) 166
- Pie (8) 74
- Pie, Cheese (12) 121
- Pommes de Terre (4) 28
- Salad (4) 28
- Salad, Camelot (8) 75
- Salad, German (8) 76
- Souffle, Gruyere (8) 75
- Potpourri, Patsy's (16) 159

Prune Cake 197
Puddings:
- Bread (12) 132
- Corn (8) 80
- Corn (16) 171
- Forgotten (16) 180
- Ice Cream (16) 179
- Noodle (8) 76
- Noodle (16) 168
- Norwegian Fish (8) 70
- Plum (8) 90
- Tomato (4) 34
- Yorkshire 188

Pumpkin Pie 208
Pyramide Dessert (8) 91

Q

Quiche Lorraine (8) 73

R

Raspberry Charlotte (16) 179
Raspberry Mousse (8) 91
Red Velvet Cake 198
Rice:
- All-in-One Risotto (16) 167
- Casserole (8) 77
- Casserole with Salmon (12) 116
- Oven (16) 167
- Pilaf, Greek (4) 29
- Spanish (16) 167
- Walnut (12) 122

Rock Cornish Game Hens (8) 64
Roquefort Salad Dressing 214
Rum Cake 198
Rum Pie 208
Rum Syrup 91

S

Sacher Torte 199
Sainte Emilion au Chocolat (4) 42
Salads:
- Antipasto (8) 84
- Asparagus and Carrot (12) 130
- Avocado Mold (8) 84
- Avocado Mold (12) 130
- Avocado Mousse (4) 36
- Beulah (16) 175
- Broccoli Ring (12) 130
- Bunny (16) 175

Salads ... Continued
  Celery Root Remoulade (4) 36
  Coleslaw (8) 85
  Cucumber Onion Mold (4) 37
  Green Bean (8) 85
  Green Bean, Zippy (16) 174
  Hearts of Palm (16) 176
  Lima Roquefort (4) 37
  Mushroom (16) 175
  Pissenlit (4) 37
  Potato (4) 28
  Potato, Camelot (8) 75
  Potato, German (8) 76
  Salmon Macaroni (4) 38
  Saturday Lunch (4) 38
  Shrimp, Molded (12) 117
  Simple (16) 176
  Sounds Awful (12) 131
  Spinach Mushroom (4) 38
  Spinach, Wilted (12) 131
  Tomato and Cream Cheese (16) .. 176
  Tomato Aspic (8) 85
  Tomato, Stuffed
    with Asparagus (12 131
  Tuna, Molded Ring (4) 40
  Vegetable (16) 177
Salad Dressings: 212-218
  Almond 212
  Blue Cheese 212
  Cooked 212
  Crowell's 213
  Horseradish 213
  Mason Jar 213
  Mayonnaise 214
  Roquefort 214
  "Salad Dressing" 214
  Sour Cream 215
  Spicy Low Calorie 215
  Sweet 215
Salami Pineapple (8) 47
Salisbury Steak (4) 14
Salmon, Boiled (8) 68
Salmon Casserole, Luncheon (16) .. 161
Salmon Casserole, Rice (12) 116
Salmon, Eggs Benedictine (4) 27
Salmon Salad, Macaroni (4) 38
Salmon Stuffed Eggs (4) 6
Saturday Lunch (4) 38
Sandwiches:
  Monte Cristo (4) 27
  Quick Dip (4) 14
Saturday Lunch (4) 38
Sauces:
  Bearnaise 216
  Bechamel 218
  Chantilly 218
  Cream 218
  Hard 40,90
  Hollandaise 216
  Hollandaise, Cream Cheese ... 216
  Hollandaise, Instant Blender . 216
  Howard's 150
  Meat, Hearty Italian 148
  Meat, Uncle Peter's 105
  Mornay 217, 218
  Mornay, Mock 218
  Smitaine 218
  Sour Cream 63
  Veloute 218
  White 218
Saucepot Meatballs (4) 13
Sauerkraut (16) 171
Sauerkraut Cake 199
Sauerkraut, Choucroute
    Alsacienne (8) 81
Seafood, listed by name.
Scallops:
  Coquilles St. Jacques (8) 68
  Easy Seafood Casserole (16) . 162
  Supreme (12) 116
Scones 186
Shortbread, Scottish 203
Shortcake, Strawberry 194
Shrimp:
  Casserole (8) 69
  Casserole, Baked Seafood (4) . 25
  Casserole and Crabmeat (16) . 162
  Casserole, Deviled Seafood (8) . 71
  Cold Paella (16) 163
  Delight (12) 117
  Dip (12) 97
  Grilled (4) 23
  Jambalaya (8) 69
  Patsy's Potpourri (16) 159
  Salad, Molded (12) 117
  San Antonio (16) 161
  Spanish Paella (8) 71
Simple Salad (16) 176
Smitaine Sauce 218
Snails in Mushrooms (8) 46
Snow Cap Spread (8) 47
Snow Peas and
    Water Chestnuts (16) 172
Sole, Broiled Fillet (8) 70
Sole, Easy Fillet (4) 24
Sole, Fillet, East Indian (4) ... 24
Sole Mousse (8) 70
Sole, My Favorite Fish Dish (4) . 24
Souffles:
  Brussels Sprouts (4) 31
  Carrot (4) 31
  Cheese-Ham (4) 26
  Cheese, Overnight (12) 119
  Coffee (8) 87
  Crabmeat (4) 22
  Lemon (12) 134
  Lemon with Strawberries (8) .. 89
  Mushroom (4) 33
  Potato with Gruyere (8) 75
  Sour Cream (8) 72
  Spinach (12) 128
  Swiss (12) 119

239

Soups:
    Almond (8) 48
    Artichoke (12) 98
    Avocado (4) 8
    Avocado (8) 48
    Beef Vegetable (16) 142
    Black Bean (16) 143
    Broccoli (4) 8
    Carrot (8) 48
    Cheese (16) 143
    Chestnut (16) 144
    Chicken (8) 49
    Chicken, Curried (12) 98
    Clam (8) 49
    Clam Chowder (4) 8
    Corn (12) 98
    Crab (4) 8
    Crab (12) 99
    Crab (16) 144
    Cucumber (12) 99
    Eggplant, Curried (8) 49
    Escarole (4) 9
    Fish Chowder, Maine (8) 50
    Gazpacho (4) 9
    Gazpacho (12) 99
    Hamburg Chowder (12) 100
    Minestrone (8) 50
    Mushroom, Clear (8) 51
    Onion (4) 10
    Onion, Cream of (16) 145
    Onion, French (8) 51
    Oyster Stew (16) 145
    Pork Butt Special (12) 100
    Spinach (12) 100
    Spinach Curry (4) 10
    Spinichicken (4) 10
    Striped (4) 10
    Tomato, Cold (4) 11
    Turkey (12) 101
    Vichysoisse (8) 51
    Zucchini and Green Bean (12) ... 101
Sour Cream Salad Dressing 215
Sour Cream Sauce 63
Sour Cream Souffle (8) 72
Spanacopita (16) 141
Spinach:
    Casserole (8) 82
    Casserole (16) 172
    Casserole with Ham (8) 55
    Casserole with Noodles (16) ... 169
    Curry Soup (4) 10
    Gourmet (12) 127
    Noodle Toss (4) 28
    Ring (8) 82
    Salad (4) 38
    Salad, Wilted (12) 131
    Souffle (12) 128
    Soup (16) 145
Spinichicken Soup (16) 10

Spoon Bread 187
Spreads:
    Chutney Cheese (4) 6
    Snow Cap (8) 47
Squares: 209-211
    Butterscotch Brownies 209
    Cinnamon Bars 209
    Coconut Delight 209
    Congo 210
    for the Gods 211
    Lemon Dreams 210
    Margaret Turner's 210
    Margo's Fudge 211
    Nutties 211
    Tannies 211
Squash: (See also Acorn Squash
    and Zucchini)
    Baked (16) 172
    Bread 186
Steak:
    Flank (16) 150
    Quick Dip Sandwich (4) 14
    Salisbury (4) 14
    Tartare (16) 141
Stews:
    Beef (8) 53
    Beef Burgundy (16) 151
    Boeuf Bourguignon (12) 103
    Company Beef (20) 154
    Gaston (8) 53
    Monte's (16) 151
Strawberry Almond Mold (12) 136
Strawberry Crepes (16) 180
Strawberry Ice Cream (12) 136
Strawberry Shortcake 194
String Beans:
    Deluxe (16) 170
    in Mustard Sauce (12) 124
    Lively (4) 30
    Puree (8) 78
    Salad (8) 85
    Salad, Zippy (16) 174
    Soup, and Zucchini (12) 101
Striped Soup (4) 10
Stroganoff, Beef (12) 102
Stroganoff, Hamburger (16) 147
Swedish Cream (8) 92
Sweet Potatoes:
    and Marron Balls (16) 166
    Casserole (8) 76
    Guatemalan (4) 29
    in Orange Shells (4) 29
    with Pecans (12) 122
Sweetbreads (4) 15
Sweetbreads Supreme (8) 58
Swiss Fondue (4) 26
Syrup, Rum or Kirsch 91

T

Tannies 211
Texas Hash (16) 150
Toast, Herb 185
Tomatoes:
   Aspic (8) 85
   Benedict (8) 73
   Cherry, Stuffed (12) 97
   Creole (16) 173
   Dutch (4) 33
   Eggplant, Spicy (16) 171
   George, Jr. (12) 129
   Pudding (4) 34
   Salad, with Cream Cheese (16) . . 176
   Soup, Cold (4) 11
   Spicy (16) 173
   Stack-ups, Broccoli (16) 170
   Stuffed (8) 82
   with Asparagus (12) 131
Torte, Mystery 207
Torte, Nut 196
Torte, Sacher 199
Torte, Zwiebach (12) 136
Trittini (20) 154
Tuna:
   Cold Paella (16) 163
   Easy Seafood Casserole (16) 164
   Ring, Molded (4) 39
Turkey:
   Casserole, Gourmet Rice (4) 21
   for a Crowd (16) 158
   Lemon (8) 65
   Sandwich, Monte Cristo (4) 27
   Soup (12) 101
   Tetrazzini (16) 159
Turkish Meat Loaf (4) 13

U

Uncle Peter's Meat Sauce (12) 105
Upside-down Cake, Pineapple 200

V

Veal:
   and Mushrooms (16) 152
   and Water Chestnuts (12) 109
   Birds (8) 58
   Chops in White Wine (4) 17
   Cutlets in Sour Cream (4) 17
   Cutlets Zinn Arturo (16) 153
   Italian and Peppers (12) 108
   Palarma (12) 109
   Parmigiana (16) 153
   Rognons de Veau (4) 17
   Vitello Tonnato (8) 59
   with Lemon (8) 59

Vegetables, listed by name.
Vegetable Patty (4) 34
Vegetable Salad (16) 177
Vegetables, Oriental (4) 34
Veloute Sauce 218
Vichysoisse (8) 51
Vitello Tonnato (8) 58
Viva la Chicken (12) 113

W

Wacky Cake 200
Waffles, Chocolate (4) 41
Walnut Rice (12) 122
Welsh Rarebit (8) 73
Wheat Bread 187
White Bread 187
White Sauce 218
Wild Duck (8) 65
Wild Rice Casserole (8) 77
Wild Rice Croquettes (12) 123

Y

Yam Stuffed Apples (12) 123
Yorkshire Pudding 188

Z

Zesty Corn (4) 32
Zucchini:
   Baked (8) 83
   Baked (12) 129
   Beef Stuffed (4) 12
   Fanned (16) 173
   in Tomato Sauce (8) 83
   Soup, and Green Bean (12) 101
   with Mushrooms and Peppers (4) . 35
Zwieback Torte (12) 136

ABBREVIATIONS

tsp.	teaspoon
tbsp.	tablespoon
c	cup
pt.	pint
qt.	quart
gal.	gallon
pkg.	package
env.	envelope
sq.	square
oz.	ounce
lb.	pound
doz.	dozen
hr.	hour/s
min.	minute/s
sml.	small
med.	medium
lrg.	large
"	inch
MSG	monosodium glutamate

TABLE OF WEIGHTS & MEASURES

Dash or Pinch = less than 1/8 teaspoon
3 teaspoons = 1 tablespoon
4 tablespoons = 1/4 cup
8 ounces = 1 cup
2 cups = 1 pint (16 ounces)
4 cups = 1 quart
4 quarts = 1 gallon